Taking Back
CHILDHOOD

Taking Back
CHILDHOOD

Helping Your Kids Thrive
in a Fast-Paced, Media-Saturated,
Violence-Filled World

NANCY CARLSSON-PAIGE, Ed.D.

HUDSON
STREET
PRESS

HUDSON STREET PRESS
Published by Penguin Group
Penguin Group (USA) Inc., 375 Hudson Street, New York, New York 10014, U.S.A. • Penguin Group (Canada), 90 Eglinton Avenue East, Suite 700, Toronto, Ontario, Canada M4P 2Y3 (a division of Pearson Penguin Canada Inc.) • Penguin Books Ltd., 80 Strand, London WC2R 0RL, England • Penguin Ireland, 25 St. Stephen's Green, Dublin 2, Ireland (a division of Penguin Books Ltd.) • Penguin Group (Australia), 250 Camberwell Road, Camberwell, Victoria 3124, Australia (a division of Pearson Australia Group Pty. Ltd.) • Penguin Books India Pvt. Ltd., 11 Community Centre, Panchsheel Park, New Delhi – 110 017, India • Penguin Group (NZ), 67 Apollo Drive, Rosedale, North Shore 0745, Auckland, New Zealand (a division of Pearson New Zealand Ltd.) • Penguin Books (South Africa) (Pty.) Ltd., 24 Sturdee Avenue, Rosebank, Johannesburg 2196, South Africa

Penguin Books Ltd., Registered Offices: 80 Strand, London WC2R 0RL, England

First published by Hudson Street Press, a member of Penguin Group (USA) Inc.

First Printing, April 2008
10 9 8 7 6 5 4 3 2 1

REGISTERED TRADEMARK—MARCA REGISTRADA
HUDSON
STREET
PRESS

LIBRARY OF CONGRESS CATALOGING-IN-PUBLICATION DATA

Carlsson-Paige, Nancy.
   Taking back childhood : helping your kids thrive in a fast-paced, media-saturated, violence-filled world / Nancy Carlsson-Paige.
   p. cm.
   Includes bibliographical references.
   ISBN 978-1-59463-043-9 (hardcover : alk. paper)
1. Children and violence—United States. 2. Mass media and children—United States. 3. Video games and children—United States. 4. Play—United States. 5. Toys—United States—Psychological aspects. 6. Child development—United States. I. Title.
HQ784.V55C375 2008
649'.70973—dc22   2007042467

Printed in the United States of America
Set in New Caledonia and Bell Gothic

PUBLISHER'S NOTE
While the author has made every effort to provide accurate telephone numbers and Internet addresses at the time of publication, neither the publisher nor the author assumes any responsibility for errors, or for changes that occur after publication. Further, publisher does not have any control over and does not assume any responsibility for author or third-party websites or their content.

AUTHOR'S NOTE
The actual names of the parents and children whose stories and quotes fill this book are used whenever possible. In some cases, however, to respect the preferences of the individuals mentioned, names have been changed.

This book is printed on acid-free paper. ∞

To the memory of Jesse McKie,
and his spirit of creativity, humor, and love,
alive in every child.

Acknowledgments

Writing a book is a collaborative venture and I have many people to thank. I am deeply grateful to all of the parents who generously agreed to be interviewed for this book and who so willingly shared their personal stories and reflections on the challenges of raising children in these difficult times.

I am grateful to the countless children I've worked with and observed in classrooms and families over the course of my career, and the many in my large extended family—I have learned from all of you, and to those whose stories and examples fill these pages, I am especially grateful. Most profoundly, I thank my grandchildren—Jackson, Miles, Alexia, and Isabella—you are the backbone of this book and without you, it wouldn't exist. For over a decade, our interactions—intimate, sometimes challenging, always precious—have allowed me to see, with the widened lens and open heart of a grandparent, how an approach guided by child development and creative conflict resolution insights bears positive fruit. Thank you for agreeing so generously to be in this book (and to your parents for their permission).

. To my sons, Kyle and Matt, you have always been my greatest (and toughest) teachers, and your wives, Lori and Luciana, I thank each one of you for supporting my work and this book. I am so grateful that you trusted me to tell your personal stories where I saw fit.

I want to express my deep appreciation to my agent, Todd Shuster, who envisioned this book before I did and stuck with it from months into years, helping to shape and hone it into a cohesive form with infinite patience. You set the bar high and held to it, always with kindness and encouragement; I am sure this book would not have reached fruition without you.

I also want to express my gratitude to those who read early drafts of specific chapters and gave me their feedback and encouragement—Lynne Hall, Ethel McConaghy, Joyce Shortt, and Roslyn Zinn. I am especially grateful to Betty Burkes and Lynne Hurdle-Price for reading the chapters pertaining to discipline and culture and engaging in a dialogue about them that without doubt resulted in a better and more inclusive book.

I feel particularly indebted to three colleagues who, through collaboration and friendship, have influenced my view of the world and my work. Diane Levin, my first source of inspiration about the thrilling potential of progressive education, who later joined me to build a perspective on media's power in children's lives and pen countless pages, makes an immeasurable contribution to this book. My deep thanks to Linda Lantieri, who has stretched me to see how children's social and emotional learning extends into brain activity and spirituality, and who repeatedly challenges me to transcend the limits of my own thinking and being. Thanks also to you, Linda, for reading and commenting on chapter 8. I am also grateful to William Kreidler, under whose tutelage I first witnessed the powerful techniques of creative conflict resolution. Bill—we are carrying on your inspired work that was so ahead of its time.

I wish to thank Joel Segel for his invaluable role in helping to structure the ideas in this book into a coherent whole. And I am truly grateful to Chris Kochansky, whose editing skill, as well as friendship and wisdom, eased me through the final stages of producing a manuscript. And for their help in tracking down specific studies and background material, I would also like to thank Joanne Cantor, Josh Golin, Susan Linn, and Juliet Schor.

I am grateful to Luke Dempsey, editor in chief at Hudson Street Press, for his support and enthusiasm for this project, and to Danielle Friedman, for her skilled and sensitive editing and careful guidance throughout production. It has been a pure pleasure to work with you both. I also appreciate the contributions of Melissa Jacoby, Abigail Powers, Susan Schwartz, Liz Keenan, Marie Coolman, and Clare Ferraro. My sincere thanks go to all of you.

For many years I received financial support from Zell Draz that allowed me to do the research and thinking that are foundational to this book. I miss you, Zell; you'd be thrilled to see this book come out.

I thank my sister Judy whose moral support, so freely given and unbeknownst to her, came at critical moments during the evolution of this book.

My deepest thanks go to my husband, Doug, grounded and wise adviser and spiritual guide. No one else read every single word of every single draft of every single chapter for more than three years running and no one has ever believed in me as you do. As I've heard you say (and who knows better than you when a Bob Dylan line is needed?), "He not busy being born is busy dying."

Contents

Contents

Prologue

*I'm riding on the subway with my son Kyle and his two sons—
my grandsons, Jackson and Miles, who are seven and four years
old. We're on our way to the Garden of Peace in downtown
Boston, a memorial established to commemorate victims of
homicide. Today we'll attend the dedication ceremony. I turn to
Kyle and ask, "Do Jack and Miles know where we're going?"*

*"Yes," answers Kyle. "I've told them we're going to a special
place to remember people who've died."*

"Do they know about Jesse?" I ask.

"Yes," says Kyle. "I've told them all about him."

Jesse was my older son's beloved high school friend, who spent almost every afternoon at our house, often sleeping on Kyle's floor at
night. The two were inseparable, clowning and cavorting together in
a way that made parents, teachers, and friends double over with
laughter at their antics. One year Jesse came with us on our family va-
cation to New Hampshire. After we arrived, I had to go to the grocery
store for provisions, and Kyle and my younger son, Matt, wanted to
come with me, but Jesse chose to remain behind. When we got back

an hour later we couldn't find him anywhere, and I was beginning to worry. But then we heard a commotion from high in a treetop, and when we looked up we saw Jesse perched on a branch, wearing a loincloth and covered in decorative body paint, hooting like a tropical bird. This was Jesse being Jesse—master of the unexpected, exhibiting once again his original, creative, and always hilarious wit.

Late one January night when Jesse was twenty years old, he was walking home from a friend's house in our neighborhood in Cambridge, Massachusetts. A van carrying five young men pulled up, and they told Jesse to give them his leather jacket, which he did. They then proceeded to stab him over and over again and left him to die in a snowbank. The lives of Judy and Todd, Jesse's wonderful parents, my life, my sons' lives, and the lives of everyone else who loved Jesse would never be the same. Now, fifteen years later, I open the newspaper in the morning and read about violent deaths by car bombings, terrorism, and war, and I know that every single death described on that one-dimensional page of newspaper holds a full-blown story of grief and lifelong sadness for family and friends just like us.

> *We're getting off the subway now and walking to the Garden of Peace. Miles is asking me questions about Jesse: "Is his body lying down?" "Are the people who killed Jesse in jail?"*
>
> *I feel grateful for my many years of study in early childhood development, which have taught me to answer Miles in concrete terms that will help him make better sense of things. And I know that behind Miles's question about whether Jesse's killers are in jail there might lie some anxiety about his own safety, so I reassure him that they are definitely in jail and not coming out.*

When I received the phone call telling me what had happened to Jesse, I was in the middle of a research project on conflict resolution among elementary school children. Since then, I've spoken with children in El Salvador who have not only lost family members in that country's bloody war but also witnessed the killings firsthand. I've visited with children in South Central Los Angeles who have seen shootings on the streets right outside their homes. I've conducted studies on violence in the media and how profoundly it affects children's play and social growth. And I've written five books and numerous articles on all of these subjects, which have occupied my mind and heart for more than twenty-five years.

Though I had begun studying children and violence long before Jesse's murder, it was his death that gave my work a new, more urgent and personal meaning. From that fateful day on, I've continually looked back at my work as a researcher and educator and asked, How did the young men who killed Jesse come to do what they did that night?

There are many factors that lead young people to use violence. Some of these relate to the social and economic inequalities in our society that predispose certain of our youth to anger and conflict. But there are other factors, too. A colleague who works with me in peace education told me that the urban kids she was working with, who genuinely wanted to change their environment and their lives, had asked her *sincerely*, "If we don't act violently, what do we do instead?"

To turn away from violence, we have to know what to put in its place. What these young people were asking for is the same thing that all children, regardless of their circumstances, need to know: how to think creatively, how to communicate with others effectively, how to see things from another's point of view, how to work out conflicts without using coercion or force, how to build relationships based on empathy and love. But there are trends in contemporary society that are making it very difficult for all children to learn these things. We have seen many worrisome examples in recent years of young people who shoot classmates or inflict pain on others without any apparent feelings for them. In this book I offer a view of how these social trends are undermining childhood today and of what you can do— the many steps you can take—to counteract them and give all children a better chance at living healthy, creative lives. And as you consider these ideas, I hope you will see that the prescriptions for "taking back childhood" are the same ones that will help bring into being a more just and peaceful world for all people.

CHAPTER 1

Taking Back Childhood

What Our Kids Are Losing—and How to Get It Back

From where I am sitting today, I am profoundly concerned about our nation's children. Life is far more challenging for children and parents than it was only a generation ago, when I was raising my kids. These days, a host of social forces and trends is putting tremendous pressure on children and their parents: Entertainment media are too often replacing active, child-centered play and social time with peers and family. Constant depictions of violence, aggression, and disrespect toward others are immersing kids in a world where "might makes right." Exposure to frightening news reports that only seem to confirm the violent messages pervading kids' entertainment leave many children fearful and insecure. Aggressive marketing campaigns aimed at kids are pushing a host of products, toys, and values on children, teaching them to value "having" over "being" from an early age. Economic and time pressures on parents are leading them to quick-fix approaches to discipline and to rely on "electronic babysitters" like TVs, Game Boys, and Xboxes. An overemphasis on standardized tests in our schools is robbing children of genuine learning opportunities and resulting in the loss of unstructured play, arts activities, and social time, all of which are essential to their well-being. Childhood as we know it is being stolen from our children, and it is time for us, as concerned parents, grandparents, and citizens, to take it back.

This book will explore how the social currents described above are threatening three basic needs of childhood—children's need for *creative play*, for *security*, and for *positive relationships* with adults and other children. It will also offer many steps we adults can take to restore these essential building blocks of healthy child development. I will share my years of experience as a child development professor and life-long observer of children—not only of my own, but also children in classrooms and communities across the nation and the globe. I will also present stories from the many parents I interviewed for this book over the course of two years, beginning in June 2003. These moms and dads—racially and ethnically diverse, young and older, from urban, suburban, and rural areas—told me about the challenges they face as parents in today's world. I gained much insight from these conversations and have many stories to share in the pages ahead—stories that I hope you will find helpful and relevant to your own experiences raising kids.

Many of the parents I interviewed described the world they grew up in as remarkably different from the one their own kids face today. Rob, a forty-five-year-old father from New York, said he played outside "all day long" as a child: "We had a neighborhood gang. We all played together—mostly I remember a game we made up called 'Capture.' The rules kept changing, but basically you had to hide and then run like heck if someone found you." Mary Kay, a mother from Connecticut with four daughters, told me how she loved walking home from school because she could "process the day and unwind. I remember the trees," she said, "when the leaves would change—and the dogwoods—when they bloomed they made a beautiful umbrella over me." J.B., a dad who grew up in Florida, said, "We played in the streets. I don't remember watching TV when I was young. Our family played games at night after dinner." And David, who drives a cab in

Boston and has two sons a generation apart (Errol is forty-two years old and Malcolm is thirteen) said, "My older kid roamed and ran outside, chased garter snakes and grasshoppers. Kids would come to the house and they'd want to go outside. But now kids want to stay inside! They aren't connecting to a lot of things. They're being fed through a screen. They want to be on the computer all the time. What the TV says, they think that's what it is."

Just as David and so many parents realize, today's fast-paced technology- and media-saturated society is undermining an integral part of childhood, namely direct experiences with the real world — with peers, with adults, and with activities of all kinds. In order to learn and grow, children need to connect—to their own creativity and initiative, to each other, to family, and to nature. When Rob and his pals played "Capture," they were inventing and negotiating the rules of their game, problem solving, and using their imaginations. New developments in brain research suggest that neurons grow and connect in the brain as children actively engage in this kind of play. Science, therefore, confirms what we know intuitively: that creative play is essential to the development of healthy minds.

But what specific kinds of experience are beneficial for our children? And how can we know how to meet our children's needs in these challenging times? In my view, the answers lie, above all, in the rich body of child development theory and research—from Jean Piaget's work on play and learning to Mary Ainsworth's ideas on attachment to Erik Erikson's articulation of the stages of life—that have guided me for over thirty years as a parent, teacher, and now grandparent. The pioneering work of these and other theorists has shown that there are universal, predictable sequences of growth and change that occur in children during the first decade of life. Of course each child is also a unique person with an individual personality, temperament, learning style, and cultural background. But knowledge of the developmental changes that occur in children can be a tremendously valuable guide in our dealings with individual kids. This child development perspective has taught me how to talk to children about difficult subjects like violence, death, and divorce. It has helped me understand why a two-year-old might be throwing a tantrum over putting on her shoes and what might help her cope; why a five-year-old is having trouble separating from his mom in kindergarten and what he might need to feel comfortable without her; why an eight-year-old is slinging insults at her friend without apparent empathy and what might persuade her to stop. Knowing more about *children's development* can be a great resource for you, too. It's not a cookbook kind of knowledge, but instead is information that will help you understand how children see the world and what they need to thrive in it. You can interpret and use the ideas differently depending on your family, culture, and personal situation. But just like the Chinese proverb says, "Give me a fish and I eat for a day. Teach me to fish and I eat for a lifetime," these are ideas that can guide you in the moment-to-moment decisions you make and actions you take with children every day.

The Need for Creative Play

When I begin to examine what's missing from contemporary childhood, the first thing I note is the absence of creative play. All of the great child development theorists, from Lev Vygotsky and Jean Piaget to Anna Freud and Erik Erikson, saw play as vital to children's social, emotional, and cognitive growth—and perhaps the most important tool our children have to work through new experiences, ideas, and feelings. Over the course of my career, I've witnessed hundreds of children using play as a vehicle for making sense of the confusing world around them. One of the most striking examples that comes to mind involves a kindergarten student I taught twenty-five years ago named Ruby. In the second half of the school year, Ruby fell ill with spinal meningitis (or "spider meningitis," as she would later tell her classmates), and was out of school for at least three weeks. Upon her return to the classroom, she headed straight to the dramatic play corner where I had set up a "hospital," put on a white coat, and was soon leaning over Sam, one of her favorite play partners and now her "patient." I remember Ruby listening to his heart with a stethoscope, giving him a "shot," and directing him to eat some "medicine"—a bowl full of plastic cubes she'd mixed up just for him. And I remember her spending much of the next few weeks in the same play area, hovering over one willing patient after another. Finally, very slowly, Ruby began spending more time in other parts of the classroom, much as she had before she got sick.

Ruby's dramatic play during this period was vital for helping her work through her hospital experience. Real play is remarkably creative: a child can be playwright, actor, and director all in one. Every child's play is different, because every child's life experience is different. As she played, Ruby was using scenes she remembered from her actual hospital stay, but mixing them with ideas from her own imagination. Ruby's play was completely original. Only she knew what she needed to do, and only through this particular play could Ruby gain a sense of mastery over what she had been through, restore her inner balance, and find her confidence once again.

Though we may barely notice it, this is ideally what children are always doing in play. They are taking aspects of their experience and transforming them into something new, moving in the direction of equilibrium and healing throughout the process. As they create their own scenarios and narratives, they come to understand and integrate what they've already experienced in life.

Given the vital importance of play in allowing children to make sense of an increasingly frightening world, it is particularly troubling that it has become so rare today to find a child who uses her imagination

the way Ruby did in the hospital corner. Along with my research partner, Professor Diane Levin of Wheelock College in Boston, I have conducted three separate studies polling hundreds of teachers across the
country, and all have shown that starting with the deregulation of children's television in 1984 (more on this below) and continuing apace,
kids' play has become far less creative, with children mimicking what
they've seen in the media, rather than coming up with it by themselves.

That play is no longer the personally inventive process it once was
is no surprise when we consider just how much time children spend
absorbing media of all kinds. According to a national Kaiser Family
Foundation survey completed in March 2005, today, eight- to eighteen-
year-olds spend an average of nearly six and a half hours per day consuming media. Even kids in the two- to seven-year-old age group now
average about three hours per day of "screen time." And even though
the American Academy of Pediatrics recommends that children under the age of two not watch television at all (because of concerns
that TV affects early brain growth and the development of social,
emotional, and cognitive skills), a 2003 Kaiser survey found that in a
typical day, 68 percent of all children under two use screen media—
for an average of just over two hours. Twenty-six percent of these
under-twos have TVs in their bedrooms.

But it's not just the quantity of media, and television in particular,
that has changed from the previous generation to this one. When my
sons were young, there were federal regulations that protected kids
from the overcommercialization of children's television. It was illegal
to market toys and products linked to television shows, so there
weren't any "single-purpose" toys like action figures and props that
are wired to say or do the very same words or actions kids have seen
on the screen (which can greatly inhibit creative play). Advertising on
kids' TV was regulated as well, so that the typical child was exposed to
far fewer than the current average of forty thousand commercials per

year. In 1978, the Federal Trade Commission (FTC) even decided to ban advertising to children under the age of eight altogether, but that same year, Congress, reacting to pressure from corporate lobbyists, voted to remove the FTC's regulating power altogether. And soon after, in 1984, came the final nail in the coffin: the Federal Communications Commission (FCC) under President Reagan rapidly removed all of the regulations it had put in place over earlier decades to protect children from overcommercialized TV. Thus were born countless popular TV shows that ultimately served as ads for entire lines of toys and products—like *G.I. Joe*, *Care Bears*, and *Transformers*.

By the mid-1980s, then, businesses were freely selling to kids through TV and profiting handsomely from it. Since then and with virtually no federal regulations since, marketing to children has escalated exponentially and is now channeled through Hollywood movies, video and computer games, fast-food chains, and even schools. Today six media conglomerates own most of the media we consume and exercise almost unlimited control over the images children are exposed to. Corporations spend $15 billion annually on marketing targeted at children—about two and a half times more than they spent in 1992. Huge marketing campaigns are tied to single themes that push a single set of characters, scripted dialogue, and mindset to children across all of the major media sectors. As my research has shown, it has become increasingly difficult for children to discover their own imaginations and create their own play in a childhood culture so dominated by these media and marketing forces.

Zoe, a young mom in a suburb of Boston, recently described to me the way she felt that consumer culture had affected her children's ability to think creatively and individually. After Zoe took Sophia, four, and Charlie, seven, to see the movie *Finding Nemo*, they encountered the film and its products everywhere. "We saw *Finding Nemo* posters on the bus, *Finding Nemo* toys, backpacks, books, coloring books, stickers; we went to *Finding Nemo* birthday parties." Zoe paused for a minute. "There's a part of you and your children that is in danger of being sucked into this machine that is going to feed you the movie, give you the hat and the T-shirt, buy you the toy, and then show you how to play with it. And that is what you are going to do—have this prepackaged experience. It will make the children less flexible thinkers. It will limit their imagination." As Zoe spoke, I thought to myself, "It may also undermine their academic progress and stymie their development into healthy, freethinking adults."

Unfortunately, if parents like Zoe turn to the school system to foster the type of imaginative play that is being stamped out by so many of the media and products marketed to children today, they may be sorely disappointed. As a professor of early childhood education who has spent twenty-five years helping dedicated people learn how to teach and encourage children, I am truly shocked by what is happening to primary education in America today. The federal government now mandates that all ninety-one thousand public schools in the United States be rated on the basis of their students' standardized test scores. Schoolchildren from grades three through eight are required to take these tests, which are tied to harsh penalties if district scores fall below a certain level. This emphasis on tests has changed the focus of our classrooms from creativity and independent thinking to rote memorization and regurgitation.

Facing overwhelming pressure to raise scores on these tests, our teachers today too often resort to "teaching to the test," a classroom strategy that ignores the aspects of learning that matter most—higher-order thinking, problem solving, creativity, and the all-important social and emotional components that are intertwined with learning. I recently met with a roomful of second-grade teachers in a large Miami public school who told me they had no choice but to spend all class time drilling kids in scripted lessons that cater to Florida's statewide standardized test. The focus on academic skills and scripted teaching, alarmingly, has pushed down even to preschools and kindergartens, where valuable experiences like play, arts-based activities, and social interactions are disappearing.

My friend Roz stopped by my house the day she decided to stop teaching kindergarten in the Boston public schools after more than thirty years. As she burst through my front door, Roz said, "I quit today. I can't stand to see what's happening to kids. Kindergarten is nothing like it used to be. The blocks, water table, science corner with birds nests and feathers are all gone—there's no time. It's all learn the alphabet and reading and writing."

What is fueling this revamping of our nation's schools is a drive to close the "achievement gap"—the disparity in test scores between blacks and Hispanics and their white and Asian peers—which so many of us want to make into a thing of the past. But we can't close the achievement gap by taking from children what we know they need for healthy development and academic success—approaches that have proven successful through decades of compelling research and experience that are now backed up by findings from neuroscience about how the brain works.

Many of the parents who participated in my recent study told me upsetting stories about the stress their children feel in this climate of high-stakes testing. Luisandra, the mother of six-year-old Beatriz, told me that the Miami public schools had informed her that Beatriz would have to begin her first-grade school year in mid-August, two weeks earlier than usual, because they needed more time to get kids ready for standardized tests.

Nothing has made sense to Beatriz and it has been almost a month of school. My mom took Beatriz to school the other day and they were having a spelling test that day. Beatriz can't spell.

She can't even read or write. How can they give a spelling test to a child who doesn't know how to read and write? When my mom turned to say good-bye to Beatriz, she saw her eyes were filled with tears. She was scared, just scared. She said, "I don't want to go in there. I don't remember anything. I don't remember any of the words." She is six and she is terrified of a spelling test.

Others parents talked about the inordinate amount of homework their kids are typically assigned—an endless assortment of drills and exercises like the ones they have to do in school. Hannah's son Warren is in the fourth grade and she said this:

> Every day it's the same. We pick Warren up at "after school" at six o'clock, come home, have dinner, and then from seven to eight it's a scene—a horrible scene. He doesn't want to do the homework—he's had no downtime, he's tired. We have to make him do it. Then he starts saying, "I can't do this! I hate math! I'm stupid!" (That's the part I feel the worst about . . . he keeps saying he's stupid.) Then he runs into his room and cries and cries.

Warren, like other children, needs school programs that nurture his mind, heart, body, and spirit. Kids need active learning approaches; they need to build, draw, and play together and to develop the many social skills critical to success in this life.

Contemplating the disappearance, in district after district, of art, play, music, recess, and field trips, I think about my two sons, both now grown and making their contributions to the world as artists: one as a sculptor, one as an actor. In first grade, Kyle brought home his drawings every day: fantastic, vibrant designs and images, many of which I've kept all these years. Matt spent much of kindergarten in the dramatic play area of his classroom, putting on dress-up items and acting out all sorts of pretend scenarios. I wonder now how they would have fared in today's schools, most of which are stripped of play areas that encourage the visual and dramatic arts. If my sons attended public schools today, they would learn that their talents are not valued; they'd also have a much harder time bringing their creative light into the world.

For years now I have been saying in my books and presentations that children's play has become "an endangered species." The play that Ruby invented—a healing kind that sprang from her own imagination and needs—has become a missing resource in most kids' lives today. Fortunately, you can do so much—when you know which toys, materials, and conditions best stimulate and inspire children's minds— to reclaim this missing resource for your sons and daughters. In the chapters ahead, I will suggest many steps you can take to help children rediscover their capacity to cope—and to thrive—through rich and imaginative play.

The Need for Security

A second bedrock of healthy childhood development is every young person's need to feel secure. Absolutely critical to children's well-being, a sense of security is rooted in the trust that babies develop from the first days of life when they learn that they can count on their caretakers. In his theory on the stages of life, Erik Erikson put trust at the very center of development—kids really can't grow and develop fully if they don't trust that adults can care for them and that they are safe and secure.

Even when children have a basic sense that they are loved and cared for, life events can shake their sense of security. I remember Gretchen, a five-year-old in my kindergarten class in the late 1970s whose parents went through a divorce. The normally effervescent Gretchen began coming to school reluctantly, crying and clinging to her mom. She was withdrawn and uninterested in the painting and building she normally loved to do. When our class planned a field trip, Gretchen didn't want to go—she preferred to remain back at school rather than venture outside and onto the bus. The world that Gretchen depended on, like that of so many kids who go through a divorce, was turned upside down for a while. Her sense of security was temporarily disrupted and she needed a lot of extra reassurance and support at school.

Of course, most children experience life events—a death, a parent's depression, the loss of a friendship—that may rattle their sense of security. But in my view, there's a toxic source of distress in the life of every child in America today: their incessant exposure to violent and scary media images, in both entertainment and the news media.

In the 1970s, violence on television was so minimal that I rarely had to worry about what my children might see on the small screen. They watched shows on public television like *Sesame Street*, and cartoons about superheroes like Superman, Shazam, and Wonder Woman, who used their super powers to rescue people. Yet today, a study by the American Medical Association confirms that 75 percent of parents in our nation are concerned about the abundance of violence shown on *children's* television. And it's no wonder: Kids are exposed to more violent content in children's programming than adults are in all of prime time, according to a 2006 Parents Television council report. The PTC analyzed entertainment programming for five- to ten-year-olds and found an average of 7.86 violent incidents per hour (as compared to 4.71 violent incidents per hour in adult prime-time programming). Analysts even separated out the "cartoony violence" many kids grew up on a generation ago (like an anvil falling on Roadrunner's head) from other types such as "physical violence" and "use of weapons." And still, even after removing the cartoon violence, they were left with an average of 6.30 violent incidents per hour on kids' TV. And it's worth repeating here that the problem today isn't just that there's more violence on children's television. It's also that the violence kids see on the screen gets a firmer, deeper grip on their psyches because it's replicated in the toys and products they interact with in their everyday lives.

When I see the extent of media violence that children are exposed to on a regular basis—through TV, movies, video and computer games, and weaponlike toys directly linked to violent media—I feel enraged that this could be happening, when there is no question that it robs children of one of their most basic needs. If only the adults who make and market these shows could understand that children don't view the violence they see on the screen as adults do. Violent and scary media are particularly detrimental for young children because during the early years, as child development theory explains, children don't clearly distinguish between fantasy and reality. They cannot be sure that what they see on the screen won't really happen to them—that the monster or the bad guy leering at them won't come right off the screen, if not now, maybe later. And especially before the age of seven or eight, it's very hard for children to understand the violence they see in a larger context of character, motive, and plot, so its impact on them is far more graphic and immediate than it is on us—and also, more lasting. Knowing this must be part of what has led Dr. Alvin Poussaint, professor of psychiatry at Harvard Medical School, to say that exposing children to violent images can have a similar impact to "physical abuse or living in a war zone." "None of us," he says, "would willingly put a child into those situations, yet we do not act to keep them from watching movies about things we would be horrified to have them see off the screen."

There is a growing body of research showing that viewing frightening media can cause increased fearfulness and mistrust in children, and this often extends well beyond the time of viewing. A random national survey conducted in 1999 reported that 62 percent of parents with children between the ages of two and seventeen said that their child had been frightened by something he or she saw in a TV program or movie, and this fear, according to other studies, can last for days, months, or even years.

I have spoken with countless children who seem upset and scared by something they've seen in the media, whether real or pretend. My own grandson Miles, who otherwise has every modicum of security in his life that I would wish for every child, has told me about TV images that frighten him. Here's what Miles told me one day when he was four years old about *Digimon*, a children's cartoon full of shooting and fighting that airs on the Cartoon Network:

Miles: Have you seen *Digimon*?

Me: No, tell me about it.

Miles: It's very scary.

Me: Why?

Miles: A bad guy has arrows that shoot out of his hands. It's scary because it has too much scary things. It has fire, and a Digimon gets stuck. When he's attacked, he jumps in the air. The lasers are very gold and on the tip it's very sharp.

Me: So it has a lot of scary things like fire and sharp lasers. . . .

Miles: When I'm in the hall, I see little footprints and when I go upstairs, I run to get my plastic sword.

Me: Why?

Miles: To fight the bad guys when I'm up there. They only come at night. They don't like the morning.

For Miles, the "too much scary things" on the cartoon upset him partly because, from his perspective, these "bad guys" aren't just contained inside the TV: they can come out of the television set and into his house at night. Miles's feeling of security is threatened by something as seemingly innocent as a cartoon, and his experience is by no means unique.

Many of the parents I interviewed in connection with the research for this book described specific instances of media violence that frightened their children. Luisa, a twenty-nine-year-old mother from Miami, told me about her seven-year-old daughter, Raquel, who was watching a children's program on TV when an ad for a horror movie for adults came on. According to Luisa, Raquel immediately became obsessed with the ad. She would sit at the top of the stairs every night, unable to go to sleep because she was afraid of the "creepy, scary voice" she heard and "the screaming."

Another parent, Jonathan, a forty-one-year-old television executive who lives in New York City, told me that his five-year-old daughter, Eliza, began having "frightening nightmares" after seeing the movie *Charlie and the Chocolate Factory*. "There's a scene in the movie where squirrels devour a little girl named Veruca Salt," said Jonathan. "A couple of days after seeing the movie, Eliza woke up in tears saying, 'I dreamed about squirrels, Daddy. I dreamed that I was Veruca Salt and that there were squirrels running all over me and hurting me everywhere.'" When I asked Jonathan how this made him feel, he told me, "I felt so bad that I had brought my daughter to a G-rated film in which the characters seemed indifferent to the violent things happening around them." As Jonathan knows, even G-rated movies can be violent. Indeed, a recent study from the Harvard School of Public Health found a "ratings creep" in movies rated by the Motion Picture Association of America: today's PG-13 movies, for example, actually have the same amount of violence as R-rated movies from a decade ago.

Even when we do succeed in shielding our children from violent pop culture, its influence can often be felt through other children. Dawn, a forty-five-year-old mom who lives in a suburb of Boston, told me about five-year-old Donte, a classmate of her son, Rodney. Donte, she explained to me, is "obsessed with the movie *The Matrix*."

His parents work and his teenage sister takes care of him; she rents and watches the *Matrix* videos over and over again. Donte is wound up, like a spinning top—he's a nervous, obsessed child. . . . He clings onto Rodney and tells him all the time about *Matrix*. Rodney gets upset that Donte won't leave him alone and he gets scared by what Donte tells him.

While there are complex reasons why kids today are exposed to so much violent media, changes in family patterns over the last generation play a large role. When I was a working mom in the 1970s, 61 percent of mothers stayed home full-time. By the year 2000, in contrast, two-thirds of the children in America had working moms. Between then and now, as hundreds of thousands of American women entered the workforce during the 1980s and 1990s, no parallel government programs emerged to support two-income families. Unlike many western industrialized countries, the United States has no system of quality national childcare or after-school care. In the hours they spend without parents, many children have to fend for themselves, filling empty hours with screen activities, unmonitored by an adult. Eliza, a third-grade teacher in a low-income community in New Mexico, had the kids in her class make charts of the TV shows they watch every day. "All of the kids in my class have working parents," she told me. "They watch five to six hours of television a day, seven to eight hours on weekends." This means, of course, that the kids in Eliza's class, like so many children in homes across America, are viewing multiple incidents of violence as they sit for long hours in front of the TV.

While it's our poorest children who are watching even more TV than the average child, more affluent parents in our country now increasingly pack their children's schedules with activities and classes from after school through dinnertime. Diaries of children's daily activities reveal that American children ages twelve and younger now spend almost twice as much time in supervised, structured settings as did children two decades ago. Many kids are therefore leading exceedingly hectic lives with very little room for unstructured activities that aren't driven by an adult agenda. These planned activities often replace "downtime"—quality daily time to play, draw, act, and re-create their experiences, feelings, and fears through symbolic play that our children need to rebalance themselves emotionally and physically (as explained in the previous section), and thus support their overall sense of security.

When parents finally do get home from work, they are often exhausted and yield to the screen to occupy their children. Betty, who for many years directed a Massachusetts elementary school, recently told me, "What parents don't have is *time*. They have no time to reflect, to take care of themselves. They are under so much pressure. They need the TV to get a break, to make dinner, to entertain their kids while they get things done." Many of the parents I interviewed for this book told me that because of their overburdened work lives, not only do they need the TV to occupy their kids, they often can't take time to monitor what their kids are watching—programs that too often entail depictions of coercion and violence.

Then, too, this prevalent reliance upon media in our homes—the television that is on during mealtimes for 63 percent of American families—and in so many of our public spaces means that kids are also constantly hearing news about frightening real-life events in the world.

I was present in a classroom in Boston in 2001 when a child blurted out to the whole class, "Did you know that a boy in the first grade shot a girl in his class with a gun?" One of the parents I interviewed for this book, Lataria, a Boston bus driver and mother of five kids under the age of ten, said she and her kids were shaken by a recent news report of a bomb threat in the subway. Her daughter Alexis was supposed to go on a school field trip on the subway and began to ask, "Mommy, should I really be getting on a train after what happened? Why do people do stuff like that? What happened to the World Trade Center?" Lataria told me, "I didn't tell her [this], but I was thinking, 'Should I really let her go on a train?' The things that my kids see, it bothers them and it has them wondering. I don't want them to worry. I should be worried for them."

Such exposure to real-world violence can be particularly detrimental to kids's sense of security because kids tend to think of it in an egocentric way. I often wish I could impress this upon adults: children do not see what we see when they watch movies or TV. When adults hear news of a stabbing or a car bomb, we can think logically about the likelihood of these things happening to us. Children, in contrast, can easily imagine that these scary and dangerous events are imminently threatening to them. They can't reason about their own safety in a larger context or separate themselves completely from what they've just seen or heard. In the next chapter, we'll discuss children's development in more depth, along with how it can shape kids' perceptions of the world at different ages.

Finally, what also exacerbates the fear-invoking media images kids constantly see is their growing inability—or lack of available time—to use imaginative play to make sense of what they've just encountered. It's a vicious cycle, with the media suppressing children's creativity and then filling their heads with violent imagery that can only be interpreted sensibly through the very cognitive process—i.e., symbolic play—that it is replacing. In the chapters to come, I will suggest many everyday steps that we can take—from restricting screen time to supporting play, from "active" listening to trying better to view things through children's eyes—to bolster the basic sense of security that our kids need to flourish even in our all too violent and frightening world.

The Need for Positive Relationships

The final essential building block of healthy childhood development is positive relationships with adults and other children.

Decades ago, the Swiss psychologist Jean Piaget, in the course of outlining his theories about children's intellectual development, recognized that children need healthy, positive social relationships in order to learn and grow into competent adults. More recently, proponents of "attachment theory" have focused in particular on the bonds that form very early on between an infant and his or her primary caregiver—most often the mother. From the first moments of life, say the attachment theorists, children seek nurturing relationships with their caregivers, and the strength of these relationships significantly shapes the way each child develops. These researchers have presented evidence that infants who don't have strong attachments to their mothers, for example, explore and play less than those who do.

Based on my own research documenting the increase of violence in children's behavior since federal deregulation of children's television, I believe it has become increasingly difficult in today's media-saturated culture for kids to create positive relationships with their parents and peers. Children today spend less time interacting with others at home and at school, and much more time absorbing antisocial messages from television programs and films, which too often glorify relationships built on coercion and force rather than on empathy and love.

I recently visited a home in Boston where two young children, having just finished breakfast, stood mesmerized a foot from the TV screen. The show that so captured their attention was *Power Rangers*, which portrays, on average, more than two hundred violent acts per hour. The boys, enthralled by the constant fighting and too young to clearly distinguish the difference between pretend and real violence, were learning some powerful lessons from this show: that violence is a normal part of your life—you eat breakfast and then you watch people fight; that violence is how you settle conflicts; that the world is made up of "good guys" and "enemies"; that not only is hurting others okay—it's entertaining and fun. Children are active learners: they take what they see and they try it out for themselves. So it's no surprise that hundreds of teachers in my research have described kids reenacting with their peers the karate chops, pushing, and fighting they've seen on the screen. All too often, kids' social relations spiral downward as they repeatedly use the negative behaviors they've seen and naturally want to try out.

Indeed, research conducted over the course of four decades has overwhelmingly shown a positive relationship between watching violent entertainment and real-life aggression. In its current policy statement on media violence, the American Academy of Pediatrics states that out of 3,500 research studies examining the relationship between violence in the media and violent behavior, all but 18 have shown a strong correlation. Other professional organizations such as the American Medical Association and the American Psychological Association have issued warnings: viewing entertainment violence increases aggression and antisocial behavior and desensitizes children to violence, hardening them to the pain inflicted on others. Nonetheless, even with these powerful findings, the media culture continues to barrage children with images and models of violence on a daily basis, and their social relationships are suffering as a result of it.

Studies show that violent video games, just like violent television programs, also serve to undermine children's ability to form meaningful relationships. Yet an estimated 70 percent of children ages two to eighteen have access to video games at home, and the Kaiser Family Foundation survey found that half of all four- to six-year-olds have played them, a quarter of them regularly. Not surprisingly, many of the most popular games are violent. Julia, who is a first-grade teacher in Cambridge, Massachusetts, can tell that the six-year-old boys in her class play violent teen-oriented video games. "I find it a lot in their writing," she said. "For example, Jeremy will write, 'Michael came over my house to play and we played video games. I was Blood Master and he was Dragon Fly and I opened the dungeon and I took the sword and I killed him.'"

I was in a third-grade classroom recently when the subject of violent video games came up. The children started rattling off the names of the violent games they've played: Dynasty Warriors 5, Helioattack II, Battlefront, Conquer, Warsmuggler, 3 Foot Ninja, James Bond. Excitedly, they described the games: "When you hit someone, their arms come off—or their legs or their head!" "You slice their legs and their stomach is cut open." "The person goes splat and it's bloody." "The kid has a sword and slices other kids." Eight of these children had seen Grand Theft Auto III—a "Mature"-rated first-person shooter game where players can shoot victims up close in the face or set them on fire with gasoline and watch them scream as they burn.

Arguably, video games foster aggression in kids even more than viewing violence on television because children playing video games are actively engaged in committing the violence. And through studies done at Kansas State University using magnetic resonance imaging (MRI), scientists have shown that playing video games alters brain chemistry: the brain treats entertainment violence as something real; it senses danger and activates the "fight-or-flight" response. In addition, the brain actually stores the violence in long-term memory, which may produce lasting ill effects on children's minds—and on their ability to form lasting, meaningful relationships.

It is no accident, of course, that entertainment geared for teenagers and adults often finds an eager audience in young children; in fact, this entertainment is often marketed directly to younger kids. In September 2000, the Federal Trade Commission published a landmark report that exposed how the movie industry routinely uses countless unethical marketing practices to advertise to children under the ages considered appropriate by the industry's *own* rating system. One common strategy to bring in young children is to promote highly enticing violent toys, which are linked to movies—for teens and adults—rated PG-13 or R. The big media companies used this approach successfully with *Star Wars*, *Spider-Man*, *The Lord of the Rings*, *The Mummy*, *Tomb Raider*, *Starship Troopers*, and *X-Men*, to name just a few. I sat in a kindergarten classroom recently next to a little boy who ate a sandwich while gazing at the lurid image on his lunchbox: the character of Wolverine from *X-Men*, with his big muscles, sneering expression, and long, curving knife blades growing out of his hands.

Many of the parents I interviewed for this book say they feel discouraged by having to fight the media culture's influence on their children; they feel as if they are living in a society that is working not for, but against them and their kids. Lee, who lives in rural New Hampshire, described the violent video games, toys, and movies that pervade her eight-year-old son's peer culture. "It's too big a force for me to go against," Lee said. "Wherever Dylan goes, he has access to everything, and I can't control it. He's playing adult video games at other houses. It makes me really sad. I feel like I'm this tiny little island in a huge sea."

Sadly, it isn't only the violence absorbed through toys and media that threaten the positive relationships children need—it's also what kids are missing out on when they're glued to the screen. At my mother's eighty-fifth birthday party three years ago, I witnessed first-hand just what is lost when children become absorbed in screen time, whether violent or not. For the first time in over a year, all of my mother's children, grandchildren, and great-grandchildren gathered in one place. It was a rare opportunity for the seven great-grandchildren to play together. Two of them, boys five and seven years old, spent much of their time playing video games in front of a gigantic screen. They therefore missed out on much of the social exchange that was going on among the cousins—the playing, inventing, and collaborating that usually occur when children are given the opportunity to inter-act spontaneously with one another. They also missed the natural learning that comes automatically when peers socialize together—figuring out how to communicate effectively, adjusting to other points of view, and solving problems as a group. These are the ex-changes that help kids build the foundation they need for positive relationships.

The increased work demands on parents today add to the problem our kids already have of diminishing time spent in relationships. Re-search suggests that parents are now working longer and harder just to maintain their living standard—and spending less time with their chil-dren. Compared to the average American worker in 1969, today's earn-ers put in an additional 163 hours per year, which adds up to an entire additional month of work each year. Then, too, the number of earners has grown exponentially, with the influx of American women into the workforce during the 1980s and 1990s. Even as we spend more time on the clock, however, wages among the working and middle classes have effectively stagnated in the last twenty-five years—and this while we see an ever-expanding gap in the distribution of wealth. (The top 1 per-cent of U.S. households now have more wealth than the bottom 90 per-cent combined.) For our children, the effects of these changes in the workplace are profound: over a thirty-year period, parental time with children has declined by 13 percent, according to a study done by New York University economist Edward Wolff. This, when we know from volumes of research that quality time with parents is at the core of a healthy childhood.

Unfortunately, I have also observed that many parents today, because they are so overworked and pressed for time, end up resorting to quick-fix approaches to discipline that inadvertently reinforce the coercion model of relationships presented in television shows, video games, and movies. Paula, a fifty-one-year-old mother from Concord, New Hampshire, told me about a recent—and typical—interaction between her husband, Jeff, and their nine-year-old son, Zach. The other night, when Jeff asked Zach to clear the dishes, Zach got mad and muttered "jerk" under his breath, Paula explained. "Then Jeff says Zach can't play his *The Lord of the Rings* video game that night. Zach gets furious and starts hitting and kicking and then Jeff says Zach won't be able to go to the movies with his friend Paul on Saturday either. One day soon after that Zach said to me, 'Mom, pretty soon I'm not going to have *anything* left.'"

Jeff was employing the time-honored strategy of trying to modify Zach's behavior by taking away his privileges. But what Zach learns in this kind of situation is that parents use their power over children when there's a conflict and that there are winners and losers in every disagreement. He learns that relationships are based on coercion, which happens to be the exact same model he has probably absorbed from the entertainment media—where a sword fight, rather than a discussion, is the modus operandi for resolving interpersonal differences.

By using his power over Zach, Jeff might succeed in changing Zach's behavior for a short time. But Jeff isn't teaching Zach anything new: How does Zach learn what to do instead of talking back and kicking? What should he do the next time he gets angry? While Jeff's approach is well intentioned, it suffers from the same basic flaw as the most popular parenting approaches today: it focuses too much on punishments and rewards, threats and consequences, and not enough on helping kids learn how to build loving, respectful relationships.

At this crucial moment in time, when the best of childhood is under attack, we have the challenge of showing our kids a different and better model for how human beings can get along. As I will illustrate in examples throughout this book, we can enhance the connection we experience with our children, and help them deepen friendships with siblings and peers, by teaching our kids to handle situations of conflict in a loving mutual way, one where power is shared rather than wielded, where ending up feeling closer takes priority over winning. In the forthcoming chapters I will show you how we can foster the genuine kindness and empathy that will bring children deep satisfaction in their relationships with others, both now and for the rest of their lives.

Strategies for Taking Back Childhood

Given that these basic needs of our children are in danger, I deeply believe that we, as concerned parents, grandparents, aunts, uncles, and educators can no longer wait for our society as a whole to become more supportive of children. Yes, we need public policies that protect kids from coercive media and marketing, including restrictions on advertising to young children and prohibitions on marketing violence to children. Yes, we need affordable national day care and after-school programs, active classroom learning approaches tailored to children's individual interests and talents, and conflict resolution programs. But while we work toward these policy changes, we can also take a more active approach as parents and caregivers. As the adults who still wage the most important influence in our children's lives, we have within our hands—right here, right now—the ability to restore the critical experiences and tools that society has slowly but too surely taken away from our kids.

As I have underscored above, to protect our children from the seemingly inescapable forces that threaten their most basic needs, I find great solace—and hope—in the literature of child development, which provides us with a deep understanding of how children grow, how they think and feel, and what their psychological and developmental needs are. This knowledge, combined with love and caring, can give us the power we need to encourage and restore children's healthy play; to strengthen kids' sense of security so they can thrive in today's often frightening world; and to teach children to create meaningful loving relationships that will help them grow and bring them deep satisfaction.

As I have stressed, one of the key insights childhood development theory provides is consideration for the child's perspective. Throughout this book, I will encourage you to try to put yourself "inside the heads" of even the youngest children in your care. And as you do this, I hope you will begin to see how it can open up new possibilities for parenting and allow you to better meet your children's needs. Let's look now at two examples that begin to show how we can guide children more effectively when we see things from their eyes.

We had a family gathering recently, and Kevin, my husband's nephew, and his wife, Sarah, came over with their two-year-old son, Will. Will spent much of the day playing with a small basketball hoop and sponge ball game, growing so attached to it that he started carrying the game around the house.

When it came time to leave, Sarah said, "It's time to go, Will," and she reached for the hoop and ball from Will's hands. This prompted a loud cry as Will clutched his prized possession. His shrieks pierced the air, as Will's parents tried to extract the ball from his fingers and get him out the door. Will was distraught, and Kevin and Sarah agreed to let me try to help. I handed the ball to Will and said, "You can carry this ball to your car, Will. Let's take it there." Will took the ball, and we immediately headed for the car and got him into his car seat. Once he was settled there, still clutching the ball, I said, "Now the ball goes back into the house with me, that's where the ball stays, and you can take your bird back to your house." (Will had arrived that morning with a little stuffed cardinal in his hand.) Will and I then calmly exchanged bird for ball, and he seemed settled and content.

Let's look at this situation from Will's perspective. It's very difficult for kids his age to transition from one place to another. At barely two years old, Will lives completely in the here and now, never thinking about the future. He doesn't understand the words "We have to go" in the same way you and I do. He can't picture getting into the car or being back at his own house playing. What has meaning for him is where he is *right here, right now*. From Will's point of view, then, the fun he was having and the objects he'd attached himself to were being abruptly taken from him. While it's very hard for a two-year-old who is playing in one location to envision going to another place—like getting into the car and going home—it's much easier to focus on the tangible ball and the task of carrying it to the car.

Using transition objects is just one example of how we can help children feel more secure by seeing things from their eyes and helping them make sense of their experience. Another important strategy that grows out of child development literature—and a crucial one for helping kids build positive relationships—is to help children understand how their actions affect others. Not long ago, for example, I was helping Byron, a kindergarten teacher in an urban public school. His student Maya, five years old and often aggressive toward other kids, came in one day with a brewing, tangled look on her face (Maya's home life was a hard one). She headed for the attendance sheet to sign in, pencil in hand, but suddenly turned and poked her classmate Anthony in the stomach with the eraser end of the pencil. I quickly took the pencil from Maya, but I didn't want to scold her; I wanted, instead, to help her learn—in a way that would make sense to her—how her actions had affected Anthony. I said, "Look, Maya!" as I poked the pencil into my own stomach, made a grimace, and said, "Ooooo! That hurts!" Then I explained, "It hurts when you poke someone with a pencil in the stomach." She looked at me for a long, serious moment, then resumed writing.

Later that morning Maya drew a picture all on her own, dictating to the classroom aide, "I poked Anthony in the stomach with the pencil. Then I felt bad." Byron was thrilled to see this expression of concern from a girl who had so often been aggressive toward other kids, seemingly unable to feel any empathy for them when they were hurt.

Again, it was an understanding of child development theory that helped me respond to Maya. A five-year-old, especially an upset and hurt five-year-old, can strike out at another child without ever thinking about how her actions will affect the other child. It is difficult for children Maya's age to "feel" what another child feels.

If I had said, "No, Maya, it's wrong to poke someone, you can't do that," or if I had put Maya in "time-out," it would not have helped her realize how she'd hurt Anthony. What did help was to *show* her the effects of her actions in a concrete way that she could understand. And this encouraged empathy in Maya, and gave her a new link to building better relationships with her classmates. At the core of the approach I'm describing is the creation of a secure space in which children can build meaningful relationships with their parents and peers.

Using many more clear, instructive examples like Will and Maya, the following chapters will focus on what we can do to reclaim childhood and ensure our children's capacity for learning, growth, and love.

CHAPTER 2

Through Their Eyes

Child Development Theory in a Nutshell

C hildren see the world differently from how adults do. Getting a child's-eye view—looking at things through children's eyes and understanding their needs—is critical if we are to help them thrive in today's society. There is no "one size fits all" children's perspective, of course—as discussed in chapter 1, each child possesses a unique personality, temperament, learning style, and family and cultural background. And while all kids go through the same general developmental stages, they do so at different rates—one child might linger in a stage for a year or two longer, another might move along more quickly; often kids straddle two stages for a long time. Still, if we familiarize ourselves with the basic developmental stages from birth to age ten, we can gain tremendous insight into how our children make sense of the world, and this will enable us to help them rediscover play, feel more secure, and form close, loving relationships with family and friends.

A child's age—and therefore his or her specific cognitive and social tools for understanding things—affects how that child perceives various relationships and events. Yet a 2001 landmark survey sponsored by Zero to Three, a national organization dedicated to advancing research and knowledge about infants and toddlers, found that the majority of parents and adults have a surprising lack of accurate child development information and that this may significantly impede their ability to meet their kids' needs. Getting a basic understanding of the sequences of growth and change in the first decade of life, then, is the first step we need to take if we want to provide healthier childhood experiences for our kids.

Sensory-Motor Learning: From Birth to Two Years

Let's start by looking at how our youngest children begin to perceive the world by listening to Larry, whose fourteen-month-old son, Oscar, is repeatedly turning the TV on and off. Larry explains, "We tell Oscar not to touch the TV, but he keeps on doing it. I ask him nicely not to touch it but he just goes up to the TV and starts pushing the on-off button in and out—and he gives me that look like he's trying to 'get' me. So I have to go over and take him away from the TV—and it makes me mad. I say, 'Find something else to do.' Then he pitches a fit and gets upset."

Just as so many parents do, Larry is interpreting his son's behavior from his own vantage point and ascribing motivations to Oscar that he is too young to have. A child of fourteen months is not capable of trying to "get" his parents—at this stage, Oscar isn't able to do an action solely in order to provoke a reaction from his parents, nor is he interested in doing so. What he wants and needs to do is to touch and manipulate things—he is busy using his body and senses to collect information about the world around him and he is literally building his intelligence as he does this. Oscar is immersed in the physical action of the button on the TV; he wants to practice this action over and over again because this is how he learns how things work on the plane of physical action. As he does this, neurons are strengthening and connecting in his brain. All of the sensory-motor connections Oscar makes by manipulating the objects in his world will lay the foundation for the mental concepts he'll learn later. Throughout the childhood years, new ideas will build gradually on earlier ones in a long, slow developmental process.

If he could see the world from his son's perspective, Larry might understand that Oscar's curiosity—the need to explore the world through his body and senses—is a natural and important part of his development. At this stage, Oscar focuses on one thing at a time, and right now he's fixated on the TV. Larry could encourage Oscar to change his focus by giving him a concrete alternative that also has knobs and push buttons to explore, like an old flashlight or telephone. This would transform a situation of confrontation into one that allows Larry to support his son's passion to explore—which in turn would strengthen the feeling of trust between parent and child that is crucial at this stage of development.

The Inner World of Two-Year-Olds

As Oscar and all young children get closer to the age of two, a profound shift, one they've been working toward for many months, takes place in them. Instead of "thinking" via their actions, children begin to be able to think about things in their minds: that is, they become able to "think" about swinging on a swing instead of actually swinging, or to "picture" a horse even if they don't see it. This new ability to think in symbols means kids can learn to talk, engage in pretend play, and use their imaginations—it literally opens up a whole new world to them! Whereas before, if a ball was out of sight it was out of mind, now kids can fully understand that when things are no longer in view they still exist. This means that when Daddy leaves the room, the child now realizes Daddy has not ceased to exist, but has just gone somewhere else. It is this new insight that fuels the favorite game of kids starting at around eighteen months, peekaboo—you hide but you're still there—and leads many twos to start methodically putting things away. And it is this insight that nudges kids to separate a bit more from their parents and fuels the strong need to express and explore their autonomy.

It is delightful to watch two-year-olds as they use their newfound ability in pretend play. Now they are able to use one thing, say a wooden block, to represent something else, maybe a telephone. Last summer I watched two-and-a-half-year-old Dana playing when her family visited my son Kyle's family. Dana had just been to the beach and when I saw her she was walking around the house carrying a plastic lunchbox. "I have a crab in here," she said to me. I asked if I could see the crab, and when Dana opened the lunchbox there was a small flower inside. Dana was using her amazing human capacity to represent one thing with another as she pretended the flower was a crab. Later Dana got onto a small kitchen stool and "dove" off (gently) onto the kitchen floor. Then she "swam," belly-down, on the floor for some time, pretending she was in water instead of on a hard linoleum surface.

Children Dana's age have discovered an amazing capacity—for creative pretend play—that can be an important source of health and healing for them throughout their childhood years. Initially, pretend scenarios are quite simple, as children are just beginning to master the basic elements of this kind of play. And two-year-olds mostly play by themselves or side by side. But cooperative play with other children—which many experts link to the development of vital social skills—is just around the corner.

Meanwhile, the realization that all things have a kind of permanence leads two-year-olds to feel more separate from their parents, and it's behind the need twos have to express their autonomy. This new expression of independence can easily lead to power struggles between parents and children at this stage. Michael, father of two-year-old Casey, tells me that his son insists on doing everything for himself. "I can't put his shoes on or peel a banana for him without him saying, 'No. *I* do it!' One day he wouldn't let me put his shoes on and we were late. I got really impatient. I forced his shoes onto his feet and he started crying. Then it was a real scene getting out the door—I felt so bad later."

It can be a challenge trying to support a healthy sense of autonomy in two-year-olds without letting them do everything they want, but we can support the need for independence in our twos while staying in charge in a way that supports their sense of security. In this situation, Michael could say to Casey, "I'll put your shoes on and you can snap them shut—show me how you can snap them closed!" When we work *with* the need for autonomy in our two-year-olds, we're helping them feel both capable and secure.

At the same time, the new cognitive advances that two-year-olds are gaining can sometimes leave them feeling insecure. They've recently discovered that they are not the center of the universe as they had previously thought. In fact, everything has a permanent existence, including their parents, who they now understand leave them and go somewhere out of their sight. Many parents of twos have told me about separation anxieties that suddenly appeared in their children, which I understand in terms of an awareness of their own separateness that crystallizes at this stage. Jane, for instance, told me how her two-year-old daughter, Lola, who had been going to day care since she was a year old, suddenly began to cry and grab on to Jane when she was dropping her off. "I don't get it," Jane said. "She's gone to the same day care for a year. Why is this happening now?" Most likely, Lola had begun to realize that Jane was truly leaving her.

I suggested to Jane that she make a book for Lola with stick figures or photos that would tell the story of their separation page by page:

first a picture of them at home, then riding to day care, then a picture of Lola at day care doing something she loves, and one of Jane at her work, then Jane coming to pick up Lola, and finally a picture of them back home and very happy to be together again. Jane made the book, writing simple words for each picture, and read it to Lola. She said that Lola loved the book and asked to read it over and over again. Jane said that she and Lola read the book every night, that Lola often looked at it by herself, and that Lola's separation anxiety began to fade away. The book gave Lola a tangible handle on the heightened separation feelings she was having at this time of developmental change and helped her regain her sense of security.

Many people label two-year-olds as difficult. But I have long thought that the description "terrible twos" is unfair. At this stage, kids are immersed in one of the biggest transformations we humans go through—moving from pure action to symbolic thought and from thinking they are the center of the world to realizing they are not. If we can remember this, and work with the behaviors that manifest as a result of this enormous change, we can support our kids through this stage of life and strengthen the trust we share with them.

A Prelogical View of the World: Three- to Six-Year-Olds

Children who are three, four, and five years old are bursting with energy to explore the world through movement and action and hands-on investigation. Now they can use symbols to talk with us, to draw, to build and create. They can carry on conversations with us about many things, which makes it easy for us, at times, to forget that they still see the world very differently from how we do.

When my younger son, Matt, was three years old he flew off a jungle gym at the park, while wearing his favorite red towel around his neck, and broke his left foot. After retrieving Matt from his caretaker and on our way to the hospital, I was comforting him but feeling very shaky myself as a young single mom in this situation. I asked Matt if he had thought he could fly when he jumped off that jungle gym. He nodded his head and answered, "Yes."

This incident still leaves me feeling disquieted, but it shows us how a three-year-old wearing a cape can believe he has the powers of a superhero because he doesn't separate fantasy from reality into neat compartments as adults do. He doesn't think logically about cause and effect, so he doesn't know that the towel/cape billowing behind him won't keep him afloat in the air.

The Swiss psychologist Jean Piaget helped us to understand this kind of prelogical thinking in young children. He observed that children in the three- to six-year-old age group can believe that they caused the thunder or that they can put out a real fire with a pretend hose. Piaget also showed us that young children are concrete thinkers: they base their ideas on what they can see and don't look beneath the surface. A four-year-old, for example, can think there are more pennies on the table if they are spread out in a line and fewer if the same number is scrunched up into a pile because the line *looks* like more. I remember when Megan, a student teacher of mine, dressed up one Halloween as a witch and the kindergartners in the class could not be convinced that it was really her underneath the hat and cloak. Even as Megan, with her green face and witch hat, said to them, "It's me—Megan!" many of the children were convinced that there was a witch present in the classroom that day.

This tendency to base their reasoning on what they can see means that kids this age don't think much about underlying logic or motives or feelings—things that we adults understand lie beneath the surface. I laughed about this one night when my grandsons Jackson, then five, and Miles, then three, were playing under the table while we were all having a long family dinner. Suddenly they started fighting. I saw Miles haul off and swing at Jack and then Jack immediately retaliate. Their mom, Lori, came in from the kitchen asking, "What's going on here?" Jack said, "Miles hit me!" I said, "Well, actually you were hitting each other." And Jack said, "Yeah, but I *missed!*" To him, the attempt to hit his brother, the *intention* to do it, didn't count because he hadn't managed to connect.

As Piaget showed, prelogical thinking leads young kids to develop many unique theories about how the world works. I think of Charlie, a four-year-old boy whose teacher, Kathy, was in my child development class at Lesley University in Cambridge, Massachusetts, several years ago. Kathy told me that one day Charlie was eating crackers at the snack table when she went over to sit with him, at which point she realized that she had never seen Charlie drinking milk from one of the small cartons provided. So she asked him, "I know you like to eat the crackers at school, Charlie, but why don't I ever see you drink the milk?" "Because if I drink the milk," he answered, "the fire alarm will go off."

Kathy realized then that the fire alarm had indeed gone off on the very first day of school that year, much to the surprise of the teachers. Charlie, she realized, had been at the snack table just starting to sip his milk when the alarm sounded. And so, for the rest of the school year, Charlie believed that the alarm would sound again if he drank milk.

Kathy knew she had to set Charlie straight. She took him over to the light switch on the wall in the empty room next door. Kathy turned on the switch and said, "This switch turns on the light—see?" She let Charlie turn it on and off, too. "There's a switch like this in the big office," Kathy said, "and it turns on the fire alarm. That's the only way the fire alarm can turn on. It won't turn on if you drink milk." Kathy knew she couldn't explain how electricity works to Charlie, but she found some concrete words and actions—things closer to his way of viewing the world—that could help clear up his confusion.

It's common for children this age to develop theories like Charlie's, and we adults don't always know about them. When the story about Charlie was told in the child development class I was leading, another student shared her childhood "theory" about why her parents had split up. Carmen told us that she had fought with her sister the night her dad had walked out of the house and that all of her life she had believed that it was her behavior that had caused him to leave. This was a belief, Carmen said, that she had held inside since childhood, never saying it out loud until that night.

In many of these stories, we can see what Piaget described as the "egocentrism" of young children. As he explained, young children usually interpret the world from their own point of view: the world revolves around them—thus Charlie thought that he set off the fire alarm and Carmen thought she caused her parents' divorce. As Piaget described, children this age tend to think of one idea at a time and often they think that everyone thinks or sees the same things they do, as when Henry, my friend's three-year-old, for example, recently tried to "show" me his new sneakers on the phone.

This difference between how children interpret the world and how we do extends to language as well. Because we share the same vocabulary, we often think that kids mean what we mean by the words they use. I remember when I was setting the table for a lunch at my sister's house with a four-year-old girl, Amy, who was visiting. My sister told us to set four places, and Amy got busy with the job, but when I looked, there were five plates on the table. I counted the plates and said, "Oh, there are five plates here." In response, Amy said, "Oh, well, four is five to me." Amy was actually *telling* me that as far as she was concerned, "four" and "five" meant the same thing. Thinking about language reminds me of another situation, in a classroom of four-year-olds in the school where I taught kindergarten, when the class guinea pig, Timmy, died. The teachers and kids had a "memorial service" for Timmy and buried him on the school grounds on a Friday. When the kids came to school on Monday, several said they wanted to dig up Timmy so they could play with him again. For these four-year-olds, the word "die" had a very different meaning than it did to their teachers. It is very helpful, then, if we can remember that children, especially younger ones, don't always mean what we mean by the words they use; doing so will help us see them more clearly and expand our ability to understand them and meet their needs.

The social relations of children who are three to six years of age are often lively and dynamic. Now in the early stages of cooperative play, children this age often love to play together, and they usually play best when their interests coincide—that is, when they like to do or play the same things. I remember two five-year-old boys in my kindergarten classroom, Malcolm and Donald, who adored building with blocks together. Every day when they came to school, they couldn't wait to start building. Sometimes they made two buildings side by side, chatting about what they were doing as they went along; other times they built something together, each adding blocks and ex- citedly describing a new door for the barn or a window to look through. Malcolm and Donald rarely disagreed—their love of blocks matched up and they could "cobuild" in synchrony.

Piaget wrote that true "co-operation"—being able to really work with each other's wants and ideas—develops very gradually over many years' time in children. But kids who are three to six years old, like Malcolm and Donald, are enjoying the first stages of cooperative play. Difficulties can arise at this age, however, if interests conflict— if children have different ideas about what they want to do. When this happens, egocentrism can make it hard for kids to understand each other's ideas. If Malcolm had wanted to make an "apartment building" and Donald was trying to make a "farm," for example, they might've run into trouble. When kids' ideas do conflict at this stage of development, they can get easily stuck in a conflict and not be able to see a way out without help from adults.

Egocentrism isn't something we can change in children, but with many years' time and lots of social experiences that help children's view of the world to broaden, it does slowly melt away. As Piaget theorized, and I believe, it's when children play together and come up against ideas that are different from their own that they gradually come to think and feel beyond themselves. We adults can contribute greatly to this process, because children's ideas change when we present them with new ideas that relate to what they already know. When Henry called me on the phone to "show" me his new sneakers, for example, I asked him, "Can you see me, Henry?" And he answered, "No." And I said, "I can't see you either. But I can hear your voice. Can you tell me about your new sneakers?" Here I helped Henry understand my point of view—that I couldn't see him or his shoes—by starting with his perspective.

Learning more about the uniqueness of three- to six-year-olds allows us to put our own ideas aside and listen more carefully to theirs. As we know more about them, we'll find ourselves appreciating the delightful ways children this age see the world. We can understand that kids this age may hold prelogical notions about how things happen, and we can clear up confusions when we see them. We can know that children in this age group are often egocentric, and we can encourage them very gradually to see other viewpoints by building new ideas onto how they already see things.

A Shift Begins: Six- and Seven-Year-Olds

Another major developmental shift begins to occur as kids get closer to the ages of six and seven. According to Piaget and other child development theorists, very gradually children this age begin to think in more logical and complex ways and realize that there's a lot that goes on beneath the surface of what they see. They begin to realize that there's a constancy to many things; for example, the number of pennies laid out on the table doesn't change just because the coins are arranged differently—it's still fifteen pennies whether they're in a pile or stretched out in a line. They come to understand that Superman can't really fly and that he's really an actor playing a role. Very gradually they begin to understand rules and they start to like to follow rules in games. They begin to cooperate more with friends and sometimes understand that other people have their own ideas that may differ from theirs. They also begin to understand intentions and feelings in relationships—that someone might mean to hurt you, or that someone can feel bad inside even if his or her face doesn't show it.

When I talked to seven-year-old Shabon in a public school in Boston, she demonstrated a lot of these budding cognitive skills as she told me how she got her brother to let her watch the TV show she wanted to see.

"My brother is three years old," she said. "He wanted to watch *Barney* on TV one day and I wanted to watch my favorite show. So I made up a game. I drew a line on the floor and you had to jump over it. I told my brother, 'If you can jump over the line, then you get to watch your show.'" Then Shabon leaned toward me to whisper, "My brother is three. He can only jump up and down. So we both jumped and I got over the line but my brother didn't. He was standing on the wrong side. Then he started crying."

In creating a game based on the logic of cause and effect and in being able to hold on to several ideas at once (that her brother has limited jumping capacity, that his failure will allow her to watch her TV show), Shabon demonstrates the sophisticated mental process that begins to emerge in children her age.

The cognitive changes that occur at ages six and seven take a long time to develop and stabilize. Children will show new abilities, but not consistently or in all situations. I saw this with my grandson Miles, at age six, when we played a simplified version of Monopoly. With his budding cognitive abilities, Miles could manage many parts of the game—he could sort his money, roll the dice, and then count the number of spaces to move on the board, and he could take turns. But at the same time, Miles couldn't quite grasp the whole set of rules that govern this complicated game—that there is one "bank," for example, and at the start of the game, we all get the same amount of money from the bank. At one point when we were playing the game, I looked over at Miles and realized that he had a big pack of additional money in his hand. He began handing this money out to all of the players with a slightly confused look on his face. I asked him, "Miles, did you take some money from the bank?" Miles nodded yes, showing no need to conceal this fact. I said, "Well, you took some extra money and thanks for sharing it with us." Miles's older brother, Jack, whispered to me, "You have to watch him, he's sneaky," but I was glad he didn't accuse Miles of cheating. In order to cheat, Miles would have had to understand the rules of the game much better than he did and intentionally bypass them for his own gain, and this was not what he had done.

In social relations, too, children are making some important advances at the ages of six and seven. As they begin to use their new logic and greater awareness of feelings, they start to understand new ways to have effects on other people. In the second-graders I studied in two public schools in urban Boston in 1991, for example, I noticed that these seven-year-olds had discovered the power of put-downs—yet, while they seemed to enjoy saying things to each other to get a reaction, they weren't yet fully grasping how their mean words might feel to the listener. When seven-year-old Danisha told me about her friend Kimberly, I could see that Kim was experimenting with getting a reaction from

Danisha. "I go over to Kimberly's house," Danisha said, "and she plays with me and then she gets smart with me and she starts arguing with me and stuff and afterwards I start crying. And she says, 'I just wanted to do that to see what you would do if we got into an argument.'"

I would assume that Kimberly's new social and cognitive abilities— such as an awareness of cause and effect and interest in motives and feelings—are behind these social interactions with her friend Danisha. But I would also say that Kim needs help in seeing how her behaviors might cause hurt. Ideally, in this kind of situation, the adults in Kim's life could use her new understanding to encourage Kim to consider how her behavior affects Danisha, and Danisha's parents could use *her* new understanding to encourage their daughter to let Kimberly know when she feels hurt.

Understanding more about this transitional period of six- and seven-year-olds can help us adults be more aware of how our children feel and what they need. We can be careful observers of our children at this age, appreciating the new connections we see them making. We can understand that children at six and seven years old may think more logically in one moment and more like their younger selves in another. And we can use our children's budding understanding of causality and underlying motives and feelings to help them make new and important connections, especially in the social arena. Doing this will support them as they play, help them consolidate a stronger sense of inner security, and encourage them to build more positive relationships with us and with their peers.

The World Opens Up: Eight- to Ten-Year-Olds

As children enter the years from eight to ten, the cognitive changes that have been developing at ages six and seven settle down and take firm hold. They are less egocentric now than they were as younger children, and better able to understand other people's points of view. While they can hang on to their own viewpoint or a single idea tenaciously at this stage, kids can think more logically now; often they can juggle many ideas at once, and integrate ideas into a larger, interrelated whole. They are noticing more abstract ideas—issues, feelings, motives, and reactions that exist beneath the surface. These new cognitive skills lead to a burst in their creativity.

Children this age are incredibly engaged in the world and eager to put their burgeoning skills to use. This is a time of industry, of active doing in the real world. Kids want to write, draw, organize, collect, make up skits, examine real problems, play actively, and follow the rules in games and sports. The psychologist Erik Erikson emphasized that this stage in life is a decisive time for mastering skills and feeling competent, stressing that children at this stage are especially vulnerable to feelings of inferiority and inadequacy.

I began noticing how this developmental change had taken hold in my grandson Jackson soon after he turned eight. He was much more interested in planning and organizing things than he had ever been before. All of a sudden he was collecting and counting money, recording where he got it, and planning what he would do with it. He started loving games with rules—board games and card games—and sticking to the rules doggedly, unlike his earlier days, when he bent them freely. He also seemed much more aware of my feelings. Instead of saying, "I want to go play with Sophia," as he had said at times when he was younger, he would now say, "I want to go play with Sophia but I don't want to hurt your feelings"—showing an awareness of my needs as well as his own. When I stayed with him during the summer that he was nine, he wanted to "plan the schedule" every day—he'd list out each activity for the day, starting with breakfast. And he wanted to "clock" his bike riding—making and breaking records for speed.

To a large extent, these changes in Jackson were the result of his new cognitive abilities—increased dynamic thinking, a deeper understanding of logic, increased attention to the viewpoints of others—that develop in all kids as they get to be eight, nine, and ten years old. These cognitive changes can look different in different children, depending on their culture group, gender, and unique personality and interests. While Jackson might be clocking his bike riding, a child in Guatemala could be making accurate change from selling wares in the marketplace. In preliterate societies, children this age were learning to hunt, farm, and make utensils. And still, in many parts of the world, the capacity to do these tasks at this stage of life enables children to make a positive contribution to the economic well-being of their families.

At ages eight to ten, the social dynamics between children become more complex. They begin to understand psychological dynamics even more deeply, as I saw with Parker, a nine-year-old girl in a Boston public school, who told me how she "psyches" her younger sister into giving her a Barbie doll. "If I want to get the doll from my sister," Parker said, "I psych her—I trick her. I say, 'I'll give you ten dollars if you let me have it,' and when she lets go, I run with it."

My eight-year-old granddaughter Alexia shows delight in psychological manipulation as she "deceives" us when we play her favorite card game, La Casa Robada. Alexia can make her face look like stone as she fools her opponents into thinking she doesn't have any winning cards. And Alexia and her cousin Jackson have both recently come to understand the underlying plots in books and movies in a way they didn't at an earlier age. For example, we watched the 1998 movie *Parent Trap* on video, and Jack elaborated later on the plot. "The twin girls didn't like their father's girlfriend," he explained, "and they wanted to get rid of her, so they tricked her into going on a camping trip and did things to make her look bad." This understanding of motive and psychological trickery is a new accomplishment, one that is common among children Jackson's age.

The advances in social development described above can easily take a negative turn in children this age and lead to bullying, as children experiment with the seductive power they can have over others. Our family learned about bullying firsthand when my son Kyle was ten years old and in the fourth grade. A group of girls in his classroom, caught up in the allure of power dynamics, began to taunt and exclude him, calling him names and sneering behind his back. The more they saw him react, the more they did it. For Kyle it was a horrid school year—one that brought on insomnia and school phobia. I tried to work with the school but with little success, and the whole terrible situation went on far too long. Today, thankfully, educators know much more about bullying and a number of outstanding antibullying programs are available for implementation in schools. (Because bullying has been on the rise nationwide in recent years and is showing up among younger children—brought on by the societal trends described in this book, I believe—it is essential that schools today have antibullying programs in place, and parents can be a persuasive force in making sure their local school has such a program.)

As the egocentrism of earlier years wanes, children in the eight- to ten-year-old age group often become more interested in the wider world. They begin to think about people, places, and issues that are beyond their own immediate lives, like ten-year-old Jenelle, a fourth-grader at a school in Cambridge, Massachusetts, who said to me, "Some baseball players get fifty million dollars to play baseball—and the only thing I think is worth all that money is world peace. Because there are lots of other people who are getting killed in war or don't have enough money to get what they need. I think people in America could be saving money for them and helping them, and lots of other countries could be helping them, too. If we were suffering or hungry, then we would want people to help us, so we should help other countries."

At ten years old, Jenelle is seeing a bigger world. In one decade of her life, she has moved from the complete egocentrism of infancy to caring about people who are in need in the world and putting herself in their shoes. This is a remarkable journey in a very short time! While almost all children Jenelle's age are capable of thinking of others as she does, not all of them do. One of the most hopeful insights we have from child development research is that children *learn* to be loving and to care about others. And it is the adults in kids' lives who have the power to instill loving kindness and empathy in children, even in these challenging times. (We'll discuss this in detail in chapter 8.)

Children in the age group eight to ten are energetically applying their new cognitive, physical, and social skills to everything they encounter. They are actively engaged in the world of doing as they exercise these new skills. Their thinking, still different from that of adults, is closer to ours now. While they are still bound to their own points of view and rooted in concrete activities and tasks, they can have dialogues with us and negotiate with us more easily than before. We adults can support children at this stage of development in several ways. We can listen carefully as they tell us what matters to them. My nephew Steven, for example, at age ten, loved to tell me tiny details about his own unique "Beanie Baby" collection—a pile of minute eggs he'd collected, each with an elaborate identity that he'd created. We can support kids as much as possible as their interests and activities expand. We can take the time to notice the accomplishments of this stage of life and remember that the need to feel competent is central now. And finally, by how we interact with them, we can help children build on the social skills we've been fostering all along. At this stage especially, when the need to feel competent is at its height, doing this will build in our kids a sense of themselves as socially competent. If we can support our children in these ways, we will help them feel more secure and create stronger relationships with family and friends at this critical time in their development.

Using the Developmental Lens as a Guide

When parents ask me questions about how to handle many of the issues they face today, I reach for child development ideas to help me answer. Here are three questions parents have asked me recently that show you how a child development lens can be used to help make decisions in the often troubling societal climate we live in today.

The first question came from a dad who attended one of my workshops on the media and how they are currently impacting childhood. He asked about the popular videos for infants called *Brainy Baby*. This dad said, "I don't let my ten-month-old baby watch TV, but I do put on *Brainy Baby* videos for her to watch. I've been told that they're very educational, but what do you think of them?"

As I thought about how to answer this dad, I reached for my child development lens to guide me. I said to him, "Let's think about what babies need for optimal development. First of all, they are sensory-motor learners," I reminded him. "They need to actively explore the environment as much as possible because they learn through hands-on, active exploration in the three-dimensional world of objects and people. They need to hold objects, roll them in their hands and on the floor, turn them over, look at them from different angles, shake them, and invent myriad other ways to explore them. As babies explore their environment firsthand, physically, they are building the crucial foundation for learning all concepts; as they explore and manipulate objects, new synaptic connections are made in their brains.

"I do know that *Brainy Baby* promotes its videos as educational for babies, describing its DVDs, for example, as helping 'stimulate cognitive development' and giving kids a 'learning advantage.' But there's no research evidence showing that screen media of any kind is beneficial for children under the age of two. In fact, the American Academy of Pediatrics advises no screen time for children under that age and research is showing that watching DVDs and videos delays language development. There has even been a complaint filed with the Federal Trade Commission against *Brainy Baby* (and *Baby Einstein*), accusing these companies of false and deceptive advertising.

"We do have decades of research in child development that tells us clearly that babies need active exploration in the real world," I told this dad in conclusion. "Given this, and the fact that there is no research showing that screen time is of value for babies but in fact may be detrimental, I think it would be unwise to put your daughter in front of a screen—no matter what's on it—before she's two years old."

Another question came from Yvonne, who is a friend and the mother of Rowan, a two-and-a-half-year-old boy. Rowan goes to day care, and recently he has been pretend shooting at his mom. Yvonne said, "Rowan has recently started pointing his finger at me like a gun and saying, 'I'm going to kill you.' I tell him, 'Rowan, we don't say that word in this house.' I don't want him learning that it's okay to *kill* anything. But what do you think I should do?"

"Let's look at this issue from Rowan's point of view," I said to Yvonne. "At two years of age, he has no idea what the words 'I'm going to kill you' mean. In order to understand the idea of killing and death, he would have to grasp the concepts of time and permanency, and these are concepts he will begin to understand four or five years from now. Rowan has likely seen someone shoot their finger or a toy gun and say, 'I'm going to kill you,' and he's doing what all kids do— he's trying out what he's seen and heard. He doesn't know that these words register so strongly and negatively with you."

As we continued talking, I told Yvonne that it seems that the natural interest in gunplay that young children have shown for generations has been showing up in children at younger ages because of the influence of media in kids' lives today. Many kids see screen images of violence and bring them into play with other kids as they try to make sense of them.

One place to start with Rowan, I offered, when he says, "I'm going to kill you," is to ask "What is that?" or "What does that mean?" This can give a parent a better idea of what a child who's repeating such a scenario thinks he or she is doing and saying. As time goes on, and the child tries out more actions and words that relate to our violent world, we can keep on trying to understand what sense he or she is making of these words and actions and encourage them in more nonviolent directions. When my grandsons pretend shoot at monsters, for example, I sometimes say, "That monster must be scared. It's saying, 'Please don't hurt me. I want to go home and see my family,'" as I attempt to humanize the "enemy" they have created in their play.

I told Yvonne that in a world like ours, where kids are exposed to so many negative outside influences, they need our help in sorting it all out. "Children build their own ideas about the world slowly over time," I told her. "If we flat-out ban certain words or actions, they won't get the help from us that they need to make sense of the world they're living in."

A third parent asked me another question recently after I gave a talk on contemporary childhood at a school in a suburb of Boston. This time it was a father who asked me a question about organized baseball for his six-year-old daughter. I had been talking about the loss of spontaneous play in childhood and the upsurge in planned activities for kids today. This dad said, "They start kids playing Little League at age six in my town. There are teams and coaches and organized games. My daughter wants to do it, but I don't know. What do you think?"

Again, it was child development theory that led the way to an answer. First I talked about six-year-olds in general, about how they are just beginning to follow rules but that they don't do this consistently. Then I talked about the importance of spontaneous play for children this age and asked this dad to picture a baseball game of six-year-olds without an adult present. The children would take turns batting, running, catching, and throwing the ball. They would not keep score in any consistent way. Children could be "playing by different rules" but not even noticing that fact, and they would be having fun making up their own rules and changing them. All of this would foster their cognitive and social skills. If the kids took a break to fool around or get a snack and then came back for more baseball, they probably wouldn't remember or care whose turn it was or how many points anyone had.

I asked the dad to contrast this with the baseball games for six-year-olds administered by adults. These situations are highly regulated as adults impose and maintain a "grown-up" regimen of rules on the game. The adults decide which children are playing and what position each plays; many kids are inactive for long periods as they await their turn to go onto the field or stand at bat. The adults continually shout directions at the kids: "Run to second!" "Throw it to Jason!" "Stay there!" The adults keep score throughout. In such games, many of the children look confused as they try to follow adult orders. They are confused because having to understand and implement the inflexible and complex rules of baseball as adults play it is not something most six-year-olds can do. While children at six years of age would not naturally focus on winning or competition, in these games they end up focusing on who "won." And, I would maintain, when they lose control over the "rules of the game" and the play itself, children's sense of autonomy and competence are seriously undermined.

I said to this dad that if his daughter wanted to play baseball at age six, maybe he could help her find ways to do it that would fit better with her developmental level and needs. I pointed out that from a developmental point of view, organized baseball and organized sports in general are better suited to children in the age group eight to ten and older.

These three examples show how it is possible to use a *child development lens* to look at many of the issues that we and our children face in these times. This lens can provide a better focus on many of the questions we grapple with today, and help us see what steps to take, often in the face of potentially threatening societal trends, that will be in our children's best interests.

STEPS YOU CAN TAKE

▶ Take the time to observe your child and think about how he or she sees things.

▶ When you observe children or play or talk with them, try to suspend your own viewpoint, expectations, and desires and tune in to what their goals and needs are, keeping in mind that these will be influenced by where in the sequence of development they happen to be.

▶ When kids seem troubled or confused, try to clarify the situation based on how they see things and using terms they can understand— that is, words and ideas that are familiar to them, concrete and tangible, and fit in with their developmental level and how they see the world.

▶ Remember that the words kids use often don't mean to them what they mean to adults—that words can mean different things to them and that these meanings may well change over time.

▶ Help children see other viewpoints and learn new ideas by connecting new information to what they already know. When you want to explain a new idea or a different perspective to a child, try to put yourself into the child's way of thinking and connect the idea to what the child already understands.

▶ Finally, when you're grappling with the many decisions that face parents today, especially those that relate to potentially harmful social trends, try to apply a developmental lens to help you make the best choices for your child.

CHAPTER 3

Building Blocks, Dress-ups, and Kids' Own Stories

Reclaiming Play and Imagination

As discussed in chapter 1, the pretend play our kids do serves a profound purpose in their lives: this kind of play is a powerful vehicle through which they can make sense of their experience, master difficult life events, and build new ideas. Let's look at a simple example to illustrate what I mean when I'm speaking of healthy pretend play.

I was giving my grandson Jack, then two and a half, a bath when a spider suddenly appeared on the side of the tub. Jack started screaming at the top of his lungs in a panic. I tried to show him how glad I was to see the spider, which wasn't hard for me because I actually like spiders, but this made no impression on Jack. He kept on screaming in genuine fright even after I removed the spider, so I quickly helped him exit the tub.

A few days later, when Jack came over to my house, I included a little plastic spider in the things we were playing with. So as not to scare him at first, I put the spider in a little box on the table and told him there was a toy spider in the box. "You open it," he said. So I opened the box to reveal the little plastic spider inside. "He's not going to move," said Jack. "No, he can't move," I said. He opened and closed the box several times, then took the spider in his hand and went into the bathroom and put it in the bathtub. Then he came back, returned it to the box, and said, "It's not going to bite me." "No, it's not going to bite," I said.

There was some play dough at the kitchen table and also a very small plastic baby doll that Jack had been playing with since his brother, Miles, had arrived six months earlier. Jack said, "The baby is scared of the spider." He made a blanket out of play dough and covered the baby. He then put the baby in the play dough container and covered it up with the play dough blanket. Then he repeated this whole scenario again, taking the baby out, saying it was scared, then putting it in the container and covering it up with the blanket.

Here's a child—just two and a half years old—using the creative play process to work out his fear of spiders. Jack was able to project his fear onto the toy baby and then make a protected space for it. When kids play in a healthy way, they do what Jack does here: they integrate their experience with their imagination and their needs. Jack created a play scene about a spider, based on an encounter from his experience; he used his imagination to invent the scenario about the baby who needed protection from the spider; and in protecting that baby he helped meet his own need to feel secure.

Jack was inventing a completely original scene as he played. No other child would have created a scene exactly like this one. When children engage in this kind of play on an ongoing basis, they are gaining mastery over the challenges of life in a way that enhances their physical, cognitive, and psychic well-being.

Is It Creative Play or Is It Imitation?

Jean Piaget described play as a process where children take reality and work on it in their own way—they fit reality to their own inner understanding and needs, as Jack did when he made up his own scene using the baby, the blanket, and the spider. Piaget contrasted this kind of play with imitation, which he called the opposite of play. Imitation, he said, involves mainly fitting oneself into reality. When a child imitates something, he tries to conform to some external model he has seen, as, for example, when a child acts out a wrestling move he's seen on TV.

Usually there's a bit of imitation in every child's play. Children who are pretending to make dinner, for instance, might start by imitating what they have seen adults do when they get out the pots and pans or set the table. But while imitation can play a useful role as a starting point, the real value of play comes about not when children directly copy an external model, but when they instead begin to bring in elements from their own experience and imagination. As children play in this more creative way, they imagine what might be instead of what is. They try on new roles. They combine elements in new ways and devise new possibilities. They invent and solve problems, and they learn.

The distinction between imitation and what I and others would define as creative play is particularly relevant today. After the deregulation of television in the mid-1980s (which resulted in the marketing of toys and products linked to TV, for the first time in history), teachers began saying that children's play was changing, looking less spontaneous and more like a reproduction of what they'd seen on TV. Over the years since then, I have heard countless descriptions like this one from Candace, who attended a workshop I gave recently: "I'm concerned because the children in my day care center don't know how to play. All of their play is scripted. It's just an imitation of whatever popular media show they're into."

It's comments like these that have convinced me and others who study early childhood development that for kids today the creative aspects of play are endangered by a combination of societal trends. As discussed in chapter 1, kids today spend more time consuming media at home and less time playing on their own; they spend more time in structured activities; they have less playtime in school. But not only do kids have less time to play, many also have a diminished capacity to play creatively: the very play process itself has been undermined by the influences of media and marketing. When kids today play, they are often drawn into imitating what they have seen on the screen, which is then reinforced by toys that further tell them what to do. This situation is robbing children of one of the most vital resources they have for growth and learning. It is eroding kids' capacity to adapt constructively to change, it undermines their creative thinking, and it teaches them to look outside of themselves for direction and satisfaction. Fortunately, though, there is much that we parents and grandparents, aunts, uncles, and caregivers can do to counteract these negative influences.

Media Impacts on Children's Play

Much of the content of what I would consider healthy children's play, like Jack's with the baby and the spider, comes from their own direct experience. Children pretend they are going to the store, they play restaurant or post office, they pretend to put their dolls to bed. But today, with more and more of the content of children's play coming from the media, it's alarmingly common for someone else's ideas to influence or even dominate their imaginations.

I recognized that media could influence kids' play many years ago, when my own sons were young, long before media came to play the big role in children's lives that it does today. Back then, my sons liked to watch a show that was on TV once a week, called *Emergency*, about two firemen who rescued people from danger. Matt, then five years old, made himself a fireman's costume from various articles he found around the house and played for much of the day that he was either "Roy" or "Johnny," the show's two rescue heroes.

One winter day during this firefighter period, I returned home from work on a snowy afternoon. The cold, dark days of winter in Boston were setting in earlier and earlier. I decided to build a fire in the fireplace of our rented apartment while Kyle and Matt were playing in the next room. But the kindling I used was far too long and brittle. In a flash, flames from the kindling leaped out of the fireplace and onto the wooden mantel that framed it. I panicked. I grabbed the blanket that was on the couch and tried to suffocate the flames. And I called, "Kyle, Matt—come quick!" (Whom else does a single mom turn to at a moment like this?) Kyle and Matt ran into the living room and saw the flames lapping at the mantelpiece. "Get water!" I called. Seconds later, Kyle, who was then eight years old, raced into the living room with a little Dixie cup of water for me. (Did he think I was thirsty?)

At this point, when the flames had begun to die down and I began to regain my composure, I wondered where Matt was. Minutes were passing by and he hadn't returned. "Where *is* he?" I thought, gazing at the empty doorway. Suddenly Matt burst into the room. He was wearing a red corduroy bathrobe, his black galoshes, a red firefighter's hat, and a sea diver's mask, and he was holding a little piece of rubber tubing connected to nothing, which he was spraying toward the fireplace in small jerky motions.

Once the shock wore off, I realized that it had made sense to Matt, with his prelogical view of the world, to put on his firefighter's costume when he saw the flames. For him, that would be what to do when flames are burning, just as they do on TV. But when I thought about it later, I realized how powerful the media's influence on children is, more than on adults: not only are children influenced by TV shows when they watch them, but the themes, characters, and actions they see enter their play to get reused and replayed many times in many different ways, and this can profoundly influence the ideas kids are forming about the world around them.

When we think of the impact of media on children's play, then, we should recognize that it has a many-layered influence. And this influence expands with increased exposure to media. If the show Matt watched as a child were on today, it would probably also be a computer game, a Game Boy game, and maybe even a Hollywood movie—so he would be seeing the same images over and over again with great frequency. And while Matt was able to use the rescue theme from this particular TV show—a theme that appeals to young children—as a basis for a lot of what I saw as healthy pretend play, much of what kids see today in the media is not at all well matched to their developmental concerns and needs.

Matt watched his favorite TV show only once a week. And he spent the rest of the week dressing up and inventing his own dramas—he made his own costumes and props, he invented scenarios where he would rescue various characters he had created from danger. For him, the TV show was an inspiration—a springboard for creative play. The hours Matt spent playing in this way gave him the healthy and healing benefits of play, and they also gave him something else—they slowly shaped his sense of self. I am a creative person, he learned: I can invent stories from my imagination, create characters and scenes, and I find deep satisfaction in doing this. I realized then, now thirty years ago, that small doses of wholesome television could in fact be a source of inspiration for kids' creative play. But I didn't know at the time that media culture would soon grow to the size of a looming giant—so huge and ever-present in kids' lives that it would overshadow or even stamp out their original ideas, personal stories, and imaginations.

Open-Ended Materials Versus Single-Purpose Toys

Not only would Kyle and Matt's favorite TV show be replicated in other media forms today, it would also most likely have a line of toys sold with it, like rescue hero figures with removable fire hats, boots, and snap-on coats. It would have fire engines with battery-run sirens and accessories such as hoses and tanks; there would be a firefighter costume to buy, identical to the outfit worn on the show; and licensed products like firefighter lunch boxes, underpants, T-shirts, sheets, and toothbrushes. Research has proven that this sea of external influence— every added toy, costume, and premade prop—takes children away from their own creativity.

In just one generation there's been a major transformation in the kind of playthings marketed to children and parents. Open-ended toys, those that lend themselves to creative play, have increasingly given way to highly structured single-purpose and high-tech toys. When my kids were young, "open-ended" toys like blocks, art supplies, and generic building materials were stacked at the front of toy stores. Now, if I can find them at all for my grandkids, I find them hidden away in the back, and often I have to ask someone to get them for me. Instead, prominently displayed on the front shelves today are single-purpose and media-linked toys and toys that run on batteries and microchips.

Open-ended toys are the kinds of basics you find in good early childhood education programs: blocks, water, sand, play dough, dress-ups, paint, collage materials, construction paper and markers, generic dolls, and animals. They encourage creative play because kids can make them into just about anything they need or want; they can bring their own narratives *to* these materials.

Single-purpose toys, in contrast, have some specific function built into them that a child activates (a Batman action figure that fires darts at the push of a button, for example). These toys are almost always linked to media and the actions of the toys usually replicate something children have already seen on the screen.

Let's look at the play of April, a child I met recently at a friend's picnic, and then Charlotte, a little girl I watched when visiting her day care center not long ago, to see how the different toys and props they use are influencing their play.

April likes to watch the *Power Ranger* cartoon on TV. She gets her pink Power Ranger action figure and walks it across the floor, saying, "I'm the Pink Power Ranger." April pushes a lever on the back of her action figure and the female head disappears and up pops a pink Power Ranger head. April walks the toy across the floor again and says, "Now I am a Power Ranger." When April pushes the lever again, the Ranger head disappears and the female head returns. "Now I'm the girl Ranger," she says. April walks her toy across the floor again, picks up a toy gorilla and knocks over the gorilla with the Power Ranger toy. April pushes the lever of her action figure a few times, making the head turn around and around, each time revealing one of the two heads.

The Power Ranger action figure directs a lot of the play that April is doing and there is very little room for her own imagination and experience to come through. She uses the toy in a repetitive way and seems to stay stuck on the surface of her play, starting out in the imitative phase but not progressing to a phase where she is actively inventing her own story. Her deepest issues don't seem to connect to what she is doing, and we don't learn much about April as we watch her. With single-purpose toys linked to media, like April's Power Ranger toy, it's much harder for kids to bring in their own experience, imagination, and needs; these toys encourage imitation and vastly inhibit what I would say is healthy, creative play.

Let's look now at Charlotte, who is playing with a set of blocks, an open-ended toy.

First Charlotte builds a rectangle shape with the blocks. "This is a farm," she says. (She visited a farm recently with her day care center.) Then she takes out a container with animals in it and puts some of them in her farm. "This is the horse, this is the pig, and these are the ducks," she says. Charlotte puts one small block in front of each animal and says, "Now they all have food." Next, she takes two blocks out, puts one on top of the other, and moves them around the floor. "I'm driving the bus. It's very, very bumpy," she says as she makes the bus rock while she moves it around the floor. Then she knocks the blocks over and says, "Crash! The bus crashed!" Then Charlotte puts the bus back together, moves it around the floor again, and puts the animals on it. "All the animals are going on the bus."

Charlotte is able to make the blocks into anything she wants because, like all open-ended toys, blocks do not have a defined identity. She makes a farm, food for the animals, and a bus —all with the same material. These different symbolic meanings come from Charlotte's imagination and her experience, and it is because materials like this aren't predefined that they foster more imaginative and personally meaningful play. Here Charlotte replays her trip to the farm in her own way, making her own meaning of the experience. As she puts one bit of food in front of each animal, Charlotte is also working on the early math concept of one-to-one correspondence. Healthy play is a fertile ground for working on many concepts that are foundational for later learning.

Another benefit of open-ended materials is that kids of different ages can play with them at different levels of complexity. A two-year-old can take one block and move it along the rug like a car. A few five-year-olds can spend all morning in a kindergarten classroom building a complex structure that's taller than they are. Kids can stay interested in open-ended toys for many years because the potential for creativity they offer is not limited by the material and can emerge endlessly from the child. Single-purpose toys, on the other hand, have a notoriously short life span, as many of us know. Kids exhaust their play potential pretty quickly and are soon asking for another toy.

High-Tech Electronic Toys

High-tech toys that move on their own, play music, make sounds, flash lights, talk, and sing have gained rapid popularity and today literally fill toy store shelves. Many adults say they buy these toys for their children because they're "educational." But let's take a closer look at electronic toys and how they affect the play and learning of young children.

I was playing with my grandson Jack in his bedroom one day when he was twenty-two months old. He picked up a ball and started throwing it and chasing it around the room. At one point, the ball accidentally landed right in the middle of the four legs of an overturned stool. Jack became fascinated with this. He tried to repeat this little accident deliberately. He took the ball out and threw it again into the legs of the stool. The ball landed within the legs of the stool a second time and Jack said, *"Stuck!"* He looked at me and we laughed with delight. He took the ball out again and walked to a different spot in the room and shot again at the stool. In went the ball. "Stuck!" he exclaimed, and again we laughed. He came close and dropped the ball directly into the stool. This ball-tossing exploration went on for a long time, with Jack throwing the ball into the stool from every conceivable angle, with differing degrees of force, and showing sheer delight every time it went in.

At one point Jack took a break from ball throwing. There was a stuffed Teletubby toy on the floor which he picked up. The toy had an image of a TV set on its stomach. He pushed the TV image and the toy said, "I'm LaLa." He pushed it again and the toy repeated itself:

"I'm LaLa." Jack dropped the Teletubby and picked up his ball again to resume the game he seemed to find more satisfying.

As Jack played with the ball and stool, he was both playing and learning. He had invented the game of throwing the ball into the stool on the spot, from his own imagination. He "played" with throwing the ball from different locations in the room and different degrees of force. As he did this, he was learning about distance, angles, and velocity. He was forming and testing out his ideas. He was problem solving: Can I throw the ball into the upturned stool on purpose? Can I get it into the stool from far away? What if I go to the corner of the room? What if I throw it really fast? In doing all this, Jack was learning that he is a problem solver: I am able to create *and* solve problems.

In contrast, the Teletubby toy, by its very design, directed Jack in how to use it and limited what he could do with it. He pushed the TV image on the doll's stomach, but he could hardly understand the causal connection between pushing the stomach and hearing the doll talk, other than that it happened. With the ball and stool, however, Jack could see the ball going into the upturned stool, see the effects of stepping sideways and throwing harder or softer. With every "experiment," he was learning new concepts and sparking new connections in his still-developing brain. Research tells us that certain connections and pathways in children's brains need to be activated through exercise and repetition if they are to be solidified and retained, so the physical kind of practicing kids do, such as Jack's repeated ball tossing, serves a vital purpose.

When children create and solve their own problems, they are learning; when they can see for themselves how things are related through action, they are building the foundation for the concepts they will learn later. Electronic toys like Jack's Teletubby doll keep kids at the surface of learning instead of helping them become more deeply engaged in exploring the world. The message gets conveyed that toys tell you what to do—rather than that you make them be what you want them to be, and do what you invent. This subtle shift can lead to passive learning. It helps explain what many teachers say about children today: they seem more comfortable when they are told what to do, they seem bored with open-ended materials and free time, they have diminished problem-solving abilities.

Because electronic toys are so prevalent today—handheld video games that travel in pockets, TV screens built into cars—they can also become an easy substitute for social interactions. They are one more influence undermining the positive relationships children today so need. Recently I saw how this can happen when I went on a hike with a group of adult friends and their children.

There were two young children on the hike and we had a wonderful time, all of us—spotting a frog, climbing onto a huge fallen tree, and arriving at a beautiful stream in the woods. On the way home in the car, we were all talking about our adventure—recapping and describing what we'd seen and done. Adriana, the six-year-old girl on this trip, was talking excitedly with us. She remembered the mushrooms she'd seen and we all described how they looked and felt. We elaborated on our group story, describing the highlights, sharing impressions, and enjoying our common experience.

But Aaron, the four-year-old on the trip, had pulled out a Game Boy for the ride home. And as young kids do, because they focus on one thing at a time, he fell engrossed into this activity and tuned out the dialogue completely. Periodically, and unaware of the discussion we were having, Aaron would shout "I won!" and he stayed lost in his Game Boy world for the whole trip home.

The toys we give children influence not only how they play but the quality of their relationships with others. Children can get lost in toys that are wired to only amuse and so miss out on valuable life lessons that are right in front of them. This is happening in American households every day. TV screens, video games, and electronic toys can easily become substitutes for the personal interactions kids need today more than ever.

Supporting Imaginative Play

Supporting children's healthy creative play begins with our appreciation for its value in their lives and our awareness of the potential hazards today's societal forces present. We can do a lot, quite easily, no matter what our resources are, to support richer and more meaningful play.

Children need certain things in order to be able to play creatively. They need time, a place to play, materials and props, and at times, some specific help from adults. If kids' lives are scheduled up from morning until night, for example, they might not have enough time and psychic space for this vital activity. And children also need some protected place in which to play. If they aren't sure that their playtime won't be disrupted, kids won't get very involved; and if every time a child's play takes off, a younger sibling grabs her toy or we ask her to move her things, she'll learn that there's no point in getting engaged. She might also get the message that her play isn't very important.

Children also need props for play, and ideally, these are open-ended materials that they can fashion into what they need for the narratives they invent. When my son Kyle was three years old, I made the lower part of the pantry in our apartment into a play space where he could be sure his baby brother, who was then crawling and standing up, wouldn't interfere. I put Kyle's play dough and small blocks on one shelf, and crayons, scissors, paper, and his favorite little animals in yogurt containers on the others. He could go into "his" pantry and close the door to keep "the baby" out whenever he wanted to.

Often with just this amount of support, kids will launch into rich and elaborate play on a regular basis. But many parents and teachers have told me that kids today need more help getting involved in doing so than kids needed in the past. So while ideally adults wouldn't interfere in children's play, today kids might need some help developing and elaborating their play—help in becoming involved, help in moving beyond imitation.

Helping Kids Move Beyond Imitation into Creative Play

One technique is to make occasional comments about what we see happening in our kids' play. The best of these simply describe what is going on—briefly, so as not to interrupt the flow—but don't evaluate it in any way. You might say, for instance, "I see that you put all the animals on one side of the blocks." Or "It looks like you made a place for the snake." Comments like this show that you appreciate what the child is doing and they also encourage conversation about it. Sometimes talk like this can lead a child to a deeper level of involvement, or spark a new idea or direction.

Another effective technique is to ask open-ended questions. Open-ended questions have many possible answers. They can lead children toward some new idea that they might not have thought of alone. For example, when April knocks over the toy gorilla with her Power Ranger toy, a parent could ask, "Where can the gorilla go to be safe?" Or "What can the gorilla do now?" Questions like these sometimes help kids elaborate on their play. But we should ask them gently and be willing to let them drop if they don't catch on.

We can also steer kids toward using materials that will extend and deepen their experience of play—and offering a simple suggestion at the right moment can lead children's play in new directions. Here's an example.

Martin is cooking dinner when his two kids run into the kitchen. Krystina has some keys in her hand and she says to her brother, Alex, "We can use these to lock the jail." Martin glances up. Alex says to him, "I need a radio."

Martin says, "We don't have a radio. But use these to make one." (He gives them a little tub of Bristle Blocks—inexpensive, colored plastic blocks in various shapes that push together easily.) The kids immediately start working on their "radios."

Krystina: This is a good one. (She puts circular nobs on a square shape.) You can really call somebody. It goes around.

Alex: Mine has buttons. You push these buttons.

The kids start pretending to call with their radios.

Alex: Get over there right away! (He makes a loud siren sound.)

Krystina: Call an ambulance! He's going to die!

Alex starts taking his radio apart. "I need a gun," he says. "A bad guy killed a good guy."

Then Alex goes back to the Bristle Blocks and gets engrossed in making guns. Krystina comes over and starts putting various pieces together. They build with the blocks for a long time and both end up with colorful guns.

Krystina: The ambulance driver is dead.

Alex: Quick, get in my truck. (He pretends to be driving.)

Krystina: I promise I won't kill you.

Martin was busy cooking and needed the kids to be occupied. When they appeared in the kitchen asking for a radio, he suggested they make one and gave them the Bristle Blocks. This was the only time Martin got involved with their play, but his one suggestion helped them become more engaged in their scenario and sustain it longer, and it helped him get more time for making dinner. If Martin had handed his kids a store-bought toy radio or gun, their play would have taken a very different direction. Here they spent a good deal of their time inventing the props they needed for their fantasy and changing one thing into another following the lead of their own creativity, even though their narrative may have involved story lines they had seen on TV. (We'll talk more about how play that looks violent can still be healthy in chapter 5.)

STEPS YOU CAN TAKE

Even in the face of societal trends that are threatening children's capacity for healthy, imaginative play, there are a great many things that we can do, every day, regardless of our resources, to help our children's imaginations and play lives to thrive.

▶ You can best support your child's creative play by carefully watching how he or she plays. When you first try doing so, there will be a lot to see. These questions might help:

What themes seem most important?
Is the child bringing her own experience into the play?
Is he making up narratives of his own?
Where do the ideas come from—from daily life, from media, from books?

▶ Think about imitation versus creative play, and about how you can help your child move beyond narrowly scripted play. Try asking these questions: Does your child seem focused on acting out something from the media and doing it just like it is on TV or in a movie, or is she willing to vary the "script?" Is the play changing over time or does it follow the same pattern over and over?

▶ Try to provide uninterrupted playtime every day, and to help your child find easy access to open-ended play materials.

The place where your child can play uninterrupted doesn't have to be available at all times, but it should belong to him or her during playtime. One parent I spoke to recently said she put a sheet over the kitchen table after lunch and her child kept herself busy there for much of the afternoon. As for toys and materials, it's a good idea to provide labeled containers so they can be easily found and later put away. (Young kids will need your help with this, but older children usually love to categorize things. The empty packages from food and household items work well—for instance, ice cream or fruit containers, coffee cans [with tape put around the top to protect from the ragged metal], empty shoeboxes. With masking tape or blank stickers, make simple labels—use pictures for younger kids—to identify what's in a container.)

▶ Make comments, ask questions, and suggest materials that will help your child expand her play. As you observe your child playing, try gently making comments or asking questions about what you see happening. If your child needs a prop, suggest he try making one with open-ended materials. Try to keep your comments, questions, and suggestions very close to what the child is doing and let them go if they don't catch on.

▶ Try to buy as few single-purpose, media-linked, and electronic toys as possible. When you consider a toy, ask the following: What is the potential of this toy for fostering imaginative play and creative problem solving? Will this plaything foster positive relationships or tend to isolate my child?

When your child is fascinated with a single-purpose toy, try to introduce a more open-ended material such as play dough or building blocks to use along with it. You can gently offer an idea that connects to what the child is already doing. For example, if your little girl is playing with the Doctor Barbie doll, you could say, "Maybe you could build a hospital with these blocks for the doctor and the sick people."

▶ Try to give your child as many concrete experiences with everyday activities as you can. Involving him in daily tasks such as cooking with you, setting the table and cleaning up, and putting out the garbage and watching the garbage truck come can provide experiences and content for rich pretend play. When you do errands, point out some of the interesting things you see; for instance, at the supermarket you might ask your child to help find items and watch how the shelves are stocked and how the checkout process works.

▶ Think about things around the house that can expand opportunities for creative play, things as simple as recycled materials, old wrapping paper, and boxes and cartons. You can learn to look at everything as a potential prop for creative play—an old flashlight, a broken telephone, an Ace bandage, a broom, fabric remnants, cardboard tubes, a collection of buttons, or any other apparent piece of junk that might become an inspiration. One parent told me that her two kids played for a whole afternoon with an old suitcase, using it as a prop in dramatizing scenes with their action figures.

▶ Keep your children's screen time to a minimum so it doesn't interfere with active play. The American Academy of Pediatrics recommends no more than one to two hours of quality TV and videos a day for older children and no screen time at all for children under the age of two. Having fewer TVs in the house and/or keeping the family TV in a central area will make the screen situation easier to monitor. In my own house I cover our TV with a piece of fabric, and I'm always surprised at how infrequently my grandkids ask to watch it when it's covered. When they do ask to watch a show or video, we talk about it and decide together to take off the fabric. This makes our viewing a conscious choice rather than a habitual activity.

▶ Try to work *with* your children when making decisions about media. You can talk with your child about screen time, explaining how you feel, listening to how he or she feels. Try to come to a shared agreement about how much screen time your child will have each day.

Look at the TV shows, movies, videos, and video games your kids see from the perspective of what we know about children's development. Does the story and its characters touch some of their deep developmental needs—for security, mastery, empowerment, connection, and belonging—in a healthy way? What lessons are children learning from this TV show or movie or game? Can—or should—a child emulate any of the characters? Can he or she use this material as a springboard for imaginative play?

▶ Talk with kids about the content of the TV programs they see, as well as movies, video and computer games, and ask questions that help them think about and reflect on screen media. Even with very young children you can ask questions like "Do you like that show? Why do you like it?" As kids get a little older, you can ask open-ended questions that provoke thinking and raise issues about the values and messages in the content of what they watch, questions like "Why does that guy look so mean" or "What do you think about how she's talking to her sister?" And you can express your own point of view, perhaps with a comment like "I don't like to see people hurting each other like they do in that video game," and you can listen to what your child thinks. (Findings from several research studies demonstrate that a show's influence on kids is minimized when parents make comments about the show's content.) Try helping your child make a list of what TV shows he or she watches, and use it as a basis for talking about the content of those shows. Above all, try to make time to engage actively with this aspect of your child's life.

CHAPTER 4

No More Time-Outs

Sharing Power with Kids

A power dynamic is at work in every interaction we have with children, though we many not always be aware of it. I have always believed that how we use our adult power with children is the single most important aspect of our relationship with them; and today, I think it's more important than ever.

Most of us use our parental power in one of two ways: either we exert our power *over* children (telling them what to do, holding the line, expecting obedience) or we give that power *away*, that is, we give in to our children's wishes and just let kids do as they want. Some of us vacillate between these two ways of using our power. But neither of these approaches can fully meet the needs of children, especially in these challenging times. Children today see far too many examples of relationships based on coercion and force—where people use power over others to get what they want. And today, because of diminished time for social interaction at school and at home, children have fewer opportunities to learn alternatives to this model of force. So if we adults use force to get kids to comply—through tactics like withholding privileges and time-out—we reinforce the already familiar models of coercion seen in the wider culture. And if we just let kids do what they want, we aren't teaching them any alternatives for mutual, positive interactions with other people.

Fortunately, there is a middle ground between the power extremes—a place where we can *share* power with children—and it is here that kids can learn what it is they need today: how to get along with others using skills of dialogue, cooperation, negotiation, and joint problem solving. And it is in this fertile middle ground that relationships based on love and trust will thrive and kids will feel most secure.

The Power Continuum

As we look at how we interact with our children on a daily basis, it's useful to think of power as a continuum: the more power we adults have, the less children have, and vice versa. I recently witnessed both ends of the power continuum in action as I sat in an airport waiting for a connecting flight. A little girl about three years old was climbing up and down and over the empty chairs in the waiting area. Her father, using what I call his "power over" his child to get her to stop climbing, threatened her with "If you don't stop climbing, I'm going to spank you." The little girl sat down and stayed there, at least for a while (I think she knew what this threat meant). A little while later I watched a young boy throw a small plastic toy across the same waiting area. His parents didn't react. He retrieved the toy and threw it farther. Still no reaction. The boy's own power was expanding with each throw of the toy. Finally, he winged the toy all the way across to another waiting area, where it came close to hitting a woman in the head! Even so, the game continued until he got tired of playing it.

It's common to think of power in a dualistic way: either you have it or you don't. But there is also a large middle ground on the power continuum that is filled with ways of working *with* children in a more give-and-take way.

Let's begin to think about that by taking a look at how power enters our relationships with our kids early on—and at how we can start what I call power sharing, even with very young children—by listening to Kevin, who told me about a recent incident involving his two-year-old son, Will, the boy who was enamored with a sponge ball in chapter 1:

> I had a bad power-struggle incident that I am not proud of. William was in the tub and he was just having fun and chewing on this washcloth with little duck heads on it, and sucking the water out of it. And it was time to get out of the tub. And the way that we get out of the tub is he lets the water out. But this time he doesn't want to get out of the tub. I say, "It's time to get out of the tub. Put the toys away. Put the toys away." And he still has this thing in his mouth and the water is draining away. And I figure, all right, I can't waffle on this because I said, "Now you need to put this away." So he needs to do it. But he's *not* doing it! So then what do you do?
>
> So then I figured that I'd take the washcloth and he'd let me have it. But he didn't. He was like a dog with a toy. So I'm pulling it and he's pulling it and I'm thinking, "Oh, no, this is *not* good." You know, it's a power struggle really—it's a tug of war. Eventually I just took it. And William was upset. He felt powerless.

Will is having fun in the bath and won't easily be able to think about making a change to another situation. At two years of age, Will tends to focus on one thing at a time—right now his whole world is filled with water, soap, and being in the tub—and he doesn't want to let go of his washcloth. Of course, Kevin can't let Will stay in the tub all night; it's time to get out. Kevin feels he can't "waffle," so he directly takes the washcloth from Will, who then gets upset. Kevin doesn't feel good about this incident; he knows Will ends up feeling powerless, and that is a feeling we don't want to engender in children, especially two-year-olds who are just trying to find their autonomy and some measure of control over their world.

What does power sharing look like in a situation like this? Can Kevin find a way to help Will exit the tub in the future without this kind of power struggle? First, when Kevin realizes that Will is going to hang on to the washcloth, he might take a second to recognize that his two-year-old is exerting his newfound will. Kevin might also remember that two-year-olds often need help making transitions; they don't understand time, so focusing on concrete objects and actions can help them through changes. Kevin might say, for instance, "Oh, you want to hang on to the washcloth. Okay. But we have to get out of the tub now. You can hold on to the washcloth while you get out." Here Kevin would be understanding Will and his needs in this moment but still be able to get Will out of the tub. Kevin could also help Will by suggesting a concrete activity to help him make the transition. For example, Kevin might say, "Can you take the washcloth out of the tub and carry it to the sink?" Or "Here's a pail, can you put the washcloth in there?"

With an approach like this, Kevin would be using child development ideas to help Will take part in managing the situation. He would be sharing power rather than either imposing it or giving it over. Doing this would show Will that his dad cares about his needs and that they can work things out together. Will's trust in his dad would strengthen as he feels "seen" by his dad. Thinking about child development issues and what children need in various situations can often help us see how we can work *with* kids to avoid power struggles and build stronger relationships.

Let's pause for a moment to consider what goes on inside Kevin, or any parent who is heading into a power struggle with his or her child. Experiences like Kevin's, if they cause us to reflect on how we use our parental power, carry great potential for enhancing our own growing self-awareness as parents. Even a small incident like this bathtub episode can be a catalyst for looking at ourselves and what happens inside us when we feel the need to unilaterally exert our power over our kids.

Betty, a grandparent who had been the director of an elementary school in Massachusetts for many years, told me what she thinks is behind the "power over" actions we take with children:

> As parents, it's easy to feel a sense of powerlessness and surprise when children resist our "authority." It seems to us as though our wisdom and judgment about "what's best" come under attack when our children claim their own autonomy. We feel inadequate, overwhelmed, and even angry in the face of "no." We take action to soothe our own feeling of helplessness, but then we shatter the feeling of connection.

Over the years, I have observed many adults whose use of power over children may be fueled by feelings of helplessness and anger. Several years ago, one of my student teachers, Grace, told me about an incident in the classroom where she was practice teaching.

> Kids come into our kindergarten class in the morning and hang up their coats in the coatroom and then come into the classroom. Last week, a little boy named Cole came into the classroom with his coat still on. The head teacher told him to go back outside and hang up his coat. But Cole just stood there; he didn't say anything. She told him again to take his coat off or he couldn't come into the classroom. He was still standing there quietly. Finally the teacher said to Cole, "Go out to the coatroom. If you want to wear your coat, you can't come into the classroom. You'll have to stay in the coatroom." So Cole went into the coatroom and sat there, and there he stayed for the entire morning.

What happened inside this teacher that made her see Cole as an adversary? Did she feel fearful? Angry? There was some obstacle inside this teacher that kept her from reaching toward Cole, understanding *why* he wanted to keep his coat on, and working *with* him to help him come into the classroom.

I believe that many of the power struggles we have with children begin inside of us—that our own feelings, fears, and reactions keep us from seeing what's really going on for kids or what we might do to keep our interactions with them creative and flowing in a positive direction.

Finding a Balance: The Middle Ground

We adults have so many ways we can use our power over children. Jane told me how she withholds privileges to get her daughter to do things: "If Kerry doesn't clean her room, then she can't go to her friend's house after school." Mike described how he bribes and rewards his kids: "I tell them that if they get their homework done, they can watch TV. And if they get it done all week without complaining, I'll buy them a special treat on Saturday."

Every time we withhold privileges, threaten kids, bribe them, reward them, send them to "time-out," or even take the extreme step of hitting them, we are using our parental power *over* our children. Jean Piaget, along with other theorists writing on children's moral development, had important things to say about the effects on children when we use our adult power over them in these ways.

Piaget was interested in how children learn to regulate themselves from within rather than as a result of coercion or punishment. He explained that too much adult power can make kids feel inferior and increase their susceptibility to domination by others, and he warned that the more authority and domination adults use, the less likely it is that kids will learn to regulate their own behavior. This is a key insight because what most of us want is a child who behaves as we would wish even when there is no adult around to monitor them. Recently I made an effort to encourage this self-regulating capacity in a three-year-old named Brian when I was at the park with him and several other children.

Brian was running around the park exuberantly with the other kids. He tore across the park at one point and bumped into a little girl who looked to be about six months younger. Brian stopped for a split second as the little girl fell down and started to cry, and then he took off running in the opposite direction. I went toward Brian, calling his name, but he picked up his pace, trying to get away from me as fast as he could. I ran faster, and so did Brian, until I finally caught up to him.

"Brian, I want to talk to you," I said; but he was already blurting out, "I don't want a time-out." Wanting to know more, I asked, "What's that?" "I have to sit still and it's boring," he said. "We're not going to have a time-out," I said. "But let's go find out how the little girl you knocked over is." I took Brian by the hand and we walked over to her.

"Are you okay?" I asked. "Brian was running fast and he knocked you over." The little girl had stopped crying. Her mom said things were all right now and thanked us for our concern. Brian didn't say anything, but he stayed there holding on to my hand and was taking part in the process of making amends. Together we had acknowledged the hurt he had caused, but without blaming or punishing him.

When Brian ran away after knocking the little girl over, he demonstrated one of the most important principles in the moral development of children: the more we punish kids, the less they learn to take responsibility for their own actions and to care about others. Brian saw the girl fall, thought he'd done something wrong, and wanted to avoid a time-out. Anticipating the punishment caused Brian to run away from accepting his part in the accident and from feeling a concern for the child he had hurt.

If I had given Brian the time-out he'd anticipated for knocking over the little girl at the park, I would have been using my power *over* him. And if I had done nothing when I saw him knock the child over, I would not have used my adult power to do anything about the situation. Neither of these responses would've given Brian what he needed. Instead, I shared my adult power with Brian. I asked him to *participate*—to follow up on the effects of his own actions, to look after the child he had hurt. Brian, and all children, need help in learning how their actions affect others and to care about how others feel.

Research overwhelmingly indicates that while techniques like time-outs may work in the short run, they ultimately diminish intrinsic motivation and rob children of the opportunity to develop what child development theorists, following Piaget's lead, call self-regulation. A mechanism of inner control whereby children are guided by an inner knowledge of what they should do, self-regulation is critically important as children mature into adults capable of sticking to their own beliefs and ideals. Using a "power over" approach with kids, while it may produce temporary compliance in certain situations, over time will actually inhibit the development of values and behaviors that grow from the inside out.

What happens when we find ourselves in the opposite situation, where it's not us, but our children who have too much power? In my first job as a teacher of young children, I learned about this from a little boy named Philip who acted very tough. Philip seemed fearless. He would go up to bigger kids on the playground and shake his fist in their face, taunting them. One day, when the class was outside, Philip tried to bolt into the street. Concerned that his "fearlessness" might put him in real danger, we talked about Philip with the consulting psychologist at our next staff meeting. At first I was surprised when the psychologist said that Philip actually felt scared inside, that he didn't feel safe in school and needed more structure and specific kinds of reassurance. But as the staff began to provide these things for Philip, his tough-guy behavior melted away. In working with countless student teachers, parents, and children since then, I've come to understand that children's sense of security depends to a great extent upon us. We have a natural authority with children. As Piaget explained, young children are predisposed to accept the authority of adults; children *want* to listen to us, to depend on us and accept our guidance. If we continually insist on obedience alone, children won't learn to regulate their own behavior; but if we don't set guidelines for them and give them direction, they do not feel safe. Often when kids "act out," or "misbehave," they're hoping we will intervene to restore for them the sense of security they need us to provide.

With the pressures parents are under today, I have observed not only an increase in the tendency to use "power over" approaches with children, but also a tendency to give in too easily to kids' whims and wants. Linda, an educator from New York City, who gives workshops to parents, commented to me recently, "I see a lot of parenting these days that seems very indulgent. Parents are extra solicitous of children's needs, always giving deference to them, and kids end up thinking they're the center of the world. It seems out of balance with understanding that there are others who have needs as well."

In the middle ground between the two power extremes we can give children the guidance and boundaries they need but in ways that make sense to them as well as to us. When my grandson Miles stayed with my husband Doug and me for a couple of days at the age of three, he didn't want to have a bath one night, but he really needed one. So I said to him, "Miles, look at your feet! They have so much dirt on them! We have to wash that off in the bathtub. Here are some animals to take with you—they need a bath, too." This was all it took to get Miles to willingly climb into the tub. By pointing out his dirty feet, I gave him a concrete reason, one he could see for himself, for why he needed the bath. I kept my voice matter-of-fact—there was no edge of power in my tone as I spoke to him. I was loving and confident, not challenging. And I gave Miles some toy animals—another concrete assist to help him make the transition into the tub. Young children do need to know that we are in charge, but we can be in charge in ways that help them feel secure and don't constitute an overuse of our power.

Even when adults have to say no to children, we can do it in a way that includes them and still shares power with them. For example, a few months ago, my eight-year-old niece was reaching for a bag of Gummy Bears to dig into one morning before she'd had breakfast. Of course I had to tell her she couldn't eat them. But could I do it in a way that still shared some power with her? I reached for the bag of candy and said to Sarah, "We can't have candy before breakfast because it won't be good for your body and you won't feel good—I want to take good care of you!" and when I put the candy away she didn't object.

When we give kids a reason for *why* we are saying no to them, we are sharing with them some of our power as adults—we are including them instead of just limiting them. And when we do this, it's easier for kids to comply because they don't feel coerced. No human beings, including young children, want to be unilaterally told what to do—it makes them angry and mistrustful. I see this as a hopeful aspect of our common humanity: that none of us like to be controlled, that we all strive for self-determination.

How Power Sharing Builds Social Skills

Today, when children are constantly exposed to models of aggression and violence in the media and have less time for social interaction in school and at home, many educators have noticed a diminishing of their social skills. Daniel Goleman, author of the national best sellers *Emotional Intelligence* and *Social Intelligence* and a leading expert in the field of social and emotional learning, describes what research studies have shown: American kids are getting worse at cooperation, at being able to work things out, and at controlling their impulses. Yet these are the social skills all people need to function successfully in the world. When we enter the middle ground of power sharing, when we talk with children and work things out with them, we are teaching them some of these vital skills.

Angie, a mom I interviewed for this book, sent me an e-mail saying this: "My husband and I do not agree about how to put limits on our seven-year-old daughter Nina's TV watching. My husband, Keith, wants to lay down the law: one hour a day of TV during the week, two hours on weekends; that's it. But I want to be more flexible. What do you think?"

I wrote to Angie that she and Keith could do much more for Nina than just limit her TV watching if they could work out this situation *with* her. I recommended that she and Keith talk with Nina about TV viewing time. "Try to listen to what she wants," I wrote, "and then tell her how you feel and what you want." I said I thought that by having this kind of a dialogue with Nina, they would be able to negotiate an agreement about her TV watching that would work for all of them. I suggested they encourage Nina to make a book of the shows she wants to watch and use the book to talk together about the content of the shows she sees. In addition, I suggested that if they asked Nina open-ended questions about her favorite shows (Why do you like that show? What do you think about how the characters act on this show?) it could help her, over time, to become more critical about television and more media literate.

Angie wrote back a couple of weeks later saying that the power-sharing approach to Nina's TV watching was working very well and that Keith was warming up to it, too. She described the following dialogue she'd had with her daughter.

Angie: Nina, let's talk about TV and how much you're going to watch on the days when you have school. What shows do you like the best?

Nina: *Fetch* is my favorite show. And I like *Arthur* and *Phil of the Future.*

Angie: Those are fun. But when you watch a lot of TV, then you don't play as much with your toys. And I don't get to play with you—and I miss that.

Nina (pleading): But I want to watch these shows every day.

Angie: You like these shows so much you want to see them every day! But we don't have a lot of time after school until bedtime and I want you to do other things, too. I'd like you to choose two shows to watch every day.

Nina: Can't it be three?

Angie: Well, how much time is that?

Nina: Each one is half an hour, so . . . that's an hour and a half.

Angie: The thing is, I don't want you to watch TV for more than an hour every day during the week. Let's start with two shows and see how that works. We can try it this way and then talk about it again. You can choose the shows—which two shows do you want to pick?

Nina: I want to watch *Fetch* every day. And then I'll pick *Arthur* or *Phil of the Future.*

Angie: So you want to watch *Fetch* every day and then you'll pick one other show?

Nina: Yeah.

Angie: That sounds like a good plan. How about if you make a book of your favorite shows? You could draw a picture of each one, then we can look at the book together and talk about it.

Nina: Yeah, I want to do that.

Angie then stapled some sheets of plain paper together to make the book, and, she reported, Nina worked on it for a long time.

Let's look at the social skills Nina was learning from this conversation with her mom. Nina learned that her voice matters; her mom's questions helped her express her preferences and feelings. Nina participated in a dialogue—she learned about having a back-and-forth conversation where two people can express different points of view and listen to each other. She learned that her TV watching affects her mother, who misses interacting with her when she's in front of the set. She learned that she and her mom can solve problems together and both feel okay about what gets decided. And Nina probably also learned through this discussion that her mom cares about her: power-sharing discussions like this one help strengthen relationships.

Working cooperatively with children, as Angie does with Nina here, opens the door for us to teach them the many social skills they need today more than ever. It offers a tremendous opportunity for us to give our kids some of the key skills they are too often lacking the opportunity to learn—seeing the effects of their actions on others, being able to communicate effectively, creating their own solutions to problems, and establishing personal connections with the people around them.

How Power Sharing Opens the Door
to Greater Intimacy

Power sharing also can open doors that lead to greater understanding and intimacy within our relationships with our children. David, a thirty-six-year-old father from New York City, told me about a conflict he'd had early one morning with his son, Mark, who was not quite three years old:

It's been several weeks since Lucas [Mark's baby brother] was born. Lucas has colic, so my wife, Sadie, has been tending to him almost constantly. This has been a huge change for Mark, who is so used to having Sadie's attention and love showered upon him. I've been caring for Mark most of the time since Lucas arrived.

This morning I fixed him a bagel with cream cheese on it, which is his favorite breakfast. But Mark started fussing: the bagel was too hot, the cream cheese wasn't right, there was too much cream cheese, too little. I was trying to accommodate by repairing the bagel for him. At one point, Mark cried, "The bagel is too hot!" I felt the bagel with my own hand and it wasn't hot at all. I said, "Mark, the bagel doesn't feel hot to me." Mark started crying harder. "Yes, it is—it *is* hot!" I kept cool and said, "Let's feel it together, Mark." I put my hand on the bagel and encouraged him to feel it along with me. Mark kept on crying and crying. Then he looked at me, tears were streaming down his face. "I don't want a baby brother," he said.

I put my arms around Mark and picked him up. I held on to him tight. He cried very, very hard. At one point he cried, "I want Mommy." I kept holding him tight and lovingly. I said, "Yes, Mark, it is really hard to have a baby brother." Mark kept on crying for a while longer. I just sat with him in the chair, holding him. After a while, his tears lessened. We sat together in that embrace in silence. After a little while he said, "I feel better."

When David told me this story, I found myself thinking how easy it would have been for him to tell Mark, "That bagel is not hot—now eat it!" But David didn't take a "power over" response; he listened to Mark and tried to see things through Mark's eyes, offering to feel the bagel *with* him, even though he knew it wasn't too hot. David's way of approaching the situation let Mark go more deeply into what was behind his distress.

A minute later, David had another big chance to use power over Mark. When Mark said, "I don't want a baby brother," David could have said, "You shouldn't say that—you should love your baby brother!" But David made room for Mark's feelings; he just let them be without trying to fix or change them. From this experience, Mark learned a lot: that it's safe to feel his deep emotions, that he can share these with his dad, that he can experience his strong feelings and move through them to feel better.

When we use our power in ways that connect us to our children, we are able to build deeper emotional bonds with them. And at a time when children need more emotional connection with others but have diminished opportunities for finding that connection, it's more important than ever for us to use our power to bring us all closer together.

Extreme Parental Power: "Spanking"

Recently a national survey of over three thousand parents revealed that 61 percent of them think that it's appropriate to spank a child as a regular form of punishment. Let's consider how spanking, the most direct form of power adults use over children, affects them.

A number of the parents I interviewed for this book shared their perspectives on this practice. Sunny, who is now a grandmother, reflected on her feelings about having been hit as a child.

> Well, my memory of it is still very clear. I must have been about nine or ten. I had been spanked several times, but this is the one that lives on in my mind. I didn't come home on time for dinner. And my father hit me with a razor strap. And this colored my relationship with my father for most of my life.
>
> He died when I was fourteen and a half. He was in the hospital for thirty days and I only went to see him once. And I felt guilty. It engendered guilt in that I couldn't love him as I would have liked to. I couldn't feel sorry for him as I would have liked to. I was outraged that he'd hit me. It fostered revenge in my heart. I felt totally resentful, so after that when he called me for dinner, I deliberately refrained from answering his call, and would sit in the bushes and listen to him try to call me over and over to come in for dinner. And I'd be really glad that he was frustrated. I will never forget. I wanted to get back at him. And I knew it was wrong. I would sit while he called me and I would torture him. I can still see myself sitting out after dark and my dad getting frustrated and calling out the window. Then I would lie. I would go in and say, "I didn't hear you."

Sunny's father tried to teach her to come home on time for dinner by hitting her with a razor strap. But instead of getting Sunny to comply, her father's punishment actually caused Sunny to do the opposite. And inside of her grew resentment and guilt rather than love for her father and the desire to respond to his wishes.

In my years of working with children and families, I have encountered wide-ranging views on spanking. I've visited countries where corporal punishment of children is seen as a violation of human rights and is banned. I've talked with religious parents who do not believe in "sparing the rod." When I spoke with Lynne, who gives conflict resolution and diversity workshops to parents and teachers all over the country, she told me that many parents in oppressed communities fear for their children's safety and spank them so they will learn to obey authority quickly, believing this will increase their chances of surviving in a racist society.

A weighty collection of research data shows that corporal punishment—by which I mean inflicting physical pain on the body of a child in order to punish the child or control his or her behavior—has a negative impact on children. Dr. Alvin Poussaint, professor of psychiatry at Harvard Medical School, has long opposed the use of corporal punishment and points to research showing that hitting kids makes them more prone to depression, feelings of alienation, use of violence toward a spouse, and lower economic and professional achievement. Several definitive studies have shown that although spanking is often successful in getting kids to comply in the short run, in the long run it increases the chances that as they grow up they will have serious psychological and behavioral problems throughout their lives.

For many family and culture groups, spanking has been a common practice for generations. When I interviewed Shelly, who has a ten-year-old son and lives in Boston, she said to me, "You have to understand spanking in a cultural context. It has different meanings for different culture groups." And Carla, the mom of two young kids who attend a day care center in Cambridge, Massachusets, said this: "What I learned in my family was, if you don't do it the way I tell you, I'm gonna spank you. So I have tried to change my style—it's a big change for me. Sometimes I want to spank my child so hard. But I say, 'No, I'm gonna take a bath instead.'"

While Shelly might be right when she says different culture groups ascribe different meanings to spanking, it is likely that it's the adults she is talking about and not the children. From a child development point of view, we know that children don't think like adults: they see the world in more concrete and immediate ways. Most likely when a child is being spanked, it's the physical hurt and immediate feelings that fill his or her awareness; the child is not thinking about spanking in a broader cultural context.

One of the parents I interviewed, Dina, the mom of five-year-old Gabriel, talked about why she spanks her son:

> I don't spank Gabriel for breaking things, but I do for disobeying. Like if I say, "Don't go outside," and he goes outside, and I can't find him, then that's ten whacks with the belt. You blatantly disobeyed me. I'm teaching him the consequences of his actions. I explain it to him. I say, "I want you to learn to listen. You have to respect authority." That's what I'm trying to teach him.

Dina, like so many parents, wants her son to learn about the consequences of his actions and to respect authority, and she tries to teach him these things through physical punishment. But as many studies have shown, using too much parental power can cause feelings of inferiority in children and keep them from learning to develop their own inner controls over their behavior. As stressed earlier, most of us want kids to be guided by their own inner sense of what they should do in any situation, even when no adult is present. We have the best chance of teaching self-regulation to our children by connecting to how they see things and helping them build their own ideas and skills from within.

When Dina hits Gabriel, she teaches him another powerful lesson. She shows him, by her actions, that it's okay to use physical force to settle a problem. This, I believe, is an even more dangerous lesson to give kids today than it was in the past. Because children these days are continually learning from the media that surrounds them that "might makes right," and because kids today have fewer opportunities to learn alternatives to violence at school and at home, the use of corporal punishment reinforces what I believe is a dangerous social trend toward coercion rather than negotiation.

I am hopeful that many parents who spank their children will come to rethink this practice in light of the societal trends that affect children today. When I interviewed Betty, the former school director and grandmother we met earlier, she told me an encouraging story of how one father who spanked his child began to change his mind:

At a parent meeting, I had parents go around the circle and share their early experiences with discipline. And this particular parent, being a kind of rough man, said that his parents had disciplined him with a belt—they spanked and beat him. And he was laughing about it; he said it hadn't injured him. And this dad said that now he spanks his own child—and he thinks it's all right.

This man sat in the circle listening to other parents tell their stories about childhood. Some parents were also spanked, but for them it was not okay; for them, it was very harmful. He heard their rage, heard about their broken relationships with their parents. When it got back to him, after hearing all these stories, this dad had actually changed his mind. Then this father began to cry. And he began to question hitting his own son, and to feel empathy for his child.

This man no longer had a relationship with his parents—they didn't speak to each other. But he hadn't made the connection that his experience as a child was related to this. It was in listening to other parents share their hurt as children, and their broken relationships now with their parents, that this change began to take place in him. I think hearing the stories let him tap into his own inner child, who was sitting there so wounded.

It was through dialogue with other adults and in a supportive community that this father was able to reflect more deeply on the whole issue of spanking. Hopefully more of us who are caregivers to children today will try to create times to talk together as these parents did—about parenting and how we use our power with children. Through honest exploration and dialogue with others, I hope many of us will discover new, power-sharing ways to relate to the children in our lives.

STEPS YOU CAN TAKE

By practicing some of the steps below, we can gradually move toward more cooperative relationships with our children, thereby teaching them the skills they will need to cope with and thrive in the challenging world they live in.

▶ Start by taking the time to notice how power is present in your dynamics with the children in your care:

> *Are you using "power over" responses? In what situations?*
> *Are you giving power away to children? In what situations?*
> *Are you using power-sharing responses? In what situations?*

▶ Are there certain situations where "power over" responses come up most often? What are these and why do you think this is?

▶ Are there certain situations where you give too much power away to children? What are these and why do you think this is?

▶ Try to "unpack" the power struggles you have with your child:

When you feel that a power struggle is beginning, try to pay attention to what you are feeling.

Try to think about what is going on for your child and what he or she needs.

Can you think of a way to meet your child's needs and yours through power sharing?

▶ Try starting a journal in which you write about these themes:

How does power come up in your interactions with your child?

How do you feel when a power struggle starts?

How do you get your child to do what you want?

Try mapping your power dynamics on the power continuum.

▶ Consider forming or joining a parent discussion group to talk about power dynamics and other parenting issues.

▶ Try role-playing power dynamics with another adult. Act out some "power over" approaches, like using threats or bribes, and talk about how these feel to both of you. Then try acting out power-sharing approaches and talk about how you experienced them.

CHAPTER 5

From *Spider-Man* to *Smackdown*

Countering Media Violence and Stereotypes

The parents and teachers I interviewed for this book, like so many polled by other researchers, expressed concern about the abundance of violence that floods the entertainment media—TV, movies, video and computer games, and tie-in toys—that the kids in their care see and play with. But just a generation ago, few if any parents expressed such a concern. It's only since the 1984 deregulation of children's television that programming and products directed at kids have become a major source of worry. Free to market violence without restraint after deregulation, the entertainment industry immediately began to take advantage of children's natural interest in action and power to sell them programs, toys, and other products saturated with violence. And today, whether it involves the physical (depictions of bodily harm and brutality) or the psychological (hurtful gender and racial stereotypes), the content of much mass media entertainment has become a widespread and negative cultural force in the lives of our children.

Because of this, it falls on us—parents and caregivers—to do our best to protect children from the harmful media messages that saturate their childhood culture. Thankfully, we have many strategies for defusing the power of this cultural influence to undermine healthy play, children's sense of physical and emotional security, and their ability to find love and kindness in relationships. In this chapter we'll talk first about the issue of violence and then about the sometimes more subtle issues of racial and gender stereotyping.

The Dilemma of War and Weapons Play

War play, which is a special form of play that children have enjoyed for generations, where "good guys" and "bad guys" pursue, capture, and/or pretend to shoot each other, has changed dramatically since the deregulation of television. Before that time, boys, and many girls, too, created original and imaginative versions of good guy/bad guy play. But in the last generation—as media programming directly targeted at children has become more violent and endless amounts of toys and products linked to this kind of programming have poured onto store shelves—educators and child development experts agree that among many of the children they have observed this form of play has become more imitative, less imaginative, and more violent.

When it springs from their own needs and imaginations, war play can be a vital resource for children. Let's begin by looking at an example of "old-fashioned" war play—the kind you don't see as much today—to understand the value this kind of play can have for children when it's driven by their own imaginations rather than scripted by the media and related single-purpose toys.

Julian and Niko, both five years old, are setting up a "spaceship" behind a big easy chair. Julian props a pillow against the chair. "Here's the ladder," he says.

Niko: I'm gonna go out in space, okay? I'm gonna lock the door from here.

He pretends to lock a door at the bottom of the pillow.

Julian: Let's both go out in space.

Niko: I'll put on my space suit. There are aliens out there. They kill people!

Both children come out from behind the chair, moving in slow motion.

Niko, screaming: Aliens! They have the electronic ray!

Both kids start squealing and jumping up and down on the floor.

Julian: We have to get in the spaceship!

Both jump on the chair.

Niko: Hide from the electronic-fonic rays! Get in the ship!

They get behind the chair. Julian takes a few small marine animals— a whale, a shark, and a dolphin—and hides them behind the chair.

Julian: Let's pretend these are the whole family—they're hiding from the alien.

Niko: We need a gun. What do we have for a gun?

Niko looks around. He takes a long whistle, points it like a gun, and resumes his "space walk."

Niko: Do we have any aliens out here?

Julian: Yes—there's one! Blast him! Blast him to outer space!

Niko points his "gun" into "outer space" and makes shooting noises.

Niko: I got him!

Julian: Even if you kill him, he comes alive.

Julian starts putting handcuffs on an alligator toy.

Julian: I caught the alien!

Julian talks to the handcuffed alien alligator. "You listen to me!" He takes a little wand and pretends to hit the alligator over and over. He pulls the alligator over behind the chair.

Julian: Now he's in jail.

Julian and Niko shove pillows in front of the alien alligator.

Niko: Now he can't hurt anybody in the family.

Julian and Niko are weaving together their imaginations and experience to make up their own story. They use all kinds of props, like the chair, a whistle, an alligator, and small sea animals, to develop their good guy/bad guy scenario. Julian and Niko feel strong and in control as they capture the alien; war play, perhaps more than any other form of play, allows children to feel a sense of mastery and power. Many kids need this kind of play, especially when they feel helpless in their lives, as so many children do when having to face scary situations such as separation from home, going to school, and, for some, divorce, illness, or neighborhood violence.

Julian and Niko's war play lets them express feelings of hostility and fear toward their imaginary foe and get some inner control over these feelings. As they lock the alien in jail, they feel safe and secure. Not only is war play especially well suited to meet these developmental needs for mastery and security, it is also a fertile ground for exploring moral concepts like good and bad and killing and death. Through their play, Julian and Niko explore these moral ideas as they talk about what makes the alien "bad" (he wants to hurt their family) and what killing is ("even if you kill him he comes alive"). And even though the theme of Julian and Niko's play is good guys against bad, their play is very social and cooperative; they are working as a team and their interactions help develop their skills for getting along.

While old-fashioned war play like this can be extremely valuable for children, we rarely see this kind of creative war play today. What most teachers and parents observe looks more like what Margaret, a preschool teacher, described when I visited her classroom just as the movie *Star Wars: Revenge of the Sith* was being released. Margaret hurried over to blurt out her frustration when I arrived. "I hate *Star Wars*," she said. "It's taken over the classroom. It's all the kids can think about—they're obsessed with it, mostly the boys. They turn everything into a light saber and start fighting. It's all they talk about and all they play."

The boys in Margaret's class were turning sticks, rulers, and building toys into light sabers so they could fight, fight, and fight some more. This kind of war play looks a lot more like the imitation discussed in chapter 3 (April and her Power Ranger toy) than it looks like real play. In contrast to Julian and Niko's war play, there is no story developing from Margaret's students' imaginations: none of their own experience is coming in, and they aren't making new props to support a story line that evolves beyond the *Star Wars* movie.

Unfortunately, in the last twenty years, the combined forces of media and marketing have profoundly eroded the healthy, creative aspects of children's war play. The repetitive, scripted play more common today makes it hard for kids to use their play to work through issues related to their own needs. And, perhaps worst of all, the primary need met by war play—to feel powerful and in control—has been channeled by media into a narrow focus on violence. Too often today children try to feel powerful not by imagining how to trap a bad guy or rescue a good guy, but through simply imitating the violent acts they've seen on the screen.

Many of the teachers and parents I talk with, fed up with the kind of play Margaret saw in her classroom or worried about its harmful influence, tell me that they don't allow their kids to engage in war play or "violent" play of any kind: they simply forbid it. But the irony is that children need this form of play today more than ever—it's an important vehicle for working through fears and confusions about frightening things they've seen or heard about in the media and in the world around them.

In recent years, I have observed that even if parents do try to ban war play, it rarely works; often, kids find ways to do it anyway. I remember interviewing six-year-old Colin, whose mother, a graduate student of mine, forbade war play at home. To me, Colin confided, "I play *Star Wars* at school. I'm on the dark side." I asked Colin, "What is the dark side?" and he answered, "We fight and win." Then Colin leaned toward me and whispered, "My mother doesn't know." Because Colin was hiding his war play from his mom, she was cut out of something important to him, something that was influencing him. Given all the other societal pressures that threaten to undermine the parent-child relationship today, I believe we are better off staying connected to our children's interests and helping them make sense of their world, especially when it has to do with violence. Our task is to try to help kids reclaim for themselves this vital form of play that has eroded out from under them. Fortunately, there are things we can do, instead of banning war play, to restore some of its beneficial aspects to our children.

Encouraging Healthy War Play

The first thing we can do, and the most important, is to vastly reduce children's exposure to entertainment violence and the toys and other products linked to it. The more we can protect our kids from media violence, the less they will need to repetitively act it out in play and the more easily they will be able to discover their own inner play needs and resources. Of course children will still engage in war play, because, as we saw with Julian and Niko, war play meets many of young children's developmental interests and needs.

Then we can encourage healthy war play in a variety of ways. Many of the suggestions made in chapter 3 for fostering healthy play (providing open-ended materials, a space to play in, and new ideas for expanding play) can help us do this. To begin with, we can observe our kids' war play and then use what we learn to guide us in where to go next. We can ask: "Is my child making up characters and scenes or does his play seem scripted and merely imitative of something he's seen in the media?" "Can I relate this play to anything going on in my child's life—some change or upheaval or disturbing event?" "Does this kind of play seem to help my child work through her experiences?"

One parent I interviewed, Jane, said that her son Wade was playing "monsters" after having seen a Saturday morning TV show about monsters. She said Wade was acting out the show a lot, but that as she watched him play she noticed the presence of deeper themes, like hiding, fear of being alone, and the desire to feel powerful. So Jane made up a story with Wade about lions and tigers and children getting chased and they retold it several times, adding funny elements from their own lives, such as feeding avocados, Wade's favorite vegetable, to the lion. Wade began to play the story out with his toys and blocks, Jane said. He would act out hiding from the lion, being scared, and then capturing and taking care of it. According to Jane, the more Wade did this, the more creative his play became and the less violent as he left the TV monsters behind.

Another way we can foster creative war play in our kids is to influence the toys and props they play with. Highly structured toys that shoot darts, fire guns, or repeat verbal insults at the push of a button will direct kids toward repetitive and violent play. So limiting children's access to such toys and encouraging the use of open-ended play materials will help them be more creative and less violent in their war play.

Most kids have at least some single-purpose toys, from *Star Wars* action figures to Bratz dolls and Transformer toys. Introducing more open-ended materials such as play dough or building materials to use along with them helps facilitate more creative play of all kinds. You might bring out small blocks or play dough to use with a Power Ranger action figure, for example. When my grandsons were playing "policemen and bad guys" I put paper-towel tubes in the play box and in the course of one afternoon they made spyglasses, guns, and telephones with the tubes. The generic nature of the cardboard tubes lent themselves to different uses and fostered the kids' own creativity.

If kids aren't thinking of new ways to use materials and toys on their own, you can offer them ideas. For example, if your child is playing with an action figure in the same way over and over, you can suggest he give it a bath or make a car or a plane for it to travel in. Suggestions like these work best if they grow out of what you see happening already. For example, if your child is pretending to shoot a bad guy, you might say, "I wonder if there's a way to capture the bad guy without shooting him." Or "It looks like that bad guy is hurt. Should you get him to a hospital?" Questions like these can help kids think beyond violence and spark new directions and inquiries. But we have to remember that play belongs to children; we don't want to be heavy-handed with our suggestions or take over their play in any way.

We can also give our kids alternatives to entertainment violence that address their needs for mastery, power, and security. Many children's books touch on these themes and can be the basis for play that meets the same needs as war play does. Martha, a kindergarten teacher I interviewed, told me that when the children in her class were consumed with *Star Wars* play, she started reading *The Wizard of Oz* to them at group time because she thought it touched on similar themes of power and security. Martha filled the dramatic play area with props relating to the story, such as a pair of red shoes and a witch hat. She said that the children gradually became immersed in the story of *The Wizard of Oz*—acting it out with elaborations, drawing it, making their own props—and their more rigidly scripted *Star Wars* play slowly dropped away. Many children's books touch on themes of mastery, power, and security but contain no graphic violence, and reading these, especially over and over again, can inspire play about mastery and power that comes closer to meeting children's real psychological needs.

As most of us know, good guy/bad guy play can get easily out of hand, especially when kids imitate scenarios from the media and use ready-made single-purpose toys like light sabers or guns. The more kids move toward creative play and away from imitation, the more self-control they will have in their play and the less they will need help from us to "keep the lid on." But when children do need our help, we can develop parameters for their play *with* them, using a joint problem-solving approach. You could say, for example, "Every time you make the cardboard tubes into swords and start fighting, one of you ends up crying. What can we do about this?" Perhaps you'll decide not to use the tubes for sword fighting, or maybe you'll put the tubes away altogether for a while. What's important is to solve the problem together and to come up with a solution that you all can agree to. This way of resolving conflicts with kids is described in depth in chapter 7 and can be a great help when you're trying to help kids play safely.

Helping Kids Process Violent Entertainment

Increasingly, an incessant exposure to violent and scary images in the entertainment media is a toxic source of distress in the lives of our children. Media-induced fears in children are well documented by researchers, and were reported by many of the parents I interviewed for this book. Most compelling for me personally, though, are the comments of the kids themselves. This is what my friend Anita's seven-year-old daughter, Tara, told me.

Tara: I don't want to sleep alone 'cause I get scared.

Me: You get scared?

Tara: Yes, of a movie, *Scary Movie 3*.

Me: What do you know about that movie?

Tara: My dad let me watch it. I said, "I'm scared." And he said, "Go play someplace else. I want to watch TV." So I watched it.

Me: Tell me about it.

Tara: A lot of people get dead and there's this scary girl named Chucky and she turns evil and she kills her parents. She gets a knife and kills people.

Me: Is the movie just pretend?

Tara: It's pretend, but for me it *feels* real.

Studies tell us that children are scared by TV and films even more often than we adults think they are, suggesting that kids may not always tell us about these fears. Our fast-paced lives may at times keep us from slowing down long enough to access our kids' deeper feelings. And too many of us still assume that if a show or movie that contains some violence is okay for us to see, it's okay for our kids, too, forgetting that children are more affected by the frightening acts they see on the screen and less able to understand them in a context of character, motive, and plot than we are. But even when we *do* try to diligently monitor our kids' exposure to violence in the media in our own households, it's simply not possible to ensure they will not encounter it elsewhere. Kids go to the homes of relatives and friends and get exposed to all kinds of things we might not want them to see. I spoke recently with nine-year-old Nelson, who told me, "One time I was at my dad's brother's house and his son was playing this video game. There's terrorists and counterterrorists and you can blow other guys up. There were images of guys throwing grenades and other guys getting their heads and guts slathered all over the ground."

Because the entertainment industry's marketing practices are so deceptive, it's genuinely confusing for many of us to know what's appropriate content for young children. When you see, for example, *Star Wars* pajamas, T-shirts, food, and toys marketed to your children, it gives you the message that this movie is for them. Children, drawn into this pervasive marketing, begin to ask to see the movie. Then the video games linked to the film are an easy next step. Even if we do keep our younger kids from seeing movies and video games rated for older viewers, they are still surrounded by violent images on

T-shirts, lunch boxes, and toys, and they hear about screen violence from other kids, and that alone can scare them.

When children have seen or heard about entertainment violence that has frightened or confused them, there are things we can do. Libby is a day care teacher who told me this:

> Geoffrey, who's four years old, came to school on Monday morning, marched up to me, and blurted out, "I saw *King Kong.*" Soon after, he was stomping around the classroom imitating King Kong—holding his arms out straight and grabbing kids. I immediately said to Geoffrey, "King Kong cannot come to school—he's scaring all the kids." But I knew that Geoffrey was scared himself and needed help working out his own fear from seeing the movie. So I encouraged him to come with me to the easel. I put on his smock and gave him some black paint. I said, "Show me what King Kong looks like."
>
> Geoffrey took the paintbrush and furiously painted black lines across the paper, back and forth and around and around until his paper was covered with black. As he painted he said, "King Kong is killing everybody. He's stepping on the people. Everybody is dead." I stayed with Geoffrey and gently said to him, "King Kong is scary. He's in a movie, but he can't come here. King Kong won't come here and hurt anybody." Then I said, "I'm going to put the King Kong picture away in my desk and we can talk about King Kong again later if you want to."

Here Libby shows us an important way to help kids process entertainment violence that has scared or confused them. We can encourage children to draw or paint what they've seen, and then follow their lead as we begin to talk about it, and then, if needed, reassure them about their safety.

As we try to support children in this way, we can remember that open-ended questions, the kind that have many possible answers and not just one "right" answer, are a crucial tool for us. By way of example, here's a conversation I had with my grandson Miles when he was four years old.

Miles: The bad guy of *Spider-Man* has a big white spider on him and he can sling webs like Spider-Man. His tongue is black and he has really, really big eyes.

Me: How do you know he's a bad guy?

Miles: Because once me and Jackson were watching *Spider-Man* at Jinny's house and when it was starting it had the *Spider-Man* song and we saw him.

Me: So you saw this guy on TV and you knew he was the bad guy?

Miles: Yeah. And I thought he was coming out of the TV, so I punched the TV. But it didn't break.

Me: So you thought the bad guy was coming out of the TV?

Miles: Yeah, so I punched it.

Open-ended questions encouraged Miles to tell me what *he* wanted to talk about. If I had asked narrower questions like "What color are the bad guy's eyes?" or "When did you go to Jinny's house?" I would not have found out much, if anything, about how he felt about what he'd seen on the screen.

Entertainment violence is particularly detrimental for young children like Miles because during the early years, as we know from child development theory, children don't clearly distinguish between fantasy and reality. They cannot be sure that what they see on the screen isn't real or won't happen to them. This makes viewing violent media genuinely threatening to young children. After I realized that Miles had tried to punch the TV to stop the "bad guy" from coming out, I was able to try to help him. "Nothing can ever come out of the TV, Miles," I said. "But you can make the bad guy go away if you turn the TV off. Or you can say to Jinny, 'I don't want to watch it—it's too scary.'"

Later, when Miles was playing with a "bad guy" action figure, I suggested "Let's make a TV with these blocks." We built a simple box with the blocks, and I put the action figure inside and covered the top with more blocks. Then I said, "The bad guy is *always* inside the TV and never comes out. You don't even have to punch the TV because the bad guy can't get out." Using this approach gave me a better chance of helping Miles understand that he was safe from the *Spider-Man* bad guy—or any others he saw on TV—than if I had tried to explain to him the difference between fantasy and reality or how the television works. Through play and using concrete materials as well as words, we can ease our kids' fears and clear up their confusions, and in so doing, help them feel more secure.

If Miles had been seven or eight years of age when he was scared by *Spider-Man*, instead of four, I would have used a different approach. Eight-year-olds can understand logical explanations and separate fantasy from reality more clearly than younger kids can, so I might tell a child that age that the *Spider-Man* bad guy is just an actor who puts on a costume and that movie makers know how to make him *look* scary, emphasizing that he's a fantasy character that doesn't exist in the real world. But if a child of eight seemed scared by something in the media, I would still encourage him to draw a picture. As it did with Geoffrey, drawing often helps children access their deeper feelings and fears when they may not be able to articulate them in words, and this can be the springboard for a reassuring discussion with an adult.

Virtually all of the educators and people who study child development whom I've interviewed agree that there should be government regulations to protect children from seeing media that is too violent or scary for them. The Federal Communications Commission was created to play this protective role, but it has outright abandoned this responsibility. The current rating systems for films, video games, and TV are managed from within the industries themselves—they call it self-regulation. The industries want it this way because outside control would undoubtedly result in stricter ratings and fewer sales. But it doesn't work for children and families.

In recent years, we have seen a steady erosion of the original rating system for movies. Both the amount and the intensity of violence in films rated okay for kids to see have increased. Movies once rated PG-13 are now PG, and movies once rated R are now PG-13. The film ratings board is made up of ten to thirteen film raters who are parents and whose identities are kept secret. (The names of the three people who oversee the ratings process were recently released under public pressure.) These film raters have no specific training in film or in child development or psychology. They have never made their criteria for rating movies available to the public and their anonymity allows them to continue to act without accountability. What is needed is an independent ratings board that operates across all media and outside of industry control, with ratings that can be easily used by parents.

But at this point in history, because no effective federal regulations exist to curb violent entertainment, it falls on us—parents and caregivers—to give our kids the protection they need. This often means having to turn off the TV while kids are in the room, not taking kids to see movies that are rated for older viewers, and perhaps missing out on seeing entertainment programming we adults would like to see. I am hopeful that this burden will not always fall on us. But until we have better protections for kids, I hope more of us will want to do what we can to keep frightening media from undermining our kids' sense of security. And when children have seen something that has scared or confused them—and this is almost inevitable—we can help them process what they've seen: first, by stopping to listen with our full care and attention to what our kids might be trying to say; and then, through play, art, and conversation, helping them process it, remembering to use open-ended questions and to be mindful of what's developmentally appropriate for each child.

Countering Glamorized Violence and Media Stereotypes

In the summer of 2000, the *Boston Globe* reported on a back page what I thought should be front-page news. Six major medical and mental health groups (the American Academy of Pediatrics, the American Medical Association, the American Psychological Association, and three others) had issued a joint statement on media violence. These six medical groups had reviewed all of the relevant research—hundreds of studies—and then issued one definitive statement: viewing entertainment violence can lead to an increase in aggressive behavior, particularly in children, and can also lead to emotional desensitization toward violence in real life.

This joint statement corresponded exactly with the voices of teachers I had polled in my own research studies over two decades, who told me that they had observed increased aggression in kids ever since the deregulation of television and often commented with concern over the lack of emotional sensitivity many kids exhibited when others were hurt. Having focused on this topic for years, I was not surprised to learn that the research of others in the field supported the conclusion that entertainment violence can desensitize kids to real violence. The violence in children's entertainment media is designed to look exciting and fun. Young kids, who are drawn to the graphic action of what's on the screen and who don't see the hurtful effects of violence, can easily get caught up in the excitement. Before they are even old enough to understand that hurtful acts cause pain, many kids have become desensitized to violence and even begun to acquire an appetite for it. This is especially troubling because researchers have shown that patterns of aggression at age eight are positively correlated with aggressive behavior in adulthood. I am sure that this early desensitization has contributed to the increase we've seen in recent years of young people who bring weapons to school and inflict pain on others without any apparent feeling for them.

Some of the parents I interviewed for this book told me that when they were put off by the violent TV and video games their kids liked they simply turned the other way. But if we do this, we cut ourselves out of the picture and ignore the impact the big media companies and their commercial allies have on our kids. I think there's a better way. We adults can actively counteract the negative messages our children get from the media, and try to reverse the resulting desensitization. But to do this, we have to get involved. The question is—how?

A group of my graduate students came up with some answers one night in class. A young woman named Claudia told us all that she was troubled because the two boys she babysits for, ages five and eight, were spending a lot of time consuming screen violence. "The younger boy watches violent TV cartoons," Claudia said, "and the older one plays violent video games like *The Lord of the Rings*. I've tried many times to entice them away from their screens, but they're hooked."

Claudia's quandary became the basis for a class discussion during which we came up with a number of ideas for her. First, we suggested, try to watch the TV shows and video games *with* the children. Ask them open-ended questions about what they see: "What do you like about this show?" "Who's your favorite character and why do you like him or her?" Later, try asking them to draw a picture of the show or the game and explain it to you. I pointed out to the students that research studies have shown that by watching and discussing violent media with kids, we can decrease the influence viewing violence has on them.

Children like to grapple with new ideas that fit with what they already know but make them look at things in a new way. We thought Claudia could also ask more focused questions that would get these two boys to think beyond the one-dimensional world presented to them by media: "What do you think about how they solve their problems on this show/in this game? If you had a problem like that, what would you do?" "Could you think of a way to solve that problem so that no one gets hurt?" We thought she might also encourage the boys to draw pictures of how the characters could solve their problems without violence and then talk about those drawings. Finally, we suggested that Claudia could ask questions and make comments to help the children think about the effects of violence: "I wonder why they don't show you how it hurts to fight with swords" or "If you really did that with a sword, how would it feel?" And she could try to "humanize" the bad guys with comments like "I wonder how that guy feels who is always getting chased and attacked" or "I wonder where he goes when he's not fighting—do you think he has a family?"

Questions like these can help kids think beyond good guy/bad guy stereotypes. And once they start thinking outside this particular box, it can spill over into more creative drawing and imaginative play as new ideas build on each other and extend to other areas.

When Claudia came back to class the next week, she had two drawings—one of a battle scene inspired by the *Pokémon* cartoon that the five-year-old had made, and a drawing full of creatures with swords and the words "Battle for Middle-earth" written across the top of the page (this is from *The Lord of the Rings*) made by the eight-year-old. Claudia said the boys had talked to her a lot about their drawings (in response to the open-ended questions she'd asked them), and that she felt encouraged that this dialogue had begun.

The good guy/bad guy world presented to kids in entertainment media is also, unfortunately, rife with racial, ethnic, and gender stereotypes. All too many kids' shows and tie-in toys convey the uniform message that violence against those who are different from the dominant group is justified.

Recently I picked up a toy labeled for children "ages 3 and up" made by Fisher-Price. It consisted of three Arab action figures in a box called Bandits, and these were clearly meant to be "bad guys." Each wore a turban that covered his eyes above a large, bulbous nose. Looking fierce and aggressive, these bandits wielded knives and guns.

I have talked with a great many young children who tell me that the good guys *have* to kill the bad guys. Here's a conversation I had with my grandson Jack when he was five years old.

Jack: Batman is a good guy and so is Spider-Man. They never kill anybody. But bad guys do kill people and talk really bad words.

Me: How do you know about bad guys?

Jack: Andy told me. (Andy is his seven-year-old friend from next door.) But there are no bad guys left. They've all been killed.

Me: Who killed them?

Jack: The good guys.

Me: I thought the good guys never kill anybody.

Jack: Well, they *have* to kill bad guys.

Many young children do pretend to "kill" bad guys in their play, but when children begin to think that the bad guys represent certain racial and ethnic groups, such as the "bandit" Arabs, they are learning dangerous lessons. In most children's programming, the "good guy" characters are overwhelmingly white and male, and the bad guys have nonwhite qualities—they wear masks, are darker in color, and may look more like monsters than people. Children learn the implicit lessons about race well. Studies show that children of all races are more likely to associate positive qualities like intelligence and being a leader with white characters on television and negative characteristics like laziness and breaking the law with minority characters, a fact that surely shapes the developing self-images of all kids. The situation is the same with video games. A recent survey of video game content by the organization Children Now found that human characters were almost exclusively white in video games for young children and that nearly all heroes were white.

Even in mainstream media offerings such as Disney films, racial stereotyping in the depiction of good guy and bad guy characters abounds, and because Disney is one of the largest institutional shapers of children's culture, virtually all kids are affected by the images it creates. In the 1992 movie *Aladdin*, Aladdin himself, who is the good guy, is depicted as an Arab, but his appearance is Anglicized and he speaks in standard American English. All of the bad guys in the animated film are also Arab, but they have beards, large, bulbous noses, sinister eyes, and heavy accents, and they wield swords. The film's opening song depicts Arab culture as "barbaric" and violent. Such an image enmeshes racial stereotyping with images of violence.

Holly, a mom with two daughters, Thalia and Taquina, who are nine and seven years old, told me about watching a Disney remake of *Little House on the Prairie*. Thalia and Taquina are biracial and bicultural. (Holly grew up, as she says, "white and middle-class," and her husband, Carlos, is "an indigenous man from Ecuador.")

"Within five minutes of watching *Little House on the Prairie*, one of the lines was 'I think we should kill all the Indians!' " Holly said. "And my seven-year-old burst into tears and said, 'Turn it off! I'm too scared, Mommy! Turn it off!' "

As an indigenous child, Taquina understandably felt scared by the threat to "kill all the Indians," and while most children may not be as visibly or immediately affected by media stereotypes as Taquina was in this case, they are not immune to the powerful messages about their own and other races implicit in the plots, dialogue, and images generated by the movies, TV, and tie-in toys.

Following on the heels of deregulation, we also saw a dramatic increase in gender stereotyping in the media as programs and toys were developed separately for girls and boys. Toy stores belonging to the major chains became gender divided almost overnight, with separate aisles for boys and girls—those with action-oriented and violent toys for boys; those for girls featuring makeup, vanity tables, and domestic themes. The colors alone could define for you which aisle you were in: black and red for boys, pink and purple for girls.

In the course of my research, I've found that teachers of young children report that boys and girls spend more of their time in gender-specific play than ever before. Julia, who teaches first grade, said this about the children in her classroom:

> My classroom is very diverse. But when I ask the little girls, "If you could be anyone in the world who would you be?" 99 percent

of them say Britney Spears. My students are five, six, and seven years old and they are emulating what they see on television. They come in and they care about fashion, the way you wear your hair; some have on lipstick and come in with little lip glosses. They wear little tube tops, off the shoulder, with their belly buttons showing. With the boys it's more physical—they act out more in an aggressive way because I think the images on television tell them "the more aggressive you are, the better you are." Everything with the boys is aggression, anger, competition.

Sadly, these gender stereotypes begin to limit how boys and girls see themselves, and one another, from an early age.

The good news is that while children take years to form their ideas about race and gender, and won't think about these things like we do, we can work with them little by little over time to counter the biases they are exposed to in the media and commercial culture.

Rachel is a friend and a teacher who told me that she was troubled by the racial stereotypes in her five-year-old son Claudio's beloved action figures.

One day when I was sitting with Claudio on his floor, I looked at his action figures and said, "Let's put all the good guys together in one pile." Claudio said, "Okay," so we started to pull out all the good guys and put them together. We lined them all up.

"How are these guys all the same?" I asked. "Like, they all have two feet."

Claudio caught right on and liked this! So he said, "They all have two arms." And I said, "And one head." We kept going back and forth naming their various features. Then I said, "They all have white skin!" Claudio looked at all the action figures and agreed. Then I said, "Let's do the same thing with the bad guys." We lined them up in the same way and described them:

Claudio: They all look mean.

Rachel: Yes, and kind of scary.

Claudio: They have masks.

Rachel: Yes, some have masks. And look, most of them are dark. They don't have white skin like the good guys. I wonder why there are no bad guys with white skin?

Rachel gives us a good example here of how we can talk with kids about stereotyping in ways that make sense to them: by using concrete materials and connecting what we say to how they see the world. Children Claudio's age love to put things into groups and talk about what is the same and different about them. So Claudio found this activity fun and Rachel helped him awaken a little bit to the racist messages in his toys. What if Rachel had said instead, "These toys are racist—the good guys are all white and the bad guys are all dark!" Then Claudio would've missed the chance to see this for himself in his own way. And her comment might have closed off communication between them and made Claudio feel guilty for loving his action figures.

When I spoke again with Holly, she expressed concern about the harmful gender messages her daughters might be getting from mass media.

"I feel like the media is an assault and I have to constantly be on guard to protect my girls," Holly told me. "I don't want them to live in a bubble, but I don't want negative media messages to get into their brain patterns telling them girls are not strong people in the world who can make passionate and sweeping changes."

My nine-year-old, Thalia, wanted to see the movie *Mean Girls*. I want her to feel part of her peer culture, but I also want her to be aware of the gender messages she's getting from the media. So

I tried to come up with a way she could see the movie that would be really thoughtful and look at it through a critical eye, as much as a preteen can be a critical thinker. So I said, "Okay, if you're going to see this movie, we have to come up with a list of questions we can talk about after you see it about the images of girls and the idea it shows about popularity." So together we made up a list of questions: Who are the mean girls? Why were they mean? What were some of the things that they were doing? What did you think about what they were doing? Then I wanted Thalia to think about body image issues, too, so I asked these questions: What do the mean girls look like? Were they considered to be pretty? Did they wear makeup? Did they wear expensive clothes?

Thalia had wonderful ideas after seeing the movie. She could identify what seemed like real friendship behavior and what girls would do to be friends that didn't feel right—things that Thalia said "made her stomach feel icky." But she saw into the movie to quite an extent and could say what she did and didn't think was good about what the girls did. After that, a friend who knew I had done this with Thalia told me that she and her husband are starting to do the same thing—they're making up questions with their daughters before they see certain movies and then talking afterwards—to help them recognize the biases and images of girls that they see. So maybe we will get more families doing this! Now I want to start a girls' group to look at issues of self-image, body image, and popular culture.

STEPS YOU CAN TAKE

We can take many steps to counter the harm that entertainment violence and stereotyping bring to our kids today; we can help restore to them healthy play, a sense of security and safety, and relationships based on love and kindness.

▶ Protect children from screen violence—on TV, in video games, and in movies—as much as you can.

   While it's almost impossible to protect our children from exposure to media violence completely, we can try. We can monitor the TV shows they watch at home and the video games they play, and carefully select the movies they see. We can let relatives and friends know that we are trying to limit our children's exposure to violence. One parent told me, "When we make a play date, I say to people, 'We don't have cable TV at our house and I prefer that there be no TV or computer time when my kids are at your house.' This is *not* easy for me to do—it's not in my comfort zone, but I do it."

▶ Watch your kids' war play to learn more about it.

   Observe your kids' war play and ask yourself some questions: Are my children making up their own characters, plots, and stories or is this play repetitively imitating something they have seen in the media? What themes seem to be important? Has my child been exposed to violence in the media? Can I relate this play to anything going on in her life?

▶ Hold the line on single purpose violent toys as much as possible.

   Most of us can't keep single-purpose toys out of the house completely. But we can avoid the movies and TV shows that have violent toys linked to them, we can avoid trips to the stores we know are full of war toys, and we can ask people who give our children gifts to steer away from single-purpose war toys.

▶ Try to facilitate creativity in war play so it can be the resource children need.

   If children's war play seems repetitive and violent, try to help them get beyond the narrow script. Try introducing open-ended materials like play dough or building materials to use along with single-purpose toys. You can make suggestions for how these materials might be used, such as "Can you make a bed/house/cave for Spider-Man with these blocks?" Try to base your suggestions on what you see happening in your kids' play. If they are pretending to shoot a bad guy, for example, you might say, "Can you figure out how to catch that guy and trap him?" When kids need help keeping their play safe, try using a joint problem-solving approach. You can say things like, "The pretend swords aren't working. You end up crying or in a fight when you use them. What can we do?"

▶ Tell stories or look for books that touch upon the same themes expressed in war play but that deemphasize violence.

Try your hand at storytelling. Pick a theme you know captures your child's interest, like feeling powerful, and make up a story about a pretend character using this theme—it could become the basis for creative play. Many wonderful children's books touch on the themes of mastery, power, and security but have no violence (a few of my favorites include *Desmond and the Monsters* by Althea, *Abiyoyo* by Pete Seeger, and *The Wizard of Oz* by L. Frank Baum). Read favorite books over and over rather than always having a continuous stream of only new books; this makes it easier for kids to reenact the story in play. Look for a few homemade props that might inspire a child to act out a favorite story.

▶ Help kids process the violent TV shows, video games, movies, and toys they do encounter.

Be aware that your child might be fearful or confused by something seen in the media. Try to be fully present and receptive to what you might hear. Try to ask open-ended questions to find out more about what your child is feeling. Encourage kids to use art and play materials, as well as conversation, to express themselves. If it seems needed, reassure children using concrete materials and drawing, as well as words; with children over the age of seven, you can rely more on logical explanations to address their fears.

▶ Counter the antisocial messages kids are getting from entertainment violence.

Try watching TV shows and video games with children and asking them open-ended questions: "What happens on this show?" "What do you think about what that character is doing?" Ask your child to draw you a picture of this show or game and then talk about it. Try asking some questions that provoke thinking: "Do you think they could solve this problem without fighting?" "What would happen if someone really did that?" "How do you think that bad guy feels when they attack him?"

▶ Help children become aware of racial, ethnic, and sex-role stereotypes in the media.

Try to talk with kids about stereotypes in ways that make sense to them. With younger children, use concrete materials to help you whenever possible and try to connect to how they see the world. You can ask younger children questions that help them begin to look more carefully at media: "What do boys do on this show?" "What do girls do?" "How does the bad guy on this show look?" "What about the good guy?" You can help older children think more critically about media by asking open-ended questions that help them think about stereotypes: "Did you notice that all the girls on this show are thin and have long hair? I wonder why." "Do your friends look like that?" "What do the girls on this show like to do?" "Is that like you and your friends?"

▶ Help both boys and girls go beyond gender-defined play and encourage them to play together.

We can help both girls and boys explore a wider variety of playthings and find common ground for playing together. One parent described watching her daughter sit on the front steps of their apartment building playing with her Barbie dolls next to a little boy who was playing with his *Star Wars* action figures. "They looked as if they wanted to play together," she said, "but they didn't know how." Here the mom could bring out some gender-neutral play material such as farm animals or play dough; or she could suggest that they make a house together with blocks where all their toy characters could live.

Another parent told me that her daughter Emma didn't like the fighting games her cousin Leo played, so this mom gave her daughter some strategies to use with Leo. The next time Leo started karate chopping, Emma put her hand out toward him and said, "I don't like to play that way." Leo said, "I want to play Power Rangers with you." And Emma said, "I don't like fighting games. Can we play something else? I want to make something with blocks." As the mom explained, Emma and Leo began to build together—they made a cafeteria for the Power Rangers.

CHAPTER 6

All Ads, All the Time

Teaching Your Kids to Talk Back to Consumerism

It has been troubling to watch the staggering increase in marketing to children that has occurred over the past two decades. In 1983, corporations spent $100 million on television advertising directed at kids; today, they pour roughly 150 times that amount—about $15 billion annually—into huge marketing campaigns that now extend beyond TV to include movies, the Internet, video and computer games, fast-food chains, retail stores, and even schools. And children have been profoundly affected by this invasion of commercialism into almost every aspect of their lives.

When corporations pitch their wares to kids, it's not just products they're selling through the increasingly sophisticated campaigns their marketers devise. It's also a mindset—one that tells kids, "You'll be happy if you have this toy, if you eat this food, if you look this way." One result is that from an early age many children get the message that happiness comes from acquiring things, which undermines their ability to find satisfaction and to meet their basic developmental needs through play and meaningful relationships with others. As we learn more about how commercialism is harming our children, we'll see that, despite its pervasiveness, there are many ways to counteract its destructive influence.

Where's the Harm in a Few Ads
for Children?

I sat next to four-year-old Troy as he watched TV. When the ads came on, the sound emanating from the TV got louder and Troy was intently watching. The spots sped by very fast, but I counted eight. There were ads for other TV shows and movies—one was for the movie *The Santa Clause* 3 and Troy immediately said, "I want to see that!" There were several ads for toys. One showed a *Pirates of the Caribbean* pirate ship you could make with Mega blocks. "I want that!" Troy exclaimed. And there was a vignette that showed very happy children at a birthday party and concluded with the announcer telling kids to have their parties at Chuck E. Cheese. "I'm going there," Troy said to me.

These ads profoundly influence Troy's ideas about himself and the world he lives in. Troy is just beginning to figure out what his own preferences are: What foods do I like to eat? What toys do I like to play with? What makes me feel happy? The ads he sees answer these questions for him, and in so doing they interfere with his own important process of self-discovery.

At four years of age, Troy doesn't know, as you and I do, that there's something behind the messages he sees that has to do with someone else's self-interest. Like other children his age, he takes things at face value and doesn't think about underlying motives. So he can't fully understand what ads are. This is why many advocates and organizations concerned with children's mental and physical health, including the American Psychological Association and the American Academy of Pediatrics, have called for federal restrictions on advertising aimed at kids under the age of eight—because, they say, the evidence from many studies shows that kids younger than this cannot understand "persuasive intent."

Of course marketing to kids has gone way beyond TV ads. All we have to do is take an inventory of our kids' clothes, sports equipment, toys, books, and food to see the abundance of corporate logos they carry. Product licensing—putting images or logos on products other than the ones they were created for, like SpongeBob SquarePants on a breakfast cereal—is a pervasive marketing tactic. (One father I interviewed for this book told me that on a family trip, when he realized they hadn't packed his five-year-old son's underwear and had to buy some, he couldn't find a pair of underpants for his son that wasn't tied to some movie or media programming.) Product licensing deceives young kids, who are swayed by what they see in the moment and can't easily consider product attributes that are less visible; they want the product, not because it is well made or of good quality, but because it carries a logo they recognize. A mother named Kathea told me this about shopping with her son:

> I took Rubin to the store to buy a new pair of sneakers. There were lots of different shoes, and I found a pair that looked functional and comfortable. But all of a sudden, Rubin was pointing to a pair of sneakers with Spider-Man on them. "Mom, I want these!" he said. "I really want these!" I tried to show him the ways that the other sneakers were better, but he didn't even want to try them on— he couldn't think about anything but the Spider-Man sneakers.

Because of his tendency to focus on visible aspects of things, and on one thing at a time, Rubin could only think about the Spider-Man logo and not about any of the attributes of the other sneakers his mom wanted to buy for him. Drawn by the logo into a world he couldn't really make sense of, Rubin didn't have the cognitive tools an adult would have to evaluate the marketing technique aimed at him. Because of their special developmental vulnerabilities, young children are easily exploited as consumers, and manufacturers capitalize on these vulnerabilities without restraint. And because we parents then often end up buying products we wouldn't otherwise buy, as Kathea ended up doing here, we parents are exploited too.

As marketers devise increasingly devious ways to advertise to kids, their ads become more and more difficult for even an adult to identify. For example, in recent years movies produced for children, such as Disney's *The Lion, the Witch, and the Wardrobe*, have been funded by dozens of sponsors per movie. Not only do they receive licenses to use images from the movie in product tie-in campaigns, but often these sponsors also have a hand in ensuring that references to their products are interwoven into the films themselves. (This is called "product placement," and it's been an often unperceived but standard feature of adult-oriented media for decades—such as James Bond checking his Omega watch or Superman eating Cheerios.)

How Commercial Culture Undermines Healthy Play

A lot of the parents I talked to commented that their children have so much more *stuff* than they had as kids. One parent, Zoe, said:

> My kids go to birthday parties and there's a ton of party favors and plastic things and hats and it's overwhelming the amount of plastic that comes into this house related to marketing to kids. I have three junk boxes filled with party favor stuff—toys that we got at McDonald's, or cheapo little things that come for free for going to the dentist. And I hate the fact that we're using all the world's resources to crank out these plastic toys.

Zoe describes the situation for many families in the United States today. Our kids *are* accumulating more and more stuff. They acquire little toys and trinkets as they go through mundane activities like going to McDonald's or a birthday party or the dentist. They ask us to buy what the marketing messages tell them they should want; at which point many of us, feeling stressed out and guilty over spending too little time with our kids, pull out our credit cards (Americans have more debt today than at any other time in history). According to Boston College economist Juliet Schor, this country constitutes 4.5 percent of the world's population, but we buy 45 percent of the global toy production, and our kids get an average of seventy new toys a year!

In the wake of the deregulation of advertising to children, marketers began pushing whole lines of toys linked to media programming, and a big shift occurred for children. Before that time, the toys they were given were likely to be open-ended ones—blocks, play dough, generic dolls and trucks and animals—and kids had grabbed whatever they could find around the house for additional props to use in acting out stories in fantasy play. But then they started getting the marketers' message: if you want to play G.I. Joe, you also need these action figures, these tanks, this equipment. The sheer number of items in each toy line grew and grew, but because these single-purpose toys were so inherently limiting (as discussed in chapter 3), kids often became bored with them rather quickly and so would ask for another new toy to spark their interest. In this way, consumerist forces have contributed to the erosion of play already under way as a result of other societal influences.

We can help our kids rediscover the kind of rich and meaningful play I've described earlier in this book by remembering that when it comes to toys, less is actually more. Children are more likely to develop their own inner resources and exercise their creativity if we give them fewer, not more, items to play with. It's the simple, flexible playthings—building materials, drawing paper and markers, clay, play dough, and craft materials—that foster the original and sustained play that our kids need and long for.

Consumerism and a Child's Sense of Self

Commercial culture also erodes the sense of inner security we hope to cultivate in our children. When they believe the marketing messages telling them their self-worth is based on what they have and how they look, children become less secure than if their sense of self is rooted in feeling good about who they are. A growing body of research shows that the more kids—both boys and girls—buy into consumer culture, the less happy they are, the more anxious, and the lower their self-esteem. They begin to measure themselves by asking how much they have relative to other people, and this is no accident: as one marketer confessed, "We're teaching them that if you don't have product X, you're not worthy."

Marketing poses particular dangers to girls, who get the message early on that above all it's their appearance that matters. Julia, the parent and first-grade teacher we heard from in the previous chapter, says that not only are the little girls in her class very preoccupied with "clothes, fashion, hair, and makeup," but the visions they strive to emulate—Britney Spears, the Bratz line of dolls—are quite sexualized. "I see a lot of sexual images with them—they want to dress like Britney Spears, wear little tube tops like the Bratz dolls. Instead of doing reading and math, they want to socialize about fingernail polish, or doing each other's hair, or the clothing they want to wear. . . . I see them competing with each other at such an early age. And they isolate [other] little girls who are not dressed the way they are."

The ideas that they need to look outside of themselves for affirmation and will find comfort through buying permeate the advertising aimed at girls. In the consumer culture that surrounds them, they see a single, stereotyped standard of what makes a woman attractive, which can easily undermine their satisfaction with their own unique beauty and abilities. Toys like the Bratz dolls, which focus little girls on shopping and sexy teenage behavior, reinforce this idea. Recently, the American Psychological Association Task Force, in its report on the sexualization of girls, expressed worry that Bratz dolls present an image of objectified adult sexuality to very young girls.

Studies show that the more a young girl is exposed to the media, the more likely she is to be dissatisfied with her body, her appearance, and herself, placing her at serious risk for eating disorders, depression, and anxiety later on. Too many of us have seen young girls get overwhelmed by this heavy socialization that starts when they are so young. Recently my friend Don lamented the influence of commercial culture on his young teenage daughter:

> My daughter is struggling with her studies at the moment and also—and this really hurts me—with her appearance. I hate, positively hate, image makers since they destroy the core of real beauty. They present us with an illusion, and sadly, and tragically, young, talented, and soulful girls, making their furtive steps into womanhood, get trapped in the illusion and think themselves ugly.

Fostering Healthy Values in Our Kids

What can we do to help both boys and girls resist the threat posed by consumer forces today? Many of the suggestions throughout this book—from power sharing to fostering creative play—will support kids' sense of self and confidence in who they are. And we can do other things, too. For one, we can help our children develop their own unique talents and interests that go beyond superficial concerns; this will strengthen their core identity and help them build the resilience needed to withstand commercial influences. We can do this in small ways by paying attention to what our children are intrigued by and lending support. For example, if a child is interested in insects, we can point out a bug or worm in the garden or we can save a dead bug found on the windowsill for her to examine with a magnifying glass. If a child seems interested in drama, we can help him collect fabric and hats for dressing up and read him stories that he can act out. In moments of free time, instead of turning to media to occupy our kids, we can suggest an activity that might fuel a growing interest. Children's preoccupations often change over time; what matters is that they learn early that to pursue one's own interests brings deep satisfaction. As a child, my son Kyle loved to draw, so I always made sure I had paper and markers for him, and I recycled various household materials that he could use for the collage creations that spilled from his imagination. Today Kyle is an accomplished visual artist whose passion and talent for art, I am sure, first took hold during those early years. Of course, he might just as well have become a teacher or a firefighter, but if we support our children as they explore the possibilities before them, we will encourage them to follow their own inner callings and discover satisfactions in life that go far beyond the surface values pushed by commercialism.

We can also show our kids that we value who they are rather than how they look or what they have. Kids are forever saying to us, "Look at me!" or "Look what I made!" What we say to them in response has a big effect on how they feel about themselves. If we make comments that evaluate, they'll be affected very differently than if we make comments that simply describe. Let's look at this example:

Annie has just drawn a picture and she says to her dad, "I made this picture for you, Daddy." Her dad looks at the drawing and says, "That's very good, I like it."

Here, when Annie's dad says the drawing is good and he likes it, he's evaluating the picture. When we make comments like this, kids quickly become dependent on our opinions, on what we think. They get the idea that pleasing us, or others, is what's important. What might Annie's dad say instead? Let's see.

Annie: I made this picture for you, Daddy.

Dad: Wow. You made a big green shape here with a long purple line along the side.

Annie: Yeah. It's a boat with a paddle. And here's the fish.

Dad: Oh, so you made a boat and you even put a fish in the picture.

Annie: It's of when you go fishing!

Here, when Annie's dad observes the big green shape with the long purple line next to it, he's describing what he sees in the drawing, which lets her know that he's genuinely interested in what she's doing. Comments that describe instead of evaluate often start with "you" instead of "I." They encourage kids to look inward for direction instead of looking only for outside approval, while at the same time letting them know that we are genuinely interested in what they do. And engaging in this kind of dialogue opens up lines of communication.

We have endless opportunities throughout the day to talk to our children—about how they act, what they build, what they draw, how they look. If we pay more conscious attention to the kinds of comments we make on a regular basis, we can help ensure that we will have a strong influence on what qualities our kids come to believe are important. With our daughters, we can be especially conscious about making comments that describe instead of evaluate, especially when it comes to appearance. Do we say, "You're so pretty," thereby giving them a version of the same message they get from commercial culture about what's important? Or do we say, "Tell me about what you made with the Legos" or "That was so kind of you to share your snack with me." These comments give another message: I value what you *do*; I appreciate who you *are*. When we have conversations like these with our children, we help them combat the marketing forces that focus them on seeking external approval rather than exploring their own unique interests and attributes.

How Commercialism Undercuts Relationships

One of the most serious ways that consumer culture is harming children today is by undermining their relationships with parents. From a very young age, kids see ads that tell them to eat, play with, or wear things that their families often can't afford to buy or don't want them to have. Betty, the former elementary school director we heard from earlier, talked about how this outside influence eats away at the primary bond of love and trust between parents and kids:

> Advertising deprives children of full engagement with the adults in their lives who have their best interests at heart. From a very early age children are programmed to think that somebody outside their most intimate relationships knows what will make them happy. A child wants a certain cereal in the supermarket and is fighting with the parent to get it. They don't trust their parents because they have seen it on television—this is the cereal to buy.

This cereal scenario is no accident. The marketing industry quite consciously aims to make an end run around parents and sell directly to kids. One senior manager at Heinz was quoted in the *Wall Street*

Journal as saying, "All of our advertising is targeted to kids. You want that nag factor so that 7-year-old Sarah is nagging mom in the grocery store to buy Funky Purple."

Getting kids to use what the industry calls the nag factor to get their parents to buy things pays huge dividends for marketers: after repeated "nags," most kids get what they want. Market researchers estimate that children ages four to twelve influence some $565 billion of their parents' purchasing each year, and children's influence on adult spending is growing at an estimated 20 percent per year. Meanwhile, studies show that kids' repeated requests often cause discord at home, something that was confirmed for me by the comments of many parents I interviewed, including Norah. "From the moment I get home from work," she told me, "my daughter starts begging me for things she's seen on TV. I get so annoyed—I feel really angry at her. I'm tired, I want to relax, she's nagging me for a new pair of jeans or a CD."

Research by economist Juliet Schor shows that the more kids buy into the culture of getting and spending, the worse their relationships are with their parents. This is an important finding because kids need a healthy, positive parent-child bond as an anchor of their sense of security, especially today with so many societal forces working against them.

And, as mentioned above, other studies tell us that children who are more materialistic are not as happy and have fewer positive relationships with their peers than those who are less caught up by consumerism. This makes sense because most marketing messages promote a "me first" way of being, where one's own satisfaction is the goal. So the more kids buy into materialism, the harder it is for them to create mutual, caring relationships. And for girls, there is the added emphasis on appearance that makes it even harder for girls to find authentic connections that transcend looks, as Julia noticed with her daughter's friends:

I went to my daughter's kindergarten graduation last Monday. I walked her to class and immediately the little girls ran to her and said, "Jalissa, what do you have on? What are you wearing?" It wasn't a matter of her being there, what mattered was what she was wearing. And from there they started comparing their clothes and jewelry and whether or not their hair was up or down.

What can we do to stem the tide of materialism that threatens to interfere with the kind of substantive, loving relationships our children need? A good place to begin is to ask ourselves what role material objects play in our own lives and how we use them in our relationships with children. Nina, who lives in Brookline, Massachusetts, with her two sons, put it this way:

I think the first step for every parent is to understand what their relationship is to all of these things. We need to understand: What do I buy? Why do I choose to buy something? What am I wearing? Because objects stand in as symbols of who we are and what we are and wouldn't that be great if we could make that conscious?

Joe, a forty-three-year-old dad from Norwalk, Connecticut, was worried that his two sons might be confusing materialism with love.

When my mother comes to visit she always brings the kids toys. I ask her not to but she keeps on doing it. Now they always say they want her to come visit and they talk about what they're going to get. Last time she arrived, my son Terry went to the door and the first thing he said was, "What did you bring me?"

Many of us use toys or material things as a way to express love to children. But we should be careful about this. If kids focus too much on things, as Joe's son Terry seems to, they may miss discovering the deeper joys that can be found in intimate relationships. Research tells us that when interactions with others are based on materialistic values, intimacy and empathy are sacrificed and relationships are more shallow and superficial.

There are also parents who use toys and presents to help soften a child's disappointment or sadness. I thought about this at a sporting event I went to last year with several families. One of the children, Ravi, six years old, was sad because his uncle, who had been visiting the family, was leaving after the baseball game. Ravi's dad, in an effort to cheer him up, told his son that he could get a toy from one of the vendors outside after the game. Ravi got excited about what he would buy and kept talking about it throughout the game, and the sadness he had been feeling seemed to fade away. But where did it go? Children learn how to manage their emotions only when they are allowed to *feel* them and learn through experience, perhaps with the help of a sensitive adult, how to handle them. If instead of trying to distract his son, Ravi's dad had listened to his feelings, talked with him about the sadness we have when someone we love is leaving, and encouraged him to tell his uncle how he felt, Ravi would've gained valuable experience in expressing and managing his emotions, and an enhanced sense of connection to both his dad and his uncle. We can help our kids develop and maintain close, deep relationships—which will be more satisfying and lasting than any toy or trinket—if we are careful to avoid using material things as a quick fix in place of genuine emotional expression and connection.

Giving money or other material rewards to get kids to set the table or take out the trash is another way we can easily undermine relationships. If we reward kids for doing household tasks, we may be teaching the wrong lesson to our kids about why we do things for each other. What's essentially a business transaction might help get jobs done quickly, but in the long run it may undermine the growth of intrinsic values like generosity and cooperation. As we discussed in chapter 4, giving this kind of reward to kids is a form of using our parental power *over* them, an approach that can inhibit the development of values and behaviors that grow from the inside. I would argue that working *with* our kids by talking to them about, and demonstrating, *why* we work together as a family—because everyone is needed, because we want to help each other, because sharing the load holds us together—will, over time, better cultivate their spirit of generosity and desire to cooperate.

One way to defend against the erosion of relationships by commercial culture is to find regular times to do things together as a family away from the distractions offered by the media. Roxanna, who lives in Boston with her partner and three children, described their routine:

> In our family we like to play cards and board games—that's something we do together a lot. And we eat together every night. If one of the kids has play practice, we work around that. When we sit down together, we talk about our day, we share what happened and how we're feeling. This time binds us together.

Carl and Hope, who live near Galesburg, Illinois, with their two children, George and Zebulon, have devised another way to bypass commercial culture and encourage empathy and closeness. Carl explained:

> For Christmas we give our two sons one present each from Santa Claus and then we give them coupons. I hand-draw the coupons. They're things like "Skip vegetables and still get your special treat" or "Have us read an extra book to you one night." Or even extra TV time. And they give us coupons, too, and they give each other coupons.
>
> When our kids were little, I gave my wife "sleep" coupons. When it was her morning to get up with the kids, if she gave me a coupon,

then she didn't have to get up and it was still my turn the next day. George, our six-year-old, gave coupons to Zebulon, our four-year-old, where he would take off Zeb's shoes for him when we came into the house, or where he would play with him. Zeb has given my wife a few coupons just recently. One is for my wife to be able to take a nap for half an hour. He even drew them—[one] has a little bed on it. Or coupons for when she's on the phone, that he'll go play by himself. George gives back rub coupons—he gives a pretty mean back rub. Once he gave me "bossy boy" coupons—he knows he gets kind of bossy—so that when he was being too bossy, I could give him a bossy boy coupon and he would chill. When it all boils down, it's a heck of a lot more work to give this kind of present than to go to the mall for half an hour and find something. But it's definitely worth it.

In giving gift coupons, George and Zeb take the time to think about what they can do to make others in the family happy—to bring joy to them through their own actions. And because we build relationships by actively engaging in them, carrying out these coupon promises takes the kids to a deeper level of empathy and commitment.

Finally, we can help our kids withstand materialism by encouraging their connection to the natural world. When children discover the harmony and wholeness of nature, they sense the larger context of life through which we are all interconnected, and this can foster an inner balance that will help counteract the pressures of an overstimulating, commercialized culture.

Luckily, we can nourish this bond to nature in all kinds of urban environments—city parks, overgrown lots, apartment balconies—as well as in wilder places. I once knew an urban teacher whose class followed a single tree on their school playground from September to June, through all of its seasonal changes. The children tracked the cycles of this tree—how its leaves changed, how its seeds grew and fell, the wildlife and insects that lived in it. Sometimes they brought leaves, bark, or seeds from the tree back into the classroom to examine, draw, paint, or glue onto paper. Through this one tree, the children became attuned to the rhythm and patterns in nature.

We can easily incorporate activities like this into our daily lives with kids wherever we live. We just have to pause and be present for a moment with our surroundings. With our kids we can observe what's around us—notice the trees, birds, insects, a seed in a sidewalk crack, how the wind blows the leaves, how the clouds change shape. At the age of three, my grandson Miles squealed with excitement to see pigeons on the back porch of our city house. It took just a minute to pause with him to watch those pigeons—how they hopped, pecked, and bent their heads to look for food, how their colors changed in the light. We can sit and listen with kids, too, to the sounds of nature. Did you hear a bird? An insect? The wind?

We can encourage kids to collect things from outside—leaves, seeds, acorns, bugs, feathers, rocks, bark, sticks. We can help them grow things from seeds in pots indoors. And we should remember that kids need to develop their own relationship to nature on their own terms, so we should try to give them unstructured time as often as we can, whether it's in a forest or a park or a backyard, for exploration and discovery.

Talking Back to Consumerism

We can also take steps that will help our kids deal more directly with commercial culture. First and foremost, as research has shown, we'll have the greatest chance to minimize the influence of commercialism in their lives if we reduce or eliminate television. When I interviewed a father named Scott, he told me how he and his partner, Renaldo, who live with their two children, Isabella, age six, and

Spencer, age three, in New York City's Greenwich Village, decided to eliminate television completely from their household.

> Renaldo and I had noticed that being in front of the TV seemed to make Isabella and Spencer either numbed out or irritable and kind of wild. So about a year ago, we decided to move our TV set to the basement and no longer allow our kids to watch it. It has improved our lives dramatically. Without the television, we find ourselves so much more connected as a family. Isabella and Spencer are way more calm and cooperative. They play together more creatively, and they've stopped begging us to buy things they've seen on TV.

Most of us won't eliminate TV from our children's lives altogether, as Scott and Renaldo did, but even if we can vastly reduce our kids' exposure to commercial TV, we'll see some of the benefits Scott describes. Beyond this, we can also help our children see through the messages aimed at them by the marketers, working differently with kids of different ages. Nina started with her two sons, Mosby and Phinneas, when they were infants:

> When they were babies, I cut out any visual stimuli that would have to do with corporate images or logos. I just didn't want the preverbal imprinting. Those images don't mean anything to a child, they're just brightly colored things, but they are actually affecting them in a powerful way in the primitive part of their brain. And to family and friends, I said, "Please don't buy them anything with logos on it."

Then, as Nina's children became preschoolers, she started pointing out ads, first on billboards. She said, "See that one up there? Wow, look at that—they want me to buy that car!" And pretty soon, she told me, her young kids were pointing out ads, too, and saying, "Oh, they want me to buy such and such, Mama."

Carl, the Illinois dad with two sons we heard from earlier, also wanted to help his young kids begin to recognize advertising and the motives behind it. So he began pointing ads out—on cereal boxes, in the previews before videos, on magazines—and telling his sons that they were there "because they want your money." Nina used a similar approach when her son Phinneas was five years old. "These people are trying to trick you," she told him. "They want your money. If you have five dollars in your hand, they want to get it." Nina's use of the idea of "tricking," a concept familiar to most five-year-olds, and the very concrete image of "five dollars in your hand" helped Phinneas understand more about what's behind an ad.

Little by little, we can encourage children to think more critically about marketing by asking questions that will help them build their own ideas. Here's a conversation my daughter-in-law Lori had with her son Miles when he was six.

Miles: Mom, you know Berry gets Doritos and corn chips in his lunch.

Lori: Those taste good, don't they? Sometimes it's okay to have them, but snacks like apples and oranges are better for you.

Miles: And they're *Star Wars* Doritos!

Lori: That's funny. *Star Wars* is a movie and Doritos is food. Why would they mix them together? One is a movie and one is a food.

Miles: I know why, Mom. Because they want you to buy the Doritos.

Lori: But Doritos aren't healthy. They're okay once in a while, but they're junk food. Why do you think they put *Star Wars* on food that isn't good for you?

Miles (suddenly thoughtful and quiet): I don't know.

Lori's questions, like all open-ended questions when they fit with how kids see the world at a given stage of development, helped Miles think more about logos and how they're used to sell products, even ones that aren't good for him.

As kids get even a little older, we can talk with them more specifically about ads. What is this ad trying to sell me? How are they doing it—are they using music, visual tricks, happy faces—to get me to want this product? Eight-year-old Hank, whom I talked to in a third-grade classroom, was beginning to get wise to the tricks of advertisers. "They're liars!" he exclaimed. "They made a [toy] car look like it jumped really high in the air and I got it but it hardly jumped at all—it didn't do anything!" Older children can also begin to understand the subtler connections behind what marketers do. Nina says that now that Mosby is nine "I'm talking to him about corporations and profits and dividends—trying to explain those as simply as I can—and he is very interested."

Some of the parents I spoke with have found creative ways to help their kids handle the yearning to buy without giving in to it. Ellen, who lives outside of Seattle with her husband, Octavio, and daughter, Ariela, told me that she thinks the advertising industry thrives on impulse buying, so she uses two techniques to help her daughter, who's seven, control her urge to buy. When Ariela asks for something, Ellen has her put it on a "wish list." Just writing down the names of the things she wants helps Ariela manage her desire. And because she sometimes changes her mind and erases an item, Ellen told me, she's learning that her initial impulsive desires may not last. Ellen also encourages Ariela to use the advertising inserts in newspapers in a similar way by cutting out ads for the things she'd like to have and pasting them on a piece of paper. "Sometimes that by itself gets her out of 'I want! I want!'" she says. "She puts it on the paper and then sometimes she stops asking for it. Also, she's looking at the prices so she's using reading and math skills. As she gets older, I'm going to give her a 'budget' (a hypothetical one, not a real one), and let her cut things out that fit that budget."

Another parent I interviewed, Brent, who lives in a suburb of Boston, used the book *The Gimmies* (a Berenstein Bear book) to give his kids, ages five and seven, a name for the longing they feel to get something new. They've learned to say that they "have a case of the Gimmies" when they want a new toy, and Brent explained that giving a name to the urge to buy has allowed him and his kids to talk about this desire without yielding to it. Nina has found a different technique to help her children step back from the urge to buy. "If my kids ask to buy something, I try to ask them questions to help them think about it: What are we going to do with that? How would you play with it? Do you already have anything like that now?"

We can also help our kids handle trips to stores and other venues that offer attractive merchandise much more easily if we tell them ahead of time what to expect. For example, if you're going to the grocery store on a quick errand, you can say before you go in, "We're just buying bread and eggs right now; we're not getting anything else." Knowing this ahead of time usually helps a child refrain from asking you to buy something that catches his or her eye. When I take my grandkids to the Boston Children's Museum, if I tell them before we go in that we're not going into the gift shop, they don't even mention it. But if I don't say this at the outset, they'll ask to go into the store.

Finally, some parents are helping their kids think more about the things we buy and use in other, even more complex ways: Where do they come from? Who made them? What are they made of? What happens to them when we throw them away? Holly told me that her daughters, Thalia, age nine, and Taquina, age seven, had learned about the concept of fair trade at church and at school. Parents at their school, including Holly, organized a fund-raiser that sold fair trade coffee, tea, and chocolate and then a farmer from Santo Domingo came in to talk with students about what fair trade means. Now, Holly says, when she goes clothes shopping with her daughters, they look carefully at the labels.

> When we go to the mall, and they find something they like, I say, "Let's see where it was made." Thalia likes the Limited Too and it's all enslaved labor. Sometimes she wants to buy something and we talk about the people who made it. I want her to be a little girl and not have the burden of the world on her shoulders, so she does buy some of these things, but I want her to understand that someone, somewhere made this thing.

As part of our effort to educate our children about our consumer culture, we can encourage them to take a closer look at their clothing and toys and we can point out where these things are made. As they get closer to the ages of Holly's daughters, we can talk with them about the people who made these items and about their circumstances. We can help them learn more about our interconnectedness with the workers in the sweatshops who produce many of the items we buy. A Gap shirt made in El Salvador, for example, sells in the United States for twenty dollars, but the workers receive just twelve cents for making it. Working on consumer issues with kids is an ongoing process. With our help, our children can slowly build conscious awareness about living in a consumer society and gradually learn to look critically at the marketing messages aimed at them.

Even in Our Schools?

In the last fifteen years, even schools have increasingly been used—or rather, misused—for commercial purposes. Marketing to kids has infiltrated schools in a variety of ways: wall advertisements, promotional samples, school fund-raising schemes, logos and printed ads on book covers, "contests" where students claim "prizes" at local franchises, television commercials, sponsored educational materials, incentive programs, and advertising on school buses.

Publicly funded schools belong to the public and shouldn't be used as vehicles to increase profits for corporations. And while any marketing to kids takes unfair advantage of them, marketing in schools is even more unethical because it occurs in a trusted public space where children are required to spend a great deal of their time. Not only do the advertisers get the opportunity to pitch to a captive audience, they also exploit the authority of the educational institution: if I saw it at school, many kids will think, it must be good.

Currently, 40 percent of our nation's secondary students are required to watch Channel One, a ten-minute daily news show with two minutes of commercials for products like Twinkies and Mountain Dew. And all over the United States, kids use corporate-sponsored curriculum kits—educational materials that companies develop. A review of seventy-seven of these classroom kits found that nearly 80 percent were blatantly biased in favor of the sponsoring company or its agenda. For example, a curriculum produced by Exxon emphasizes the earth's resilience in responding to oil spills, and a Nabisco math curriculum has children estimate how many chocolate chips are in a bag of Chips Ahoy.

Tina's son Maurice, age eight, attends a public school in New Hampshire, and when I interviewed her she was distraught over its reading incentive program.

Every night we get a homework package and in it is a calendar. I'm supposed to fill out a form to show how many hours Maurice reads. He is supposed to read for fifteen to twenty minutes a day and I'm supposed to write it in and send it in at the end of the month. Then I get a "reader's coupon" for a kid-sized pizza at Pizza Hut.

I wrote to the school that I don't want Maurice to get something free for reading. And I hate families being manipulated by the school into going to eat horrible food. The teachers want Maurice to get the coupon so he won't be the only one not getting it, so he brings the coupon home.

While many parents like Tina are discouraged by the commercialism invading our nation's schools, there are signs of hope from parents in communities across the country who have been organizing to rid their communities of this kind of marketing. Parents in Seattle, Washington, for example, joined together into what became a broad and powerful coalition advocating for commercial-free schools in their city. In the last chapter of this book, you can read about what those parents did and how you can begin a similar grassroots effort in your community.

STEPS YOU CAN TAKE

▶ Keep it simple with toys. Remember that fewer is better, simpler is better.

▶ Help children explore their own unique talents and interests, and show your interest in their activities by making descriptive rather than evaluative comments about what they do.

▶ Avoid substituting material things for emotional expression and connection.

▶ Find regular times to be together as a family and encourage children to contribute to family life as a way of caring rather than a means to getting a material reward.

▶ Reduce or eliminate television, especially children's exposure to commercial TV.

▶ Help children find peace and sanctuary through connecting to the natural world.

▶ Point out ads, talk about why they exist, and ask open-ended questions that encourage children to think more about marketing, keeping children's ways of seeing the world in mind.

▶ Help children learn how to handle the urge to buy without giving in to it.

▶ Prepare kids ahead of time for visits to a store.

▶ Talk with children about our interconnections with the people and conditions that produce the items we consume.

CHAPTER 7

Might Does Not Make Right

Resolving Conflicts Creatively

Taking back childhood also means helping our children find peaceful rather than aggressive or violent ways of solving problems in their relationships. As we explored a bit in chapter 5, children today are inundated with examples of "might makes right" ways of resolving disagreements and differences. Teachers tell me about the rising number of kids with "short fuses"—kids who punch and kick classmates and use mean-spirited, hurtful language with other children and with adults. And when I talk with kids about the conflicts they have, many of them sound like seven-year-old Elvin, a second-grader in a Boston public school: "Me and my brother had a fight and he pushed me, so I pushed him back and then he fell and broke a chair. Then he got angrier and the more he got angrier, the more I slammed him on the floor."

A convergence of societal trends—economic stress on parents, increased academic pressure on children, overexposure to models of coercion and force on TV and in other media, the loss of creative play time and spontaneous social interactions among kids both inside and outside of school—is making it very hard for children today to develop the positive skills necessary for getting along and settling disputes. At the same time, the results of one of the biggest research studies ever done in the field of conflict resolution, a two-year study conducted by the National Center for Children in Poverty (NCCP) at Columbia University's Joseph L. Mailmon School of Public Health including approximately five thousand second- through fifth-grade children in fifteen New York City public schools, showed that children *can* learn these skills and put them to use in resolving conflicts peacefully. In order for this to happen, however, kids need to see and experience positive alternatives to aggression and coercion in their everyday lives. By how we handle the conflicts we have with our children, we can begin to teach these skills to them from the time they are very young. And as we do this, we'll help our kids feel more secure and pass on to them the relationship skills they urgently need now and for the rest of their lives.

To many of us, it doesn't come naturally to handle conflicts with our kids in a cooperative way. Most of us grew up in families where disagreements got resolved by either aggression or withdrawal—by fight or flight. As Duane, a dad of two preschoolers in Cambridge, Massachusetts, said, "I can remember my mother screaming and yelling multiple times. She used time-outs with us, but mostly we were hit." And Ernestine, another parent at the day care center Duane's kids attend, said, "If there was an argument in my family, for whatever reason, if one person didn't get their way, we didn't talk. I didn't talk to my father for one whole year when I was sixteen."

When we get into conflicts with our children, the power dynamics we discussed in chapter 4 come up front and center. The urge to use our adult *power over* kids intensifies when they do things we don't like, but when we use our adult power during conflicts, we create an adversarial relationship—it becomes "we" versus "them"—and the emotional distance between kids and adults expands. How can we bring conflicts into the middle ground of *power sharing*, and transform the disputes we have with our kids into win-win situations that don't disconnect us from each other?

We can start by thinking about our own earliest experiences with conflict. We learn a lot about how to deal with conflict from our family and culture, and most of us carry these patterns into our own parenting. As Luisa, who lives outside of Boston with her two young children, said, "When I scream to my children I feel like I'm going back into my background. I'm going back to when I was a child and my mom was screaming to me. And now I'm using the same words my mom said to me."

In the family I grew up in, I didn't hear screaming like Luisa did because conflicts were never discussed or expressed out in the open. Different culture groups handle conflict very differently, but I believe that for all of us, a collaborative approach—involving dialogue, negotiation, and joint problem solving—will enable us to meet our children's needs and help them learn how to build strong relationships.

I spent many years trying to learn new ways to handle conflict that were different from what I learned in the family I grew up in, and I'm still trying today. It can be hard to break the old behavior patterns, and sometimes there can even be pressure from those around us not to. Lynne, the conflict resolution and diversity trainer we heard from earlier, lives in New York City with her husband and two young sons, and is very attuned to this issue.

What I want to do is to look at the cultural norms we grew up with. What was good and what was bad about them? And where do we want to make a change? There are a lot of good things that we want to keep. But what are the things that we really feel like—You know what? I don't have to do that just because I grew up with that. I can look at it and see what it did in my life and I can decide that it's something I don't want to bring to my children's lives.

There's a lot of pressure to raise your kids the way you were raised in the African American community. And if you're doing things against that, then you get a lot of pressure. Particularly you can get a lot of pressure that says, You're acting white. You're raising your kids the white way. My boys were "labeled" by some family members and elders when they were younger, simply because some of the methods my husband and I chose for handling conflicts with them were not considered the "norm" for our culture. They were called "spoiled" and we were told that our children were "running the show" in our household. We still occasionally get challenged on these differences, but the proof is in the pudding now in terms of the wonderful and respectful people they are. I think there are many of us who really do need the courage to say, "No. I'm just raising my kids my way. This is how I want to do it." If you really feel like there are some new ideas out there for you that you want to try, then I think you can try those. It doesn't mean you're abandoning your culture.

No matter what our family or cultural backgrounds, we can become more conscious about how we handle conflicts with our children by asking ourselves, as Lynne suggests, What are the aspects of the family patterns we grew up with that we would like to keep and what do we want to change? With this in mind, we can look at our most recent conflicts with our kids and ask some questions: What exactly happened? How did I feel? What did I say? Did I get angry and aggressive? Did I withdraw and shut down? Did anything get truly resolved?

Getting on the Same Side

When our children are doing something we don't like, how can we handle things so that we don't become opponents but instead stay connected and work together? Often we can see how to "get on the same side" of a conflict with our kids if we ask ourselves, How is my child feeling right now and what does she or he need? Then we can try to reframe the conflict in a way that captures both their needs and ours.

Here's an incident I had with my grandson Jack that will show you what I mean by "getting on the same side." Jack was playing at my house one summer day when he was three years old when he accidentally cut his toe. The toe was bleeding and Jack began to wail. I went to get a washcloth and some antibacterial ointment and walked back into the room with these items in my hand. When Jack saw them his face grew more panicked and he screamed frantically. I sat down next to him and spoke gently.

Me: We need to get your toe washed and put this cream on. How can we wash the blood off your toe and put some cream on it?

Jack kept on screaming and seemed really frightened.

Jack: No, no. *Don't touch it!*

Me: Okay, I won't touch it. But I wonder, how can we wash off the blood and put on this cream? The cream doesn't hurt at all.

Jack reached for the washcloth. He lightly began to wipe the blood from his toe.

Me: Oh—good idea. *You* can do it. Here's the cream, too.

Jack took the tube of cream and took the top off. Then he squeezed some out and rubbed it on his toe.

For me there are some important ideas in this story. First, it was plain that Jack felt scared when he saw the red blood trickling down his toe. And I think he felt powerless, too, as I came toward him with the washcloth and the cream. So what Jack needed was to feel more in control in this scary situation, and if I could get on the same side of the problem *with* him, he'd feel less overwhelmed. By framing the situation as one we could deal with together ("How can *we* wash the blood off your toe and put some cream on it?"), we were looking at the bloody toe as the problem we had to solve together rather than a conflict where I would use my adult power over him and intensify his feelings of fear. When Jack, still scared, blurted out, "No, no. *Don't touch it!*" I reassured him right away. "No, I won't touch it," I told him, giving power back to him. And then I added that the cream did not hurt at all, hoping that this information would help him feel less apprehensive about what we needed to do. Then I posed our common problem to him again: "But I wonder, how can we wash off the blood and put on this cream?" and by then Jack was able to move forward and work with me to take care of his toe.

Language and Listening

The words we use with one another can create or prevent conflicts and make them better or worse. I thought about this recently when I sat in the waiting room at the dentist's office next to a father and a little boy who looked to be about three years old. The boy was taking out all the magazines from the rack, and when the father told him to stop he reached for still more magazines. With a tone of annoyance, the father said, "Can't you keep your hands to yourself? You always have to touch everything!" The little boy moved to a table with books on it and started putting them in a pile. The father grabbed the child and forcefully put him in a chair, and then said sternly, "You sit here and don't move. If you move, we won't get any ice cream later."

This conflict began when the little boy's dad viewed him as the problem instead of "getting on the same side" of the situation with him (what can my child do while we're waiting in this boring office?). And then the language the dad used made the conflict grow worse. (*Can't you keep your hands to yourself? You always have to touch everything!*) This statement of criticism put the boy down for expressing his need to explore, and it fed the "me" versus "you" struggle they were already in. Then, the dad threatened his son by saying, "If you move, we won't get any ice cream later."

Criticism, blame statements, put-downs, and threats are "power over" ways of using language. When we use them, we create emotional separation between ourselves and our kids. "Power over" statements carry the message that children are doing something wrong. "You're trying to make me late." "You're always messy." "You make me mad." "You" comments like these cause hurt and defensiveness and almost always escalate a conflict. But if we don't say things like this, what can we say instead to express our feelings to our kids and get them to cooperate with us?

One of the biggest challenges in all of our relationships is to reframe a problem in a way that opens up the possibility of dialogue, and an important first step is making the shift from blaming someone else to looking within. An "I" statement transforms blame onto another person into an expression of our own feelings and needs.

Using "I" statements can be a first step in solving all kinds of conflicts and problems with children. Lynne, the conflict resolution and diversity trainer we heard from earlier, told me a story about how when she shifted from using a blame statement to an "I" statement, the escalating tension between herself and her son and niece turned into understanding and connection.

I remember we were in Philadelphia. We had gone on a trip, and I had driven. I was tired and we had to go back, and we'd stayed a lot later than I'd wanted to stay, so by the time we left it was like ten o'clock at night and I was really exhausted and Jabari and Sekai were hyper about the trip back. I don't remember exactly what they were doing, but whatever it was, it got on my nerves. And I said, "The two of you are just getting on my last nerve." And the look on their faces—they were just crushed.

And I said, "You know what? You have been wonderful on this trip. I'm just tired. I'm scared about going back, having to drive by myself because I'm getting tired." And Jabari, who was eight at the time, said, "I understand, Mommy. I understand how you could be frustrated. You aren't really saying that we got on your nerves. You just said that because you were really frustrated." And I said, "Yeah."

It was incredible. I was able to lay myself out in front of them and say, "That's not what I meant to come out of my mouth. I'm scared about something."

So one thing we can do to reduce conflict with our kids begins with examining the language we use when we talk to them. Are we criticizing them and putting them down? When we don't like what they're doing, can we express this in terms of our own feelings and needs instead of as blame, as Lynne did? In the following pages, we'll see more how "I" statements can be helpful in other conflict situations.

A second bedrock communication skill that can help us create trusting, positive connections with our kids, and is especially helpful in conflict situations, is called "active listening"—it's what we do when we listen with full attention and, for a short time at least, suspend our own ideas and opinions. When we practice active listening with our kids in our ongoing relationships every day, our bonds with them strengthen and we prevent many conflicts from ever occurring in the first place. And when we use active listening in conflict situations, it usually promotes understanding and de-escalates the situation. Here's an example of what active listening looks like. Carrie, who was then ten years old, came to visit me just after her grandmother died. One morning we had this conversation:

Carrie: My grandma died.

Me: Yes. Your grandma died. . . .

Carrie: She used to visit us in the Malcolm Road house. (Carrie's family had recently moved.)

Me: So she came to visit you when you were in the old house. . . .

Carrie: Yeah. She used to sit with me in the mornings.

Me: Oh. So that was a time you two had together.

Carrie: I'd come downstairs first every morning and Grandma would be sitting in the rocking chair with a green blanket.

Me: So you were the first one down and she was already there. . . .

Carrie: And I would get on her lap and we would just rock and talk.

Me: So you had this time together to rock in the chair and talk. (Carrie began to cry.)

Me: It's sad, isn't it? You loved your grandma a lot. . . . It's so sad. I feel sad, too.

Carrie: I heard my mom on the phone with her sister. She was crying and I didn't know how to help her.

Me: That must've been hard if you heard your mom crying and you wanted to help. . . .

Carrie: She was crying and crying, but she was talking to her sister on the phone, she wasn't talking to me.

Me: So you didn't know how to help because she wasn't talking to you. (Carrie nodded her head and reached for the little frog sitting on my windowsill. She got down on the floor.)

Carrie: Come down here with me. (I got on the floor with Carrie and she put the frog on my shoulder and leaned her head there.)

When we practice active listening, it often means we reflect back the essence of what the other person is saying to us, as I did here with Carrie. For example, when she said, "I'd come downstairs first every morning and Grandma would be sitting in the rocking chair with a green blanket," and I said, "So you were the first one down and she was already there," I am accepting what Carrie says without judging it or interpreting it in any way—I simply rephrase what I hear. When we sincerely reflect back to children the essence of what they are saying to us, they often feel closer to us and want to tell us more. And that closeness and sharing can lead to healing and peace.

The Buddhist monk Thich Nhat Hanh describes active listening as a deep practice requiring the full presence of our whole being. Because active listening requires total attention, it is often difficult for busy parents to practice it. But again and again I have seen how a few moments of focused, genuine listening can prevent hours of behavior problems and conflicts later on.

It can be a lot harder to practice active listening when we're in conflict with our kids, but it's often an important first step toward resolving things. Kids can't start to cooperate with us until they feel they've truly been "heard." But once children feel genuinely listened to and understood, they can work with us much more easily. That's why active listening is always a vital part of creative conflict resolution.

Here's an example of how active listening and "I" statements can de-escalate a conflict and help create a win-win situation.

I went to the park one day with four children—two who are part of my large extended family, and two of their neighborhood friends. Before we left, I reminded everyone that we would walk together and cross the streets together. But on our way back, seven-year-old Owen broke away from the group and started running toward home on his own. I called (at the top of my lungs) after Owen to wait for us, but he kept going. I saw him come to an intersection and then cross on his own. I screamed as loud as I could for him to stop and wait, but Owen, already two blocks ahead, kept going. "Okay," I thought, "he's really feeling his oats—showing his competence by walking by himself on city streets, but this is *not* okay with me." When we all got back to the house, Owen was waiting. "Owen," I said, "I am really upset. We were all walking together and you ran away. I was calling you but you didn't stop. You crossed the street and I was worried about your safety because of the cars."

Owen: I can walk home alone. I did it with Cheryl, my babysitter.

Me: So you walk home alone sometimes? You do that with your babysitter?

Owen: She lets me go ahead sometimes.

Me: So your babysitter lets you go ahead of her when you're walking outside?

Owen: Well . . . I can go to the next street.

Me: Oh, so you can go ahead to the next street but then you have to wait for her?

Owen: Yeah.

Me: But this time you crossed streets without anyone with you. I was worried about cars—I didn't want you crossing streets without a grown-up. If a grown-up says to stay together, that's what we all have to do.

Owen: I don't want to get a punishment.

Me: You think you're going to get a punishment?

Owen: Yeah.

Me: Owen, I'm not going to punish you. But I want to make sure you understand. If you run away and I call you to stop, I want you to stop. I need to keep you safe. Do you understand?

Owen: Yes.

Me: What can we do now to make sure this never happens again?

From here, Owen and I negotiated a new agreement. He said he would not run away from me or other grown-ups again, and if one of us called him, he would stop. We both said we felt good about our talk and what we'd agreed on. We were sitting very close together by then, and we gave each other a hug.

The language that Owen and I used in this dialogue helped us to de-escalate the tension between us and get to a win-win solution to the problem. I tried to listen to what Owen had to say, and as I reflected it back he realized that he'd gone beyond what his babysitter had permitted in the past. When I told him I was upset, I used an "I" statement to say how I felt and why ("I was worried about your safety because of the cars"). This brought down the tension and helped Owen be less defensive, take some responsibility, and work with me rather than against me.

Choosing Age-Appropriate Approaches

Keeping in mind the sketch of developmental stages discussed in chapter 2 can help us find the most effective tools to handle conflicts—or head them off—depending on how a child of a given age is most likely see the world. By way of illustration, here are three examples of how different approaches are appropriate to take with children at different stages of development.

The first example is one I witnessed not long ago when a dad and his little girl pulled up next to me in a parking lot. The dad got out of the car and began to take his little girl, who looked like a two-year-old, out of her car seat. When he took the child's hand once she was on the ground, she grabbed it away and shouted, "No!" (Now I was sure this child was a two-year-old!) The dad then seized her hand forcefully and gripped it. "You have to hold my hand," he said, and he began walking toward the stores bordering the parking lot, half dragging his little girl, who had started crying.

What would it look like to "get on the same side" with a two-year-old in a situation like this? Ideally, a parent would frame the problem to himself as something like, "How can my daughter and I get across this parking lot smoothly and safely?" If he had some child development knowledge about two year olds   that they are in the process of realizing that they are truly separate from other people and have a strong need to express and explore their autonomy—this might help him. The dad could give his young child a choice. He could show her both his hands and say, "You can choose this hand to hold or that one, but you have to hold one of them when we walk—which one do you want?" This would allow his daughter to express her need for autonomy while still complying with his wishes. I have always found that if I work *with* a two-year-old's need for self-determination, I can negotiate us both toward the goal I have in mind. I am best able to do this when I hold in mind and heart what the child needs and how she or he sees things.

The second example of how choosing one's approach with a child's developmental skills and needs in mind comes from another one of my "field observations." This time I was in a park in Boston with my grandkids and there was a boy playing near us who looked to be about four years old. The boy's mom, who was sitting on a bench nearby, began calling to her son that it was time to go home and the boy kept calling back, "No. I don't want to go." The boy had a large ball that he was kicking around the park and bouncing against a wall. The mom kept yelling at him, her voice growing more impatient and angry, but the boy was not responding. What's a mom to do in a case like this? How does she get her son to leave the park without using coercion or force? If we think about what we know about four-year-olds, we remember from chapter 2 that they are concrete thinkers—they base much of what they think on what they see. Kids this age are usually caught up in what they are doing in the present moment and they tend to think of only one thing at a time, so when they're playing in one place it's hard for them to think about being somewhere else, which can make it difficult for kids this age to transition from one activity or place to another. In this case, some concrete form of assistance is likely to help the boy make the transition, and knowing this might give the mom a few ideas. She could suggest another activity to do with the ball as they leave the park: "Can you bounce the ball across the park all the way to the subway stop?" She could suggest an activity to do when they get home: "Let's go, and when we get home we can play a round of Animal Bingo." Or she could give her son, who does not yet understand logical time, a concrete way to see when it is time to go: "I have two sticks here. When I hold up one, we have three more minutes and when I hold up the other, it will be time to leave—and then you bring the ball over to me." Concrete suggestions like these are very helpful to children at this stage of development and prevent many a potential conflict because they convey our adult expectations in terms children can understand.

My third example comes from an interview I did with Ruth, a single mom with a seven-year-old daughter, Kayla. Ruth told me, "Kayla has been talking back to me a lot in a very nasty voice. I can't believe the disrespectful things she says to me. The other day, she even told me to shut up. I told her, 'Kayla, if you talk to me that way again, if you disrespect me again, I'm going to take your toys away.'"

If Ruth takes Kayla's toys away for verbal disrespect, she'll be escalating the conflict she and Kayla are already having. How can Ruth defuse the tension and begin to work *with* her daughter? Let's think for a minute about this problem. Many of the parents I interviewed, and many teachers, too, have told me that mean, nasty put-down language among children has increased greatly in recent years. As I've stated before, I believe that one reason for this is the influence of mass media. Many of the popular TV shows that children watch today are filled with nasty language delivered in a disrespectful tone of voice, especially toward adults, and many kids who hear this language then try it out in their own interactions, experimenting as we know kids do as part of their learning process. I think the way to help children with the language they are testing out is to explain to them, in ways they can understand, how and why these words are mean and hurtful.

At seven, Kayla is certainly able to grasp that words have an effect on others. In fact, as I mentioned in chapter 2, many of the seven-year-olds I've studied were fascinated with the power of put-downs without really grasping how their mean words felt to those on the receiving end. Yet kids Kayla's age are capable of engaging in dialogues, listening to others, and reflecting on their own behavior, especially with our adult help and when they are offered concrete examples. Given this, I think Ruth could initiate a dialogue with Kayla. She might pose the problem like this: "I've been thinking about some of the words we use when we talk to each other and how they make us feel. Can we talk about this?" Ruth could ask Kayla if there are words she says that make Kayla feel bad, and practice active listening, accepting and reflecting back what she hears. Then Ruth could tell Kayla, using an "I" statement and being specific, about the words and tone of voice Kayla uses and how they make her feel. She might say, "When you say to me, 'shut up,' or 'I'm not going to listen to you,' it makes me feel really bad." Once Ruth and Kayla have talked in this way, they could try to come up with an agreement about how they will speak to one another in the future. For a while, I would expect, Ruth would have to help Kayla see how certain words or tones relate to their agreement. She might have to stop and ask, "Can we think about what you just said and how it fits with what we decided?" or perhaps "Can you find another way to say that?"

Putting It All Together

Let's look now at a simple conflict between a parent and child and put together all the elements of a creative conflict resolution process. We don't always go through all the steps of this process—sometimes we need to focus on only one aspect or skill, such as active listening—but it's helpful to see how the whole process can work from beginning to end.

Five year-old Derrick's mother, Vareen, sees a bunch of toys on the floor near the table where the family eats supper. Vareen walks over to where Derrick is playing a board game with his older sister and speaks to him in a neutral tone of voice.

Vareen: Derrick, your toys are on the floor by the table and we're having supper soon. The toys are in the way. How can they get picked up?

Derrick: I'm playing Chutes and Ladders with Tania.

Vareen: I really want these toys picked up before dinner. Someone might trip on something when they come to the table. How can they get picked up soon?

Derrick: Can't you pick them up, Mom? I'm playing.

Vareen: No—that doesn't feel fair to me. I don't want to pick them up. I didn't even play with them! (She laughs.)

Derrick: Can you do it with me?

Vareen: You want someone to help you?

Derrick: Yeah.

Vareen: Does it feel like a big job?

Derrick: Yeah.

Vareen: Can you ask Tania if she'll help you?

Derrick (turning to Tania): Will you help me pick up the toys?

Tania: Okay—if you put the game away.

Derrick: Okay.

Vareen: So that worked out—you're both picking up. But when?

Derrick: Soon as we finish this game, right, Tania? (Tania nods.) We're almost done, Mom.

Vareen: Okay. Sounds good. Because we're going to have supper soon.

Vareen's example shows us all of the steps in the conflict resolution process and illustrates the skills involved. First, Vareen gets on the same side of the problem with Derrick, stating that the problem is the toys on the floor. It's important that she doesn't say, for example, "Derrick, you've made a mess," or "Derrick, pick up your toys." Instead she poses the question, "How can the toys get picked up soon?" Presenting problems in this way encourages children to take responsibility for solving them and fosters their problem-solving abilities. Because Derrick is five years old and so tends to see things in very concrete terms, Vareen describes the problem in a way that will make sense to him: "Someone might trip on something when they come to the table."

Then Vareen and Derrick start looking for a win-win solution to the problem. At five, Derrick is still quite egocentric and he tends to think of one idea at a time, so he needs his mom to lead him through the process, and she helps him think about solutions to the problem one at a time. Derrick's first idea is that his mom should pick up the toys. Vareen gives a clear "I" statement back to Derrick that no, she doesn't want to pick up the toys, and she helps him see, with some humor, that it wouldn't be fair because she didn't even play with them. Then Derrick has another idea—can she do it with him? Here Vareen uses active listening. "You want someone to help you?" she asks, and then guides the negotiation toward a solution that they can both agree to, with a little help from Tania. And once they have a win-win solution, Vareen helps her kids figure out how to implement it. This last step is important because many children need help putting their ideas into practice.

Let's recap the steps Vareen used to resolve this conflict:

▶ Vareen gets on the same side of the problem with Derrick.

▶ She talks about the problem in concrete terms that a five-year-old can understand.

▶ She negotiates with Derrick using active listening and "I" statements.

▶ She helps Derrick focus on possible solutions one at a time, which fits with how a child of his age thinks.

▶ She pushes for a win-win solution—one that can work for both of them.

▶ She helps both children think about how they will put their solution to the problem into practice.

Of course, not all interactions will work out quite so neatly. When I first began presenting this model for resolving conflicts in parenting workshops, some parents returned to the next session saying, "I tried your approach and it didn't work." True enough, working with kids in this way takes time—and patience. But as kids learn how the process works, they come to trust that their needs will be met and, over time, they get better and better at using these conflict resolution techniques. I've seen many times that parents who stick with this approach find that it eventually leads to fewer conflicts at home and that it enables them to iron out more easily those that do arise.

Managing Anger

Ines confided during our interview that she gets "horribly angry" with her two young children. "I get so mad at them sometimes, mostly when they fight, that I end up screaming—no, screeching—at them. I even told them I hate them one time recently. I feel so out of control when I'm like that. I know I scare them. Then I feel so bad for unleashing my uncontrollable temper onto my kids."

When we're in an emotional state, we can't communicate or problem-solve constructively—our feelings hijack us and block our capacity to focus. We need to find ways to reduce the anger so that we can begin to communicate again.

Learning to deal with our own anger is an essential skill for conflict resolution and for life. Educators for Social Responsibility, an organization I have worked with for many years, does workshops for parents and teachers on managing anger. You might find some of their suggestions helpful. First, it can help just to notice that you're getting angry. What's happening in my body? Is my breathing more rapid? Does my face flush? Is my voice rising or my heartbeat increasing? Then you can ask yourself, What is it that's triggering my anger? Next, see if you can lower the intensity of your feelings by breathing deeply, using "self-talk," such as repeating a key calming word or phrase, taking a step away for a moment, or just simply pausing and waiting. Then try to communicate your anger in an "I" statement—using words that say what you feel, what is making you angry, and what you need.

It's worth noting here that anger is often a secondary emotion—that is, it can arise as a response to other emotions such as fear, sadness, or insecurity—and it can be a challenge to go inward and try to find the underlying feeling or need. Marshall Rosenberg, founder and educational director of the Center for Nonviolent Communication, explores anger deeply in his nonviolent communication (NVC) approach, set out in a body of work that may be very helpful for many parents. In his book *Nonviolent Communication* (published by PuddleDancer Press in 2005) Rosenberg explains that often what triggers our anger is not its true *cause*; that is, it isn't what people do that makes us angry but something in us that responds to what they do. He encourages us to try to go beyond what triggered our anger and become more conscious of the need that is at its root. His belief is that we get angry because our needs are not getting met, but often we are not in touch with those needs and instead of recognizing them within ourselves we focus on what's wrong with other people. Perhaps some of you reading this book will recognize that your own anger is interfering with being able to engage in the conflict resolution process and skills described in this chapter; if so, you may want to go further in looking for resources that can help you explore and manage it. The Center for Nonviolent Communication and the books of Marshall Rosenberg are good places to start.

On the other side of the equation, what happens when we're dealing with a child who is angry? First, if the child is acting aggressively, it's vital before anything else to ensure the safety of everyone involved. I remember a time when my grandson Miles was furious with his brother, Jack, and swung a baseball bat dangerously close to him. My husband, Doug, immediately took the bat from Miles, explaining that it wasn't safe to swing it at another person, that the bat was only for baseball, so he was putting it away. Once you've made sure everyone is physically safe, try to listen attentively while the angry child expresses how he or she feels. Try to reflect back the essence of what you hear. Sometimes this alone is enough, especially for a young child, to enable him or her to move beyond being upset. My younger son, Matt, for example, used to get intensely angry at his older brother, and he would storm into the house from outside and scream about what awful things Kyle had done and how terrible he was. Whenever this happened, I would sit with Matt and practice active listening. I would reflect back his anger and the statements he made to express it, like "I'm never playing with Kyle again." And always in a very short time Matt would calm down and say, "I'm going back out to play." With younger kids anger often passes quickly, as it usually did with Matt, especially if they know they are being listened to and respected for how they feel.

For a child whose anger is not dissipating, suggest that the child try one or two of the calming techniques mentioned above. I tried this recently with my grandson Jack, who at age nine was in a peak state of anger at his younger brother, Miles. I sat with Jack and tried to repeat back calmly the words he was screaming. But after I'd listened for a while, he was still upset, so I said in a quiet voice, "Jack, try to focus on your breathing. Breathe in and out slowly and gently." Jack really tried to do this, and slowly he did start to calm down. Then we were able to begin to try to resolve the conflict he was having with his brother. After they were reconciled, Jack came up to me in the kitchen and put his arms around me, and with a lot of love in his voice he said, "Thank you, Nanny, for helping us solve our problem."

Very recently, two experts in the field of social and emotional learning, Daniel Goleman (author of *Emotional Intelligence* and *Social Intelligence*) and Linda Lantieri, have developed a series of calming strategies to do with parents and kids. In their book and CD, called *Building Emotional Intelligence: Techniques to Cultivate Inner Strength in Children*, these authors guide parents and children in doing exercises that help kids become aware of their inner selves by learning how to calm their bodies, quiet their minds, and focus their attention better. The authors say they are encouraged to see how many children embrace the activities and want to practice them on their own. I believe that by helping kids develop inner life skills, we're putting in their hands new tools that will help them manage all kinds of life situations. And when there are conflicts, or kids are angry, they can call on these skills to help bring down tension and restore peace.

STEPS YOU CAN TAKE

There are a great many ways we can help our children learn skills to use in resolving conflicts effectively and creatively. Using power-sharing ways of working on the disagreements we have with them will deepen our kids' sense of security and help us forge close, trusting relationships. And when we help our children learn these skills, we are giving them a great gift that they will carry into their lives now and for the future.

▶ Reflect on what you learned about conflict from your family and culture.

▶ Try to get on the same side of a problem with your child.

▶ Explore what is behind your own anger and practice techniques for managing it.

▶ Let your knowledge of the stages of child development guide your choice of approach in conflict situations.

▶ Practice active listening.

▶ Reach for "I" statements instead of "You" statements.

▶ Look for win-win solutions.

▶ Help kids think about how to make their solutions work.

CHAPTER 8

Love Above All

Encouraging Empathy and Caring

Given the antisocial models that surround our children, and given their limited opportunities for social play both at home and at school, kids today need more help learning social and emotional skills than children did in the past. Parents tell me that they want their kids to be emotionally healthy people who will be kind and caring toward others. But how do we teach these things to children? We can't *make* them feel empathy or be kind. No, they have to learn these things in the same way they learn everything: by having firsthand experiences that help them develop their own awareness and skills from within.

In recent years there has been a growing recognition that children's success in school and in life depends to a large extent upon their social and emotional skills: self-awareness with regard to one's own feelings, being able to handle difficult emotions, having a capacity for empathy with others and the ability to "put oneself in their shoes," and dealing effectively in relationships. Daniel Goleman reports that these "human skills" are far better predictors of success and well-being than any other single factor, including IQ. We know, too, from the field of neuroscience that social and emotional factors in a child's surroundings affect brain development on a physical level, and that we can actually do a lot to influence and strengthen the neural connections in the brain that represent these skills by how we interact with our kids. It's ironic, then, that so many of our nation's schools, in the current climate of academic testing, have pushed aside play and activities that promote social and emotional skills. Fortunately, we parents and caregivers, through our everyday interactions with children, can give them what societal influences threaten to take away. But we have to go slowly; teaching our children to be emotionally and socially competent individuals is a long, slow process, and one in which the results and future benefits are not often immediately apparent.

When we ourselves use the power-sharing approaches I advocate throughout this book—such as dialogue, negotiation, and finding win-win ways to solve conflicts—we are teaching our children a wide range of social and emotional skills in the process. As we discussed in chapter 4, "power over" approaches like time-outs and punishments fall short not only because they don't encourage our children to develop inner controls, but also because they don't teach them any new skills. I talked about this recently with my friend Nadine when she called to ask advice about an incident that happened at the family day care site that her son attends. Curtis was riding a tricycle and he bumped into another child, who then fell off his bike. The teacher made Curtis sit on the steps for a time-out. Later Curtis was back on a trike, and this time he bumped into a little girl named Madeline, who fell off *her* tricycle and got a bloody nose. The teacher then told Curtis that he couldn't ride at all anymore. Nadine's question was, "Is this a good way to teach Curtis how to get along with other kids?"

When Curtis got back on the tricycle the second time, he did just what he'd done earlier. The time-out hadn't given him any new ideas about what to do instead of driving into other kids. It seems to me, I told Nadine, that making Curtis sit on the stairs or taking away his chance to ride a trike wouldn't teach him what he needed to know in order to become more socially competent.

What Curtis needed in this situation was to learn how to interact more positively with other children. After first helping Madeline, the teacher could have brought Curtis over and said in a matter-of-fact voice without blame, "Curtis, Madeline got hurt and her nose was bleeding. She got hurt when you bumped into her. Can you do anything to help her feel better—can you say any words to help her?" The teacher might also have asked Madeline, "Do you want to say anything to Curtis?" or "What can Curtis do to help you feel better?" When we ask questions like these of children, we stimulate their thinking and help them build social skills. As Jean Piaget wrote, "to understand is to invent." What he meant by this is that real learning happens when children build their own ideas. Here, Curtis has a better chance of learning how to make someone feel better if he invents the words to say and tries them out with Madeline instead of being directed by an adult to "tell Madeline you're sorry."

For me, the point in this situation would be to help Curtis make a connection between knocking into Madeline and hurting her that could spark the beginnings of empathy and caring, to help both children learn how to communicate, and, in Curtis's case, make amends. Three-year-olds like Curtis, as we've mentioned before, tend to focus on only one thing at a time and don't yet think logically about cause and effect, making it possible to crash into other kids on a tricycle without any real understanding of the hurt this could cause. Children Curtis's age need adults to point out, in concrete terms that make sense to them, how their actions affect others. And here, if the teacher had encouraged Curtis to help Madeline feel better, he would have felt better about himself, too, and more socially confident; her punitive approach not only didn't teach Curtis new skills, it also most likely made him feel bad about himself. Especially today, as we see so many children in great need of social and emotional learning, we have to find constructive rather than punitive ways to teach them how to build positive relationships.

In addition to implementing the power-sharing strategies discussed throughout this book, there are other steps we can take to help our kids become the genuinely caring, socially skilled, empathic human beings we hope for.

Social and Emotional Coaching

There are many times, of course, when children need direct feedback about their behavior. The question is, What form will that feedback take? When we act as social and emotional coaches for our kids, we help them understand what they and others involved may be feeling, why a certain behavior is not working, and how they can change it. We look at the feelings and behavior *with* them—as allies working together—and we urge them on as if they were learning to swim or ride a bike. We don't blame, but instead use language that describes what we see and offers the possibility of new ideas and strategies. Here are three examples from my experience that can show you what social and emotional coaching looks like.

When my grandson Jack was three years old, he suddenly started repeating a very troubling phrase whenever something, or more typically somebody, made him angry. In a vicious and cruel tone of voice I would not have believed Jack capable of (and a tone that no one, to my knowledge, had ever used with him), he would scream, *"I hate you!"* at the top of his voice. This was hurtful and somewhat shocking to the poor person on the receiving end, and we all wondered where this ugly behavior came from and why Jack was acting this way. Jack's parents, my son Kyle and his wife, Lori, felt terrible, and they told him repeatedly not to say these words. But Kyle and Lori's advice was not sinking in.

I eventually discovered that Jack had been playing with older kids in the neighborhood who, when they got into fights, had been screaming "I hate you!" at each other. In that moment I understood:

three-year-old Jack *had* heard these words—he had not invented them—and he was doing what all children do as they grow and learn: taking what he had heard and trying it out for himself. It was as if he'd said to himself, "When you get really angry, you scream these words at somebody. I'll try that the next time I'm really mad."

Faced with this situation, I asked myself not only "How can I get Jack to stop this behavior?" but also "How can I get Jack to *want* to stop this behavior?" I felt it was critically important for Jack to understand, young as he was, how his words made the recipient feel. How might I do that?

One afternoon I went into Jack's room with him, picked up two action figures, and started acting out a little scene. The action figure in my right hand said, "I want to play with the motorcycle" (Jack loved toy motorcycles at the time); the action figure in my left hand said, "I want the motorcycle." I made the two action figures argue briefly: "I want it." "No, I want it." Then one of them said in a very nasty voice, "I hate you!" to the other. I made the doll who got yelled at slowly fall facedown, *showing* Jack that he was hurt, while I said these words: "I feel bad when you say 'I hate you.' Those words are mean words. They hurt me. Please don't say those words anymore."

Jack watched, fascinated. He looked at me and said, "Do it again." So I repeated this little role-play exercise, and he watched a second time. When I finished, he said once more, "Do it again." This went on several more times as Jack continued to ask me to repeat the little drama, an indicator that I had tapped into a hot spot for new learning. After we'd completed the dramas, I put the dolls down and said to Jack, "We aren't going to say 'I hate you' anymore, Jack—those are mean words and they hurt people." And from that day on, according to Lori, Jack didn't use the words "I hate you" again.

We have a much better chance of helping a child make sense of any situation if we can figure out how to put it into terms they can understand. As a three-year-old, Jack needed help *seeing* the effects of his words. When the action figure slowly went facedown to the floor and said, "That hurts me," it *showed* him those effects. Using concrete actions, dolls, and dramatic role-plays like this can help young kids understand emotions and the dynamics of relationships far better than words alone can do.

This exchange between Jack and me took place at a level of social and emotional development that went beyond merely stopping his unwanted behavior. Our challenge as parents, especially today, is to do more than "get kids to behave." If we are to help our children grow socially and emotionally—if we are to instill in them a true sense of empathy and caring—we have to help them build a network of connections about how their actions affect others and how we humans get along. Only in this way can we encourage children to build their own internal sense of right and wrong and come to rely on their own inner compass.

The next example of social and emotional coaching I have to offer lets us look further into what underlying need a child might be expressing by a particular behavior. As kids try to meet their needs, they sometimes use strategies that aren't very effective. When I interviewed Betty, the former school director, she told me, "I always assume that a child is doing the best they can in any moment—that if they had other choices they would've made them." I thought about Betty's comment when I went with my friend Zadie to her grandson's third birthday party. When I got there, a number of families with young kids were arriving. Zadie's grandson Jake's older brother, five-year-old Liam, was there, too, wearing a pair of cowboy boots with a very pointy toe. As the party guests began to arrive, Liam started going around the party kicking his leg up very high and bringing those points perilously close to the party guests. Zadie kept yelling at Liam, "Stop that!" This went on for quite a long time. Finally, I went over to Liam, a boy I had never met, leaned close to him, and gently put my hand on the toe of his left boot. "That's a really sharp end on your boot, isn't it?" I said. "That could hurt if it hit somebody." Liam looked at me with a very intense and knowing expression. "Are you looking for someone to play with?" I asked. "Yes," said Liam.

Me: Is there anyone here you like to play with?

Liam: Nina.

Me: What do you do when you play with Nina?

Liam (smiling): We play cheetahs.

Me: Why don't you go ask Nina to play with you now?

Liam went over to Nina, they began playing together, and there wasn't any more boot kicking after that.

It seemed to me that Liam was having difficulty as the guests were arriving and giving birthday wishes and presents to Jake. "He must be feeling left out, or unseen, or maybe jealous of his brother," I thought. "Maybe he needs to regain a sense of belonging—to feel that he matters, too." Liam's strategy for getting his needs met—the boot-kicking behavior—wasn't getting him what he wanted. And when I spoke to him, I assumed that he hadn't fully understood that his boot jabbing might really hurt people. As we've learned earlier, young kids often don't understand the effects of their actions on others. But I also knew that if I could talk to Liam in the concrete terms that would likely make sense to him, he would probably realize that his kicking could hurt someone and should stop. I also wanted to give him a strategy that would help him feel a greater sense of belonging at his brother's party—one that would work better for him than getting noticed for kicking. If we can think about what it is children need in any given situation—keeping their developmental level in mind—

and come up with a more effective way to meet that need, we can usually find ways to coach them toward more prosocial behavior.

When kids aren't acting as we would want, many of us just flatly tell them, as Liam's grandmother Zadie did, to *stop.* But, as I've mentioned earlier, "power over" approaches like this are profoundly limited because they don't teach kids what to do *instead* of the unwanted behavior. What kids need from us are alternative strategies they can use to meet their needs and help them build more positive relationships.

This is why coaching may also involve suggesting new behaviors that a child might try. I made such a suggestion to eight-year-old Toby last summer at a gathering of our large extended family. There was a lot of excitement and high energy among the children that day, but I noticed that Toby was having a hard time. Twice he hauled off and hit his cousins, which led to a downward spiral of negativity toward him. Wanting to help him, I looked for a chance to speak with Toby alone.

Me: Toby—I saw you hit your cousins twice.

Toby: I was mad at Johnny.

Me: You were mad at Johnny, so you hit him?

Toby: Yeah.

Me: You know, when you hit people it hurts them. That's why we can't do it. It's not okay to hit someone, even if you're mad.

Toby: He's a jerk. He wouldn't give me the Frisbee.

Me: So you wanted the Frisbee. Is there anything you can do when you get mad besides hit?

Toby: I could talk, but I'm too mad. That's why I hit him.

Me: Yeah, you can feel so mad you want to hit. But the hitting has to stop because it hurts people and then they don't want to play with you. Did you ever try just saying the words "I'm really mad!"? (Toby shook his head no.) It can work better than hitting. You say, "I am really mad." Then say what you want—like, "I want a turn with the Frisbee." Can you try that?

Toby: Okay.

Me: See if you can do it next time you're mad instead of hitting. We'll talk again later to see how it worked, okay?

Toby: Okay.

I noticed Toby didn't hit anymore for the rest of the day. Before bedtime, I grabbed a chance to talk with him when the other kids weren't in the room.

Me: Toby, how did it go for you the rest of the day? I didn't see you hit anybody again!

Toby: I didn't.

Me: Wow! Did you try saying you were mad?

Toby: I told Johnny I was mad. I said I wanted to bat.

Me: You did? You told him you were mad and you wanted a turn to bat?

Toby: Yes.

Me: What happened?

Toby: He gave me a turn.

Me: Wow. So you tried saying words instead of hitting and he gave you a turn?

Toby: Yeah.

Me: So that really worked out! (I gave him a hug and we were both smiling.) Do you think you can keep on doing that? (Toby nodded his head yes.) I think you can, too.

At eight years of age, Toby is able to reflect on his behavior in a conversation and talk about what makes him mad and why he hits his cousins. He is capable of understanding how his actions affect others and of using words instead of fists, but he needed some coaching on finding a better strategy than hitting. I looked for private times to talk with Toby about his behavior, directly and without blame. Toby and I have had a special connection since this incident—when we work *with* children to help them solve problems, we build bonds of trust. Social and emotional coaching lets us participate in children's development by providing the crucial building blocks they need at the time they most need them and in a way they can respond to. Over time, working in this way with children will increase the likelihood that they will act with kindness and care for others even when no one is looking over their shoulder.

Nurturing Emotional Intelligence

Children are emotional beings from the moment they are born. I will never forget my granddaughter Isabella's arrival into this world—she was so full of expression, her face scrunched up in a look of annoyance as she emerged into the world, letting go with a bellowing cry. The first relationship we have with our infants is an emotional as well as physical one. We learn to "read" our babies' cries and nonverbal cues. My son Matt told me, when his daughter Isabella was six months old, that when she met a new person, if she didn't want to interact with them or if she felt overwhelmed, she looked away and made eye contact with her mother. Indeed, babies show us through their body language and actions, as well as their voices, what they need and want. And they begin early to learn about emotions from their interactions with us. We can amplify an infant's positive emotional states and reduce uncomfortable emotions like fear, anxiety, or sadness with our voices, facial expressions, and body motions. Matt and my daughter-in-law Luciana, for example, respond quickly when Isabella is distressed; if their baby daughter shows fear of a person or a situation, they reassure her by smiling, by touch, and by speaking in a soothing voice, that the situation is safe. When these experiences are repeated over time, they help a child build an internal sense of what John Bowlby called, in his book *Attachment and Loss*, a "secure base" in the world.

As babies become toddlers and start to talk, they can begin to express their feelings in words, and this is an important step toward managing emotions—using language is one way that children begin to gain control over their impulses. But we need to remember that it's a major task for kids to learn to put words to how they feel, and it takes time to learn what words match up with which feelings. We can do a lot to help even our youngest children identify their feelings and talk about them, something I saw lots of chances to do in the first few years of my grandson's lives. I remember one hot summer day, for example, when Miles was two and a half and was trying to investigate the rotating fan we had on the floor. I went over and said, "Miles, I don't think we can play with this. See how the blade goes so fast? It could hurt your finger." Miles gave me a grumpy look and said, "I'll put you in jail." I felt the urge to laugh (where did he get *that* line?), but wanted to respect his sincerity, so I said, "Oh. You're *mad* at me. You want to play with the fan, but it's not a toy. Let's find something else for you to do."

The best way Miles knew to describe his annoyance with me was to say he'd "put me in jail." Often young children will have feelings that they can only approximate in words—so we can help by giving them language we think matches up with what they feel. And if we can acknowledge a child's emotions matter-of-factly and accept them without judging, we send a powerful message that it is okay to feel the way you do.

As children get a little older, we can continue to talk about feelings and help them understand more about *what* made them feel as they do. For example, for the first several years of his life, my grandson Jack came to our house one day a week. He loved our time together and was truly attached to both me and my husband, Doug. During his third and fourth years, the transition from our house to his home got to be emotionally difficult for Jack. We used transition objects a lot—he would carry something from our house into the car (like Will from chapter 1 carrying the sponge ball)—but it was still hard for him, and often he would cope by getting a glazed look in his eyes and withdrawing. One day, as I was about to drive Jack home and Doug was saying good-bye to him, the by now familiar look of vacancy came over Jack's face. So, as we pulled out of the driveway, I said to him, "Whenever we have to say good-bye, we feel sad. We have to leave and say good-bye and we have a sad feeling."

Jack: Do you have a sad feeling?

Me: Yes, when I have to say good-bye to someone I love, I feel sad. You might feel sad right now, too, because you're saying good-bye to Doug.

Jack: I'm sad.

Me: Yes—it feels sad when you have to go home. (I paused for a moment.) But you know what? We'll be together again very soon—you'll come back to our house and we'll play.

Later, when I told Doug about this conversation, he told me that as a child he was often discouraged from feeling his emotions and that this had set him back in life and relationships for many years. Unfortunately, this is still the case for many young children—for boys even more than for girls—who get the message that they have to act strong and not show vulnerability. When we help children notice, label, and talk about their feelings, we are strengthening their emotional intelligence. When we encourage our kids to feel their emotions instead of disconnecting from them, we are giving them a crucial base for healthy emotional *and* social development—after all, we can't begin to connect with how someone else feels if we don't connect to those emotions within ourselves.

In this situation, after acknowledging Jack's sadness, I also reassured him that we would be together again soon. I did this because young children, who tend to focus on one idea so completely, can get pulled into an emotion like sadness, fear, or anger and become overwhelmed by it. This is why I believe it's important not only to help children feel their emotions—especially the hard ones—but also to help them move beyond them.

For children, learning about their own impulses and feelings is directly connected to the even more complex capacity for understanding how *other* people feel.

We know that even infants and toddlers are able to show empathy, as many parents, caregivers, and professionals have observed. Still, I remember feeling surprised when I saw this one day, while sitting on my daughter-in-law Lori's front porch. Jack was twenty months old at the time and was playing nearby. I was telling Lori about my father, who was suffering with Parkinson's disease. I was feeling very sad about Dad's situation and I started to cry. Suddenly little Jack, who had come over to stand next to me, began patting my shoulder. Much of the research on empathy has shown that, yes, even infants can pick up on other people's feelings. But it's a very long road from those first empathic understandings and impulses to full empathy that involves not only emotions but thoughts as well. Because children are egocentric, they have a hard time seeing someone else's perspective; typically, it isn't until well into adolescence that young people acquire the capacity to truly "put themselves in someone else's shoes."

Even though awareness of how others feel builds very slowly in children, we can begin to work with them from an early age to nurture this understanding. Feelings themselves can't be seen, of course, but we can try to make their manifestations more visible for young children. Here's how Joyce, for example, a forty-four-year-old mother of two from Boston, helped her three-year-old son, Khalil, to "read" his sister's feelings.

While I was talking on the phone with Joyce, Khalil was playing with his five-year-old sister, Tara, when he suddenly hit her on the head with a small truck. Tara screamed, and after Joyce excused herself with a quick "Be right back" and put down the phone I overheard the following:

Joyce: Khalil. Look at Tara's face. Look at her eyes. How do her eyes look?

Khalil: Sad. She's crying.

Joyce: Yes, she looks sad. Let's ask Tara how she's feeling.

Tara: I'm sad. *And* mad.

Joyce: Yes, you're feeling sad and mad. Khalil, what made Tara feel sad?

Khalil: I hit her.

Joyce: Yes, she's sad because you hit her. Can you do something to help her feel better? (A pause.) Oh, yes . . . a big hug. And can you say any words to help Tara feel better?

Khalil: I sorry, Tara.

Tara: Okay. I'm only a little mad now.

Joyce was using Khalil's concrete way of seeing the world to help him understand how his sister felt. With the question, "How do her eyes look?" she asked him to try to figure out how his sister was feeling by "reading" her facial cues. Joyce then went on to help Khalil understand that Tara was sad and mad *because* he hit her, and to help him think of a way to make her feel better. I was amazed when I listened to this little exchange that one mom could pack so many emotional and social skills into one short interaction.

As children get older, more toward the ages of six, seven, and eight, they can understand how someone else feels even when they don't have the visual cues that tell them, and they realize now that someone might look one way but actually feel another—that a person could be looking happy but really feeling sad. Because children's thinking at this age is becoming more complex (they see more easily how ideas are related) and logical, they can get very interested in social dynamics—who said what to whom and why and how it made them feel. You can see this in a conversation I had with Taisha, an eight-year-old girl in a Boston public school, typical of many conversations I've had with children her age. Taisha was complaining about the problems she was having with her friend Jessica.

Jessica accused me of stuff that I didn't even do so that she could win and that Mrs. B. wouldn't yell at her. And I don't think that was fair because I was in tears. I was sad for the whole day. But she feels happy and joy for when I was bad off. We were friends, it was like we were best buddies, but today she comes over and bothers me. And I don't like that. I do not like that. And she better stop it because that really makes me so mad.

Here Taisha is aware of feeling sad and mad and imagines that her friend feels happy and joyful when she's "bad off." She's also thinking that Jessica has the ulterior motive of trying to influence their teacher, something younger children are rarely capable of thinking about because ulterior motives can't be seen but only inferred. And Taisha is involved in trying to understand all the complex dynamics of her relationship with Jessica, but mostly still from her own point of view—which is not surprising considering where she is on the developmental continuum. I find that sometimes I can encourage children Taisha's age to make new connections if I ask questions like "How do you think Jessica feels when you're mad at her?" or "Did you ever do anything that made Jessica feel bad?" At the age of eight, Taisha is capable of understanding that her behavior also affects her friend, although it will take her a very long time to fully comprehend what these effects are or might be. The truth is that it will take years for our children to become aware of their own emotions and the feelings of others and they will need support from us throughout childhood as they gradually build this understanding.

Threats to Social and Emotional Growth

As I've expressed throughout this book, I am concerned that the media culture that surrounds us poses a threat to children's healthy development and to their social and emotional growth in particular. Not only are children seeing antisocial models in the media, but the electronic toys, games, and screens that occupy their lives from infancy on are affecting them in other ways, too. In chapter 3, on reclaiming creative play, I discussed how electronic toys can undermine children's early conceptual learning and problem-solving skills—but these toys can also impede the crucial social and emotional learning that begins in infancy. Another anecdote will show you what I mean.

When my son Kyle was six months old, he used to lie on his back in his crib and vigorously kick his feet to make the animal mobile that was attached to the crib's side shake and bounce, and he'd give out a big belly laugh every time he moved the mobile by kicking. Not only was he learning the important concept of causality (in action), Kyle was learning other things, too: I can do something active to amuse myself, I can be happy when I'm alone, and I can make myself laugh! This wasn't a conscious kind of learning, but it was a crucial first building block in emotional awareness and self-regulation.

I thought a lot about those early days with Kyle when I saw the device, a descendant of the simple mobile, that was sent to my granddaughter Isabella recently by a well-meaning friend. It's a floor mat arched over by a canopy with a star in the center that turns on by a switch to show four flashing lights that rotate in a circle with on-and-off patterns while music plays. When Isabella was placed under the canopy and the switch was pulled, she stared fixedly at the rotating, flashing lights. (Her parents, becoming concerned that she looked mesmerized and dazed, stopped using the thing.) This toy, and electronic toys in general, can pacify babies, stop them from crying, and capture their complete attention for a time, but is this good for them? With toys like this, the stimulation comes entirely from the toy. The infant is not active, is not learning that she can make something interesting happen or initiate an activity to make herself happy.

As electronic toys have increasingly replaced more traditional ones, many parents, not realizing that such toys can actually hamper cognitive, social, and emotional learning, have become enamored with them. The fact that such toys can occupy, distract, and entertain children offers a seductive lure to busy caregivers. Early habits set in on both sides: for the child, learning to be passive, to look outside of oneself for happiness and fulfillment; for parents, learning to rely on toys instead of our own ingenuity and creative parenting to soothe and occupy kids.

I thought about how electronic toys can be a substitute for genuine emotional and social experience two years ago when Doug and I took Jack and Miles away on a weekend trip for the first time. We were all packed up and ready to go when Miles's eyes (he wasn't quite five years old then) began to fill with tears. "I have to say good-bye to Mama," he said, struggling. I could see the powerful sadness sweeping over Miles now that the concrete reality of our leaving was upon him. I felt a wave of empathy for Miles and gently rubbed his chest. I said, "When we go away from Mama, we have sad feelings." I waited a couple of seconds—I wanted to acknowledge the feelings he was having, but I also wanted to help him. "But you know what? We're going to New York, we'll sleep one night, then we come back the next day and Mama will be right here waiting for you!" Miles looked reassured. I was trying to explain things to him in concrete terms, to let him know what would happen and to reassure him about returning and seeing his mother again. I wanted Miles to know he could feel sad but also that he could cope with this transition. If he got through this, he was going to have a big accomplishment in his repertoire that would help him deal with other emotional transitions he'd have to make in the future.

What if when Miles had started to cry I had handed him a Game Boy to play with to distract him from his sadness, or offered a DVD to watch on my computer? "Want to watch *Finding Nemo*?"—that would've cheered him right up because kids get absorbed so quickly in electronic media. Meanwhile Miles's mom, Lori, knowing he was struggling to cope, came out of the house with two small photos of their family of four, one for each boy. As we drove away, Miles and

Jack sat looking at their photos for a while, then asked me to hold them. Over the next couple of hours, they asked to see their photos two more times. At one point, I heard them talking together in the backseat about their mom and dad and I heard Miles say to his brother, "Jack, Mama is thinking about you right now." I was struck by how, with the help of the photos and other supports, Miles and Jack, although they were feeling the pangs of separation from home, found the tools within themselves to cope with those emotions. And as they did this they were also sharing as brothers, deepening their own relationship. It's experiences just like this, with the support of adults, that build emotional intelligence and foster social growth in children.

I am concerned that many children today are learning to cope with their feelings and relationships by distraction and substitution, and that these temporary "fixes" will not serve their emotional and social development well, now or in the future. Across America every day, TV screens, video games, and electronic toys have become easy substitutes for the inner life experiences and personal interactions children need now more than ever. We can make choices about the role we want electronic toys, games, and screen activities to play in our children's lives. Whenever we are considering turning to them in any moment, we can ask ourselves, How will this activity affect my child's emotional and social growth? What might the alternatives be?

STEPS YOU CAN TAKE

Even in a climate where outside influences threaten to undermine our children's emotional and social learning, we have many choices to make and steps to take that will strengthen these aspects of their lives. By what we choose to do, we can help our kids become emotionally healthy people who have the tools they will need to build positive, creative, and lasting relationships.

▶ Help children notice, label, and talk about their feelings, including why they feel as they do.

▶ Think about the underlying needs expressed by what children do and help them find more effective strategies for meeting those needs.

▶ Use power-sharing approaches such as dialogue, negotiation, and win-win conflict resolution, which promote social and emotional learning.

▶ Encourage young children to use visual cues to "read" other people's feelings and help them understand how their actions affect others. Using dolls, concrete actions, and dramatic scenarios is especially appropriate with younger children.

▶ Coach children on their feelings and social behavior by working as partners, being direct, nonblaming, and using a problem-solving approach. Suggest new behaviors for children to try, and reflect with them on how these are working.

▶ Give children feedback about their behavior that is at their level of understanding and makes sense to them.

▶ When considering using electronic toys, games, or screen activities, ask yourself, How will this activity affect my child's emotional and social growth?

CHAPTER 9

When to Step In

Helping Your Kids Build Positive Relationships

Valora, who lives with her two young sons in Cambridge, Massachusetts, described the conflicts her kids get into this way:

> They argue about everything. They even play pretend football—there's no ball, but they keep arguing. "I've got the ball!" "No, I've got the ball!"
>
> I want them to be close. Me and my brother weren't so close. It probably had a lot to do with the way my mother dealt with things. When we fought she'd say, "Go to your rooms"—and they were at separate ends of the house. And we stayed there for a long time. I think with my boys if I help them work things out they'll be able to stay friends even if they have arguments.

While it seems like a natural part of growing up for kids to fight with each other, as discussed earlier in the book, many teachers and parents tell me that children today are fighting more and in a way that too often quickly spins out of control. Indeed, we have seen an increase in aggression among children in the last decade and more of it at ever younger ages. Considering the antisocial messages and models that kids see in the media and absorb to use in their own fights, and the increased stresses on many children from other societal factors, this is no surprise. The question is, How can we counter those influences and help kids learn how to resolve their conflicts in a peaceful way?

In chapter 7 we discussed how we can transform our own conflicts with children into win-win situations; in this chapter we'll take a look at how we can use this same approach to help kids resolve the disputes they have among themselves. When we help children learn how to become collaborators instead of adversaries, we nurture the healthy peer relationships that are so important to their development.

When Kids Need Our Help: Acting as a Mediator

On a sweltering Sunday last summer, along with scores of other people, I headed to the beach for relief. Sitting on a crowded stretch of sand about an hour north of Boston, I noticed two moms nearby with two little girls who looked to be about four years old and whose names, I soon overheard, were Nicole and Maria. Both girls had shovels and they were happily digging in the sand.

Nicole and Maria were dumping shovelfuls of sand onto a spot that they were starting to call a house. They kept at it for a long time, they seemed really content, and the mound of sand was getting higher. Then Maria broke the spell. She had a small bucket next to her. She picked it up and started pouring water on the "house." This sent Nicole into a frenzy. She started screaming, "No! No!" and crying loudly. The cries turned into wails. Nicole's mother ordered, "Stop crying, Nicole. Stop it!" Then Maria's mother grabbed Maria by the hand and pulled her aside (over toward me), saying to her, "Do you want me to take that bucket away?" Nicole began to quiet down and then stopped crying. Each girl sat back down on the sand, but they sat much farther away from each other than before. They both started digging again, but neither said anything. And this time each girl made her own separate pile of sand. For the rest of the time we were at the beach, Nicole and Maria played separately.

It's very rare for young children to play and interact without any conflict whatsoever. A big reason for this, as I've explained throughout this book, is that they mainly see things from their own point of view: in this case each child had a different idea of what the house of sand should look like and eventually their different ideas collided. As we've also noted, young children like Maria and Nicole tend to think of one idea at a time, which makes it very easy for them to get stuck in conflicts and not be able to see a way out.

Nicole and Maria's moms did what so many of us do when kids argue—we try to stop them from fighting. But just ending the conflict, as we saw here, won't necessarily help kids continue playing or teach them any of the skills they need for getting along. For me it was sad to see Nicole and Maria withdraw to their individual spaces that afternoon and not reconnect.

If I had been more than just an observer at the beach on that sultry Sunday, I would've stepped in to help Nicole and Maria. I can imagine a scenario something like this:

Me: What's happening here?

Nicole: She's putting water on the house!

Me: Let's stop a minute. (I might take the shovels and hold them.) Let me help you. Maria, tell us what you want to do.

Maria: I want to make a swimming pool.

Me: And Nicole, what is it you want?

Nicole: I want a house but no water on it!

Me: So we have a problem, don't we? Nicole wants a house without any water and Maria wants to make a swimming pool. What can we do?

What I would be doing here is using the win-win approach I outlined in chapter 7, but instead of an adult getting on the same side of the problem with a child, as we can try to do when we have our own conflicts with kids, here I would be helping the two children get on the same side with *each other* and look at the problem they share. While at four years of age these girls can't easily do this for themselves, they can do it with the help of an adult "mediator." Once kids get a bit of help in looking at the problem they have *together*, they can usually begin to think of how to solve it.

There are many occasions when children fight and are able to work things out on their own, allowing us to stay back and uninvolved. But there are other times, when things break down or are escalating quickly, where our intervention can make a critical difference. Let's look at three other examples to see how we can help children move toward resolution and learn social skills that they will eventually be able to use on their own. I'll start with a fight that erupted one day at my house between my grandsons Jackson and Miles.

When Miles and Jack were three and five years old, they saw the movie *Peter Pan* and then went through a long phase of acting out the story. They would switch roles between being Peter Pan or Captain Hook, inventing scenarios that usually involved hiding and finding each other. I had found a little plastic hook in the shop of a "pirate museum" and brought it home for their dress-up box. But when they saw this, they were both overcome with the desire to have it right away, and both reached for it, setting off an instant fight.

Jack: I got it first.

Miles: No, I did!

At this point they were both grabbing feverishly at the hook and screaming. I snatched the hook back.

Me: Guys, I'm really sorry. I should've realized this would be hard for you. I bought one hook but there are two of you and you both want it. Let's sit down. What are we going to do?

Jack: Give it to me.

Miles: No!

Me: We have one hook and you both want it. What can we do?

Jack: I hate sharing. I want it.

Me: Miles, is that okay with you?

Miles: No.

Me: So we have to find some way that you both feel good about. Does anyone have an idea?

Miles: We could have two minutes and two minutes.

Me: What do you think, Jack?

Jack: That's okay.

Me: Who'll go first?

Jack: I want to.

Me: Miles, is that okay with you?

Miles: Yeah, I guess so.

Me: I'll tell you when the first two minutes is up, Jack, and then it's Miles's turn.

Miles (beaming with a big smile across his face): My idea worked!

In my neutral role as a mediator, I used three simple steps to help Jack and Miles resolve this dispute. First, I helped them get on the same side to look at the problem they needed to solve together: there is one hook and you both want it. Second, I encouraged them to think of ideas they could *both* agree to about how to solve the problem; I tried to show them that we were looking for a win-win solution by asking for agreement on the suggestions each made. It was Miles who came up with a solution they both liked: "We could have two minutes and two minutes." And then came the third step. To help them put this idea into practice, I asked, "Who'll go first?" It was important to make sure they agreed about this, too.

You'll notice that at the end of this episode, after we'd found a win-win solution, Miles grinned broadly and said, "My idea worked!" Here was Miles, only three years old at the time, discovering that he could think of a way to solve a conflict with his older brother. This realization surely became part of Miles's evolving sense of self—"I am a person who can solve problems"—and both he and his brother, through their active engagement in solving this problem, took another step in learning vital social skills. And there's an even deeper lesson, in my opinion, that children learn from this kind of positive process, which is that it's okay to have conflicts because we can be creative in solving them in many different ways that don't involve aggression or force.

The three basic steps I used to help resolve this fight between Jack and Miles are often all it takes to help children settle a dispute: getting on the same side of the problem, searching for a solution both can agree to, and seeing how to put their idea into practice. I have used this approach countless times with children and have found that, with younger kids especially, we often move through these steps and arrive at a solution quite quickly. But sometimes the arguments, especially as children get a little older (closer to the ages of six and seven), get more complicated, and the mediation process can involve some additional steps.

By way of illustration, here's a vignette in which a father named Wilfredo intervenes with his two children, seven-year-old Calvin and his five-year-old sister, Maya, who are fighting over a puppet. Before looking for solutions to the problem, Wilfredo elaborates on the first basic step cited above by setting "ground rules," getting the kids' stories out, and using active listening. Let's take a look at this conflict to see how Wilfredo incorporates these additional elements into the process.

Wilfredo hears Maya and Calvin fighting in the next room— "Gimme that!" "I had it first!"—and he calls to them, "Do the two of you need help in there?" Both kids are yelling and Wilfredo hears things escalating. He comes into the room to find Calvin and Maya in a physical tussle over a puppet.

Wilfredo: Whoa, whoa, whoa. Take it easy, guys. I'm gonna help you both solve this problem. We're each gonna talk and we're not gonna interrupt each other.

Calvin: She's dumb.

Wilfredo: No, we're not going to put each other down either. Let's start with you, Calvin. What happened?

Calvin: She was playing with Ralphie but she left him on the floor and went outside, so I started playing with him, and now she starts crying because she's a baby.

Wilfredo: Calvin, remember I said we're not gonna put each other down. Let me see if I understand what you said. Maya was playing with Ralphie, but then she put him down and went outside, so you started playing with him.

Calvin: Yeah.

Wilfredo: Maya, what happened here?

Calvin (interrupting): Ralphie's trying to say something—"She's dumb!"

Wilfredo (taking the puppet from Calvin): I'm going to hold Ralphie so he doesn't say things like that anymore. (Wilfredo nods the puppet's head up and down to show that the puppet agrees with him.)

Maya: I put him down for a minute. I had him first, and I didn't go outside, I went to the bathroom.

Wilfredo: So you put Ralphie down for a minute when you went to the bathroom, but you didn't go outside.

Maya: Yeah, I didn't go outside.

Wilfredo: It sounds like we have a problem here. We only have one puppet. How can the two of you play with it when we have only one?

Maya: I want to play with him!

Calvin: I want to play with him!

Wilfredo: So that's something we know—you both want to play with Ralphie. What can we do so each of you gets a chance?—there's only one puppet.

Calvin (in a mocking tone): Take turns.

Wilfredo (ignoring the sarcasm): There's an idea. Let's find out if that's okay with Maya.

Maya: Yeah, take turns. I want to go first!

Wilfredo to Calvin: How much time would you like?

Calvin (who's learning to tell time): Fifteen minutes.

Maya: Yeah, fifteen minutes. I want fifteen minutes.

Wilfredo: So are we saying the way to solve this problem is that you each get fifteen minutes with Ralphie?

Both kids: Yeah.

Wilfredo: And Maya asked to go first. Is that okay with you, Calvin?

Calvin: Yeah, she can play with Ralphie first. But how will we know when it's her turn and my turn? Adults always say share, but how do we know?

Wilfredo: Well, remember the other day we were practicing with time and you held my watch? Why don't you take my watch now and you can see when the fifteen minutes is up

Calvin (looking pleased): Okay.

In this situation, before the problem solving can begin, the children have to explain to Wilfredo what happened. But to enable them to do this successfully, Wilfredo has to lay out some ground rules: they will each get a chance to talk, there is no interrupting, and there are no put-downs. Keeping to ground rules is very important to the success of a mediation—and if the rules always stay the same, kids learn them easily and can count on them every time. In this situation, for example, Calvin calls his sister "a baby," and Wilfredo reminds him that this is not okay and eventually takes the puppet. Wilfredo then asks each child to tell their story and he uses active listening, which we discussed in chapter 7, as he listens and rephrases what each child says. In this case, it's then that the problem solving can begin.

Here is a summary of the steps Wilfredo used with Maya and Calvin to help them resolve their dispute.

▶ Setting the ground rules (both kids will have a chance to talk, but there's no interrupting and no put-downs)

▶ Getting the stories out

▶ Active listening and rephrasing the stories

▶ Getting on the same side of the problem

▶ Looking for a solution both can agree to

▶ Helping kids put their solution into practice

In both my research and my personal experience, I've noticed that some children's disputes are not only over toys or actions, such as we've seen in the examples above, but also about their relationships and the feelings that arise when they disagree. As children get older and become more attuned to emotions and motives that lie beneath the surface (and especially, I have observed, with girls) their conflicts can be layered with anger, hurt, and more complicated relational dynamics.

When my granddaughter Alexia was seven years old, I was staying with her in Miami, and Terry, a family friend, was also visiting with his nine-year-old daughter, Maeve. Alexia and Maeve had several wonderful days playing happily together, but on the fourth day of Maeve's visit things took a turn for the worse. That afternoon, Alexia came to sit beside me and said, "I'm mad at Maeve. Don't tell her." "Can you tell me more?" I asked, and Alexia said, "She's being mean to me. She ate eight lychees and only let me have four. She ate four and then she ate four more and she said I could only eat four." (A lychee is a small, sweet fruit.) "Can you talk to Maeve about how you feel?" I asked, and she answered, "Come with me." Minutes later I saw Terry, who told me that Maeve had been crying in their room all afternoon because she and Alexia were fighting.

Soon after this and most fortunately, I thought, both girls came into the living room from their separate directions. I said, "Come sit. I want to talk with you two. Come on over here." Alexia and Maeve came and sat down on either side of me.

Me: You're both unhappy today, and you've been fighting. Let's talk about it and try to figure it out. You can each say what's happening and we'll listen. Who wants to start?

Alexia put a piece of play dough over her mouth and pointed to Maeve.

Me: Maeve, can you start? What's going on?

Maeve: She came in my room and took a lychee. I had one in a dish and it's gone.

Alexia (peeling the play dough off one side of her mouth): No, I didn't!

Me: We'll let Maeve talk and then you can talk. (I turned back to Maeve.) So you think Alexia came in your room and took your lychee?

Maeve: Yes.

Me: Alexia, can you tell us what you think?

Alexia: I didn't take the lychee. I only took her play dough and I put it back. She ate eight lychees and only gave me four.

Me: So you didn't take the one lychee from the dish, just the play dough, and you put that back. And you think Maeve ate eight lychees and gave you four.

Alexia: Yes.

Me: Maeve, do you want to say more?

Maeve: I had four lychees. I broke them in half and ate them. I had two that I broke in half, then two more. It looked like I had eight but I only had four.

Me: So you really only had four lychees but it looked like eight because you broke them in half.

Maeve: Yes.

Me: Alexia, does that make sense to you?

Alexia: Yes.

I glanced at Maeve and she still had a very upset, angry look on her face.

Me: So how are we feeling now?

Maeve: Mad.

Alexia: Mad.

Me: Maeve, can you say more about your mad feelings?

Maeve: When we were playing, Alexia made this sign at me. (Maeve crossed her fingers in a T sign.) It means "I hate you." (Maeve's face began to quiver and tears welled up in her eyes.)

Me: Oh. So Alexia made a very strong sign that made you feel how?

Maeve: Mad and bad.

Me: So you feel really bad about the sign she made. And Alexia, how about you?

Alexia (to Maeve): I did it because I was mad at you then.

Me: You were so mad at Maeve then, and you made a strong sign at her.

Alexia: Yes.

Me: So you both thought the other person did something she didn't do: Alexia thought Maeve ate more lychees than she did, and Maeve thought Alexia took a lychee from her room, and you both felt very mad, and Alexia made the "I hate you" sign and Maeve felt bad and mad about that, too.

Here we paused for a breath, and then I addressed them both.

Me: Well, how are we feeling now? Are you still mad?

Alexia: I'm this. (She put her hands apart and then drew them closer together, to show she was not as mad as before.)

Me: So your mad feelings are softening?

Alexia: Yes.

Me: How about you, Maeve? Is your madness softening? (Maeve nodded yes.)

Me: Okay, so it's getting a little better.

Alexia: Who wants to play bouncy ball?

Maeve: *Me!*

They jumped off the couch and started playing.

As became clear, the conflict between Alexia and Maeve was about more than just lychees; it also involved anger, hurt, and their relationship. With them I used the same first few mediation elements Wilfredo used, but here we didn't need to brainstorm to find a win-win solution to a problem. What these two friends needed in order to reconcile was encouragement in getting their full stories out and having the support of a neutral adult who could actively listen and rephrase what they said and felt. In this conflict, the solution was not merely about sharing, but also about repairing a relationship. As we guide children through the conflict resolution process, we'll often be taking our cues from them, as I did here when I asked Maeve to talk more about how she was feeling. When children get the chance to express and hear about emotions in a mediation, we strengthen not only their conflict resolution skills, but also their emotional intelligence and their capacity to build deep and positive relationships with others.

It may seem a bit daunting to read these mediation steps on paper. (How many are there? Do we need to go through all of them every time?) It's easier to see them in action, which is why I've relied on anecdotes to illustrate how conflict resolution strategies—from basics to elaboration—can work. I do know that we adults get a lot better at this with practice and that, with time, using the steps I've outlined gets easier for children, too. They come to rely on the mediation process because they know the adult is neutral, treats both kids equally, and is helping them find their own fair solution. When kids can trust that their viewpoint will be heard, they get good at seeing the bigger problem, and they often enjoy searching for win-win solutions. Maybe not all fights or disputes can be resolved this way, but a great many can. And I find that the more children experience mediation, the more they come to use its basic elements on their own, needing our help less and less.

Too Mad to Talk: Additional Tools for Helping Kids Get Along

Of course, mediation doesn't work every time. Sometimes kids really can't resolve a dispute—they're just too tired, they need to separate for a while, or they simply *want* to fight.

Luckily, there are other specific techniques that we can use to support children in the moment as they learn to work things out with siblings and friends. Having kids focus on the cues they're getting from their own bodies, for instance, can help them calm down. "How does your body feel?" you might ask. "Your breathing? Let's make your breath go slower. Let's count." Asking a child to sit quietly for a minute until he or she feels calmer seems simple enough, but it often works as a start.

One simple and useful tool is to encourage kids to draw a picture of what has gone on when tensions in a conflict are high. Drawing a story can be just as useful (and sometimes more) as speaking in helping kids get some distance from a conflict and preparing them to talk directly about what's happened—and it provides an oasis of calm. Here's a story that Gena, a thirty-three-year-old mother from Medford, Massachusetts, told me about her five-year-old twins.

Raun and Angie came barreling into the house one day, screaming at each other. They were really angry and explosive, so the first thing I wanted to do was help them calm down. Karla, their teacher, said that when kids are close to blowing up, she gets them to make a drawing of what happened. So I tried that. I said to both kids, "Here's paper and markers. Make a picture of what happened and then we'll talk about it." I was surprised how easily both kids got into the drawing—they made pictures fast and furiously. But they did seem to calm down as their energy poured onto the paper.

When they were done, I asked Raun first to tell us what he had drawn and I told Angie we would hear about hers next. Raun had drawn a person with one long arm coming out of the body and a great big fist. He'd colored in the fist bright red. He'd written the words "mad" and "stupid" and said Angie wasn't letting him use the soccer ball. Then Angie talked about her picture, which showed a soccer ball, and said she was going to give Raun a turn but then he got mad. They had calmed down a lot and seemed to be listening to each other, and I could feel the mood changing. So I said, "Do you think you can figure out a way to solve this so you both feel okay?" Angie said, "I'll give you a turn. Let's go play," and they went running back outside.

Gena told me that she was surprised that things had worked out so well in this situation. Doing the drawings helped Angie and Raun step back from their conflict and start to resolve it as they talked about their pictures. When we help siblings work through difficulties and find ways to keep on playing together, we nurture and strengthen the precious relationship they have.

Another helpful suggestion comes from Craig, who has a four-year-old and a six-year-old and also teaches preschool. When I interviewed Craig, he told me that he uses a "talking rock" to help his preschool children as well as his two kids at home resolve conflicts. "The rock really helps young kids listen to each other without interrupting," Craig said. "They can see the rock and whose hand it's in and it helps them take turns talking. At home I keep the rock in a dish on a table and when my kids fight, I say, 'Why don't you two get the talking rock?' Or, if I have to intervene to help them, I get the rock and give it to one of them, signaling who should start talking and who should listen. When we switch the rock to the other person's hand, they get their turn to talk."

Many teachers also use simple sock or hand puppets and storytelling to help young children work on conflicts, and these are things parents can do, too. It's easy to make a few puppets out of socks, with buttons for eyes and tufts of yarn for hair, or you can use action figures or dolls to tell your kids a "conflict story." Let's say your children love to play dress-up but have recently been fighting over certain props. You could put two sock puppets on your hands and try storytelling.

You might say, "This is Paco and this is Jenny and they're fighting because they both want to use the red scarf." You can make Paco say, "Give me that. I want it!" and Jenny say, "No, I had it first!" and Paco say, "You're a baby and you stink."

Then you could stop and ask a few questions: What do you think about what Paco just said? How does Jenny feel when Paco calls her a baby? And how does Paco feel when he says this to her? Can you think of some way that Paco and Jenny can figure out what to do? They have only one red scarf and they both want it.

Setting up a little puppet play like this, one that is similar to—but slightly different from—a conflict your children are having can be very engaging for them. They are one step away from their own dispute, which makes it easier for them to reflect on the argument and brainstorm ideas. Then, when children get into their own real-life fights, you can gently interject ideas they came up with during the storytelling, maybe by asking, for example, "Can you think of a way to solve this like Paco and Jenny did with the red scarf?"

As children get older, more toward the ages of six and seven, you can encourage them to try role-playing, something Lynne, the conflict resolution trainer we heard from earlier, told me she does often with her eight-year-old son, Jabari, and his cousin, Sekai, who is nine.

Jabari and Sekai, as much as they love each other, they do fight a lot because they're always together. So we might do a role-play called "How do we talk to each other?" I usually start by saying, "Do you want to do a role-play?" (They like to act out things, so they'll say yes.) And I'll say, "What part do you want to play? Who wants to play what?" And we figure that out and then we'll say, "Where are we?—maybe we're on the school playground or at the park." So we figure that out, too, and then we just go into it. They use their imaginations.

Lynne went on to tell me that she also suggests role-playing scenarios to help her children learn how to handle potentially difficult situations outside the family.

We might role-play a conflict they get into with someone in the park, for example, and we talk about the use of violence or not using violence. That comes up a lot because Jabari and Sekai live in a culture where violence is really a big part of the game. They might use violence in a role-play (if they do, I let it go) and then we talk about it later. I might ask, "Why would you use violence?" And, "What'll happen if you do?" Or I might suggest, "In this role-play, we aren't going to use any violence—so how would you handle the situation without it?"

Recently we did a scenario about "standing up for each other," and how you do that. Because sometimes it's hard for them—they see all these images of how you have to push people out of the way or be mean to them. We role-played that someone was picking on Nai'im [Jabari's younger brother]. One of them would play the person picking on him and the other one would say, "What's going on? What are you doing?" and try to talk with the person instead of hitting them.

And then I helped them do next steps. I said, "Okay, it seems like you're not going to be able to handle this by yourself, so what do you do then?" Then they said, "Go get Auntie or you or another adult." So in a role-play they see not only what they *can* do, but also what they can't do and when they have to call somebody else to help them.

Bullying

A role-play scenario such as the one Lynne devised called "standing up for each other" is the kind of activity children do in the good antibullying programs that exist in some (though not enough) of our nation's schools. Children practice, as they did with Lynne, how to step in and challenge a child who is picking on another. This is an extremely effective strategy for dealing with bullying: when peers have the courage to step in, bullying behavior stops 57 percent of the time within ten seconds.

Bullying has become an escalating problem in U.S. schools today, and according to some observers it is more frequent and more problematic with children at younger ages than in the past. According to a recent study funded by the National Institute of Child Health and Human Development, more than 16 percent of U.S. schoolchildren said they had been bullied by other students during a school term. With boys, bullying tends to be physical, while with girls—who some researchers say are bullying each other at increasing rates—it is more often verbal or psychological. Bullying seems to increase throughout the elementary school years and peak in middle school, as children explore the boundaries of their power in peer relationships, but the damaging effects of bullying can last well into adulthood.

When it comes to bullying, the initial challenge for us as parents is to find out that it's going on in the first place. Studies show that most children who are bullied don't tell their parents, and in my experience, kids tend to be more reluctant to talk about it as they get older. As we've emphasized throughout this book, creating a climate of open communication with our children is always important, and it can be crucial when it comes to detecting a bullying problem. We can also be on the alert for symptoms in our child such as reluctance to go to school, difficulty sleeping, vague complaints like headaches and stomachaches, or belongings that are missing or coming home ripped. We can ask open-ended questions that will help us learn more: What's it like on the school bus? What happens on the playground? Are there any kids at school who are mean to other kids? As we emphasized in chapter 7, listening with complete attention and being fully present while our kids talk to us will let us learn more.

Like many parents I've spoken with, Patti, who lives in a town outside of Boston, was worried that her son, Rex, who is seven years old and in the second grade, was being bullied.

Rex is physically smaller than other kids. He has asthma and he doesn't run as fast as the other kids. He literally ends up being the kid who always finishes last. The problem is that in the public school, there aren't enough resources. They just cut the number of lunch monitors in half, so there are only three for a hundred kids, and they're outside and inside.

It seems like some of the kids are trying out their power. One kid came up behind Rex and punched him in the back. And then, on the playground, another kid came up and just pulled his sweater off over his head and ran away with it. Rex said he chased after him and he eventually dropped it, but he couldn't stop him. That really threw Rex for a loop. It was the first time he ever realized that someone could do something to him and there was nothing he could do about it.

I told Rex that I wanted to talk to his teacher about this and he said, "Mommy, don't tell anyone." Because he was afraid that these children would attack him or get mad at him. He said, "Mommy, no, no, no! Don't say anything because then they'll be mad at me."

I know some of these boys who are doing the bullying. They're good kids. If someone talked to them about their behavior, they'd understand and stop doing it. But nobody's there to talk with them. One day when I was dropping Rex off at school, I saw maybe five boys pushing each other. And then behind them I saw one kid punching another. Punching and punching and punching and punching until the weaker kid fell to the ground.

Patti's story is distressing and is similar to many I've heard from parents. Bullying becomes a problem in schools when there are few resources and no prevention programs in place. Once parents find out that their child is being bullied, most kids, like Rex, beg them not to do anything out of fear that things will get worse. But the reality is that in most cases adults do need to step in. You can encourage your child to talk to a teacher or another adult, or you can do it, but the earlier the better, because bullying usually escalates with time. If you're not happy with a teacher's response, don't give up. Speak to someone else, perhaps a guidance counselor or the principal.

The best way to prevent bullying at school is to establish a climate throughout the entire school community where respect and nonviolence toward others are valued and practiced. Usually a climate like this is fostered when there are bullying prevention and peer mediation programs in place for all children and staff. In such programs, kids who might be potential bullies learn alternative skills for getting along with peers and get the message that bullying others is not accepted. Other children learn, through role-playing and a host of other activities, how to stand up when they see peers acting like bullies, and when and how to turn to adults for help. When schools have programs like this (and parents can organize to insist that they do), bullying rarely occurs or continues for long.

Win-Win Decision Making

Up until now, we've been using a conflict resolution approach where two children, or an adult and a child, are encouraged to look at a problem from the same side. But you can easily broaden this to include more than two people who look at a problem or issue together. That's what we do when we include children in making decisions in our family. Of course there are situations where kids can't have a say and have to simply comply with what the grown-ups have decided, though as we discussed in chapter 4, we can give children reasons even if we can't give them choices—"You have to zip up your jacket because it's thirty degrees outside and I don't want you to get cold," for example. But there are many decisions, often more than we think, that kids can have a voice in making. I have learned that even though it can take more time to include children in family decisions, in the end they participate in the outcome more fully and without resentment because they were part of deciding what would happen. Here's an example of what this kind of everyday family decision-making process can look like.

My husband, Doug, and I arrived at Jack and Miles's house to spend some time with them on a Saturday morning in February.

Jack: Can we go ice-skating? (We had been teaching them to skate at a small urban rink near our house.)

Doug: I'd love to go skating.

Me: Me, too.

Miles: I don't want to go.

Me: You don't, Miles?

Miles: No.

Jack: Miles, if you don't practice skating, you'll never be able to skate when you grow up.

Miles: I want to do play dough.

Me: Hmmm. You love play dough. We haven't made it for a long time.

Jack: If we don't go skating, I'm not doing anything else.

Doug: We're trying to figure this out, Jack, to find something we all want to do.

Miles: It's three against one.

Me: No one is against you, Miles. We want to find something to do that we all want—you, too.

Doug: We have four people who want to have fun. What can we do that everybody would like?

Miles: I think skating.

Me: Are you changing your mind?

Miles: Yeah.

Me: Are you sure?

Miles: Yes.

Doug: That would be great.

Me: And, Miles, maybe next time we can make some play dough.

Of course we could've used our grandparent power over Miles, telling him that, yes, it was three against one and he *had* to go ice-skating. But if we had done that, Miles would've felt diminished or angry, as if his voice didn't count. And, perhaps more importantly, he would've understood that we were choosing the activity Jack wanted, which could have easily led to feelings of competition toward his sibling and alienation from us. When we assured Miles (and Jack) that we *all* wanted to agree about what we did, we strengthened the trust and spirit of cooperation that was growing among the four of us. When we make consensual decisions in the family, we build relationships and give kids social skills that they can take into many other situations.

Family Meetings

Another way to support children's relationships with siblings and peers, as well as with us, is to have family meetings—that is, regular times when the family gets together to talk about issues of concern to any of them. Meetings provide a support system everyone can count on, and they are a way to build a deeper continuity into the family—to strengthen what is shared, build commitment, and learn many skills along the way. Lynne, who showed us earlier about role-playing, gives workshops on family meetings to parents. When I interviewed her, Lynne described the meetings they have in her own family.

What I like about the family meeting and the way we do it is that we just do it as a regular way of building communication and building relationships and understanding each other. It brings issues that you're dealing with in the family into a new light. So you're not responding to something just in anger or frustration. You're actually coming to the table to say, "This is something that keeps coming up so let's have a conversation about it and let's really listen to each other." Maybe we can get some new insight, some new information—and preferably from the kids. I think that it's important to hear their point of view on a lot of things, and it's just as important for them to hear from us.

When my sons, Kyle and Matt, were young we had regular family meetings on Sunday nights, and they could count on this consistent family time. I "facilitated" the meetings, making sure that everyone got a chance to talk, and I used the same ground rules that mediators use: listen to each other without interrupting and no put-downs allowed. Lynne's format, as she describes it, is a bit more elaborate.

We open family meetings with a song. Whoever has a song they want us all to sing, they tell us, and we do. And then after the song I say, "Okay, let's build our agenda. What do we want to talk about?" And then we say what it is we're going to talk about. And then we talk about those things. And then we do some kind of closing.

One closing I love is that we take turns and say whatever we like about the other people there. I might say, "Okay, so what I want to do when we close is for each of us to say something that we like about each person here in the meeting. Who wants to start off?" So someone else will say, "This is what I like about Jabari." And then I'll say, "What I love about Jabari is that he is a terrific person. He really shows that he loves other people and I love that about him. He has just got a good heart and spirit." Sekai might say that Jabari is the best cousin anybody could ever have and he's always there for her and she's got his back. We'll do it with Nai'im, too, even though he's only a year old. They might say, "Nai'im is really sweet and he will let you hold him and he loves people."

I was struck when Lynne told me this by how important it could be for a child to hear family members say explicitly what it is they like about him or her. Hearing that you are loved and appreciated for who you are will certainly engender feelings of security and self-esteem in any child. Building a web of care through family meetings can be a tool for strengthening all of the relationships in the family and fostering in everyone a deep sense of belonging and cooperation.

STEPS YOU CAN TAKE

▶ Try to mediate when kids need help resolving their conflicts:

> *Lay down the ground rules.*
> *Get the stories out.*
> *Actively listen and rephrase the stories.*
> *Frame the problem as shared by both kids.*
> *Ask kids to help find a win-win solution.*
> *Help kids implement that solution.*

▶ Try using a talking rock to help young children communicate.

▶ Use drawing to help kids calm down and resolve a conflict.

▶ Encourage older children to try role-playing to solve and/or prevent problems.

▶ Keep communication lines open and watch for signs of bullying.

▶ Find teachers or other adults who can help resolve a bullying problem.

▶ Practice a win-win approach to making decisions within the family.

▶ Have regular family meetings or make sure to set aside less formal time for discussing issues within the family when they arise.

CHAPTER 10

When Real Life Intervenes

Nurturing Children's Sense of Security and Hope
about the World

T he increasing presence of mass media in children's lives has
meant that they have more and more exposure to disturbing and
frightening material, not only through entertainment programming
but also through the news.

Children today hear about murders, kidnappings, terrorism, war,
and other alarming events from the TV and radio at home, from newspaper and magazine headlines and photographs, from TV monitors in
public spaces, and from talking with other children. One study has
shown that almost four in ten parents say their children have been
frightened or upset by something they've seen in the news and concerned that what they saw or heard about could happen to them or
their families; as a result, according to some researchers, children today
feel less safe than kids did in the past. And of course, for those children
who have witnessed tragedy or violence firsthand at home or in their
communities, fears about the world's dangers are greatly magnified.
Not only does hearing about disasters and violence in the wider world
make children feel less secure, but when they see government leaders
modeling threats and aggression—including warfare—as the way to
settle disputes, they get the message once again that relationships are

built on force and the principle of "might makes right," rather than on dialogue, understanding, and negotiation.

Many of the techniques and tools you have read about so far in this book—such as supporting imaginative play, seeing the world from a child's point of view, asking open-ended questions, and active listening—will be of great help as we begin to ask how we can help children feel more secure, hopeful, and empowered in a world that often feels scary and uncertain to them. As we find ways to do this, we'll not only help our children feel safer and more hopeful, but we will also show them how relationships can be built on power sharing and cooperation, instead of on winning versus losing, and how their own actions can bring about positive change.

When Real-World Events Intrude

Most of us want to protect children from hearing about world events that can frighten them, but that seems like a near impossibility in today's media-saturated environment. A grandmother from Providence, Rhode Island, described to her daughter a conversation she had one afternoon with her eight-year-old grandson, Charlie, about a year after the war in Iraq had started. ("Vovo" means "grandmother" in Portuguese.)

Charlie: Vovo, I know why we're getting bad weather. It's because God's punishing us because we went to war in Iraq.

Vovo (surprised): What? (A pause.) Oh, I don't think God would punish just one part of the country. It's raining here, but in other places they're having good weather. And, anyway, I don't believe God punishes people that way. What do you know about the war?

Charlie: George Bush made the war and Mom and Dad are not going to vote for him next time. I'm against the war and I made a sign to put in my window. I made a mistake—it said "War No" instead of "No War"—but I put it in my window anyway. And I know that more than two thousand people have died already.

Vovo: Charlie, the war is far away, and no one will come here and have a war because we are a very strong country, and I don't want you to worry about that.

Charlie: Yes, they will come, because they came to New York and they blew up the two towers and they killed lots of people.

Vovo: Well, that's true. (Another pause.) But now we will watch more carefully, and none of those people are going to come back and hurt us.

Charlie: Oh, yes, but I know about North Korea.

When Charlie's mother recounted this conversation to me, she said, "We were just so shocked, because we don't have a TV. We get the *Boston Globe* once a week and it's kept in the corner. He can read at this point, but he wouldn't have read the paper! So then we all wanted to know how he got this information."

I have a stack of stories told to me by teachers who report similar conversations with children that reveal how much they know about the dangers, both near and far, that exist in our world. One example comes from Janice, a preschool teacher in Garden City, Michigan, who told me about a four-year-old who asked her, "Are they gonna shoot me with bullets when I go to the big school?" And about a six-year-old who asked her, "Will the mean people knock down the building if I go in it?"

And of course we adults are not immune to similar worries and fears. Many of the parents I interviewed for this book described feeling a vague, low-level anxiety about their children's safety, and others mentioned the threat of terrorism. A father named Todd talked about the sense of powerlessness he felt in wanting to protect his daughter,

Sophie, from outside dangers. Todd was living in Brooklyn and working in Manhattan on September 11, 2001, when Sophie was two years old. He went to work on the subway that morning but was soon one of the many New Yorkers caught up in the unfolding tragedy of that day. Todd described putting Sophie to bed the same night.

> So that night I have a very distinct memory of singing the lullaby song to Sophie, and just breaking down. Because I felt like it wasn't true. This song is all about "all is well." It's meant to comfort a child. And I had this sense that as I was singing to Sophie—it's the tune that's also on her little mobile—it's a routine that we have, and I felt . . . well, I wasn't sure what kind of world she was going to inherit from us. It was a very sad moment.
>
> I know I can protect Sophie as best I can from a car when we're crossing the road, or all the things parents do have some control over, but that random violence, whether domestic or international, so-called terrorism, I really can't protect her from that.

As difficult as it may be for us, when we acknowledge how we ourselves feel about raising children in an uncertain world, as Todd does, it actually makes it possible for us to better support them. By recognizing our own anxieties, fears, and feelings of powerlessness, we can see more clearly what it is our children feel and need, and we can begin to explore ways to help them.

We can't protect children completely from hearing about real-world disasters and violence, much as we might like to, but we can make a concerted effort to shield them as much as possible, especially when they are very young. Because of how they see the world, young children can easily become confused about what they hear, which may heighten their anxiety. As we've pointed out throughout this book, they sometimes put ideas together in unique ways that can surprise us. One mom, for example, told me that her four-year-old daughter didn't want her dad to go on an airplane, and it turned out that she thought all airplanes carried bombs. But as children get older and develop more logical thinking, they slowly begin to understand more about how the world works—to comprehend concepts like geography, "countries," governments, and even probability. Some of the confusions and fears of earlier years fade away, but school-age children, influenced by the media and particularly by how the news is reported, may continue to have anxieties that we need to address. For example, one study conducted in Ohio with elementary school children reported that 43 percent of the kids in the fourth through sixth grades thought it was "likely" that they would be kidnapped at some point in their lives. So children of all ages will need help in sorting out what they hear about the world around them and feeling safe and hopeful living in it.

Talking with Children about War and Violence

One of the best tools we have for helping children make sense of the wider world is to talk with them. When my granddaughter Alexia was six years old, my daughter-in-law Luciana told me of a conversation they had after seeing a uniformed soldier one morning in a restaurant. After breakfast, Alexia began asking lots of questions: "Why was there a soldier there? Why was he dressed like that? What do soldiers do?" Luciana tried her best to answer. Here's the conversation as she recounted it:

Alexia: What do soldiers do?

Luciana: Soldiers go and help if there's a problem or if people are in trouble or if there's a war.

Alexia: What war?

Luciana: We've been at war with other countries—Vietnam, Iraq . . .

Alexia: Do they kill people?

Luciana: Sometimes people do die.

Alexia: Why do they have war?

Luciana: Stupid reasons . . . money or power, but they always say it's to help people.

Alexia: Do they blow up buildings?

Luciana: Yes. Bombs get dropped and buildings get blown up and people do get hurt.

Alexia: Children?

Luciana: Sometimes.

Alexia: Do children get killed?

Luciana: Sometimes that happens. We don't want it.

Alexia (as she started to cry): I don't like war.

Luciana: I don't either. Your family doesn't support war.

Alexia: Have I been to Iraq?

Luciana: No.

Alexia: Are we ever going to go there?

Luciana: I hope someday we can visit but it's not safe now.

Alexia: I don't want to go there. I'm scared.

Luciana: We wouldn't go if it's not safe.

As Luciana later told me,

It was a hard, hard conversation. I had a lot of doubt. I tried to answer her questions but through the whole conversation I was having my own battle: Am I saying the right things? Does she need to know any of this? I don't want to lie to her but I don't want to scare her. At some age you have to start telling them there are things in the world that are not good. I want her to be aware of the world—to have compassion about what's going on. But I don't want her thinking about this in school. . . . It's so hard raising a kid!

Luciana's struggle captures what so many of us feel when we try to talk with children about difficult issues. We face the tension she describes between trying to be truthful and not scaring them—and there are no perfect answers for how to do this. But there are some tools that can help.

The first thing that can help an adult in Luciana's situation is to take a deep breath and remember that we don't have to have all the answers: what will help most is to find out more about what a child knows and thinks. When Alexia asks early on, "What war?" Luciana could ask her, "What do you know about war?" It will be easier for a parent like Luciana to answer her child if she has a better idea of what this complex concept means to her. I've learned over the years that when we ask children open-ended questions early on in potentially hard discussions, our adult worries about how that conversation will go are often taken care of when children take it in their own direction.

I remember a conversation I had with my son Matt when he was eleven years old. I was tucking him into bed one night and he asked me, "Do you think there's going to be a nuclear war in my lifetime?" This was during the Cold War, when nuclear buildup was frequently in the news. I remember clutching up as I struggled to find an answer. Then I remembered what I could do. "What do you think?" I asked

Matt. And with absolute confidence and enthusiasm, he said, "No! I'm positive! There will not be a nuclear war in my lifetime!" So, as we enter these challenging exchanges with children, our first tool is re-membering to ask them open-ended questions that will give us a win-dow into what they know and what they need from us. Then, based on what they tell us, we can continue to talk, all the while trying to keep what we say close to their level of understanding.

This last is the second helpful tool for talking with children about their fears: to remember to look at things from their perspective. As we've said throughout this book, children do not think like adults. When we're talking with them, even when we're using the same vo-cabulary, the meanings they make of words and ideas is often differ-ent from ours. I remember being in a first-grade classroom one day when the teacher was talking on and on about "peace" and a little boy asked, "A piece of what?"

From a child development perspective, a six-year-old like Alexia doesn't yet have a logical understanding of time and space, and be-cause of this she doesn't understand where Iraq is in relation to her home. Also, most children at the age of six are still quite egocentric: Alexia can't easily separate the harm that she hears is facing other chil-dren from her concerns about her own well-being. That, coupled with her still fuzzy sense of geography, means that she can't be sure she's safe from the dangers that threaten other kids continents away. Taking Alexia's worldview into account can help Luciana as she emphasizes that the war in Iraq is far away and that Alexia is safe at home.

Luciana and I also talked about how important it is for children to feel a sense of hope and empowerment. We agreed that it would help Alexia, or any child in a conversation like this, for us to emphasize the proactive steps people are taking to make the world a better and safer place. For a young child, it's helpful to describe such steps in concrete terms. Luciana might say, for example, "I called our congressman to say I want him to vote to stop the war. Lots of people are calling and telling the government to stop the fighting so all the children everywhere will be safe . . . and that will help."

As children get older, as we saw with eight-year-old Charlie in the first example of this chapter, many become increasingly interested in understanding the events of the wider world in more specific ways. When we talk with them, we can use the same tools that guide our conversations with younger children: asking open-ended questions to help us see things through their eyes and giving them reasons to feel hopeful and empowered. But our discussions with older children will also hold new challenges. Kids Charlie's age and older understand more about geography and countries and why things happen than younger kids do, so we can talk with them in terms that are more complex and logical. But we have to be careful. We don't want to assume they think like us or can handle what we know. While they can comprehend more about the complexities of the world around them, they still see things subjectively, and thus can become fearful and anxious about how world events might affect them and their families.

In the dialogue between Charlie and his grandmother, he tells her he knows about "the two towers" and North Korea, but we aren't sure exactly what information he has or what it means to him. Here active listening would help an adult who wants to find out more about what sense Charlie is making of these events. Is he scared? Does he need reassurance or more information or clarification? When Charlie says, "I know that more than two thousand people have died," we might say, "So you know that many people have died already," and then wait for Charlie to say more. Or, when he says, "They came to New York and they blew up two towers and they killed lots of people," we could say, "So you know that there was an attack in New York and many people died . . ." and wait for him to continue. If it seemed appropriate, we could ask an open-ended question: "How do you feel about that?"

Or "What do you think of that?" This would help us get a fuller sense of how Charlie understands the potent things he's said, and about what more information and/or assurance he needs.

One of the best ways to help children in the elementary school years to feel hopeful and empowered about their world is to help them take some positive action. Eight-year-old Charlie did this: he made a sign for his window that said "War No." Taking an action step like this helps someone Charlie's age feel like he is doing something positive to help with the problems he's learning about in the world. (You'll remember from chapter 2, that the years from eight to ten are a time when active doing and feeling competent are central.) If I were talking with Charlie, I would want to say to him, "People will go past your house and see your sign, and it might make them think about war and decide that they want to help stop it." And I would also tell Charlie something about what adults are doing to make the world safer for children, because kids his age also need to know that we are working to make the world better and more secure and that the burden of solving the world's problems does not fall on children.

Encouraging Expression through Play and Art

As I've discussed in earlier chapters, children often need more concrete ways than just words to process their experiences and express themselves. Both dramatic play and art materials are wonderful vehicles for helping children make sense of their experience and build resilience, and it's often through play and fantasy scenarios that we learn what kids know or feel about some event they've heard about. It was through play, for example, that I first learned that my then four-year-old grandson Jack knew about the terrorist attack on the World Trade Center. Two months after September 11, he was pretending that he was driving a car to Mexico when suddenly he said, "I'm really flying a plane. I'm flying a plane and we're going to New York City." My ears perked up because with children this age we often find out what they know and feel about some event in just this seemingly out-of-the-blue way. "Did anything happen in New York City?" I asked.

"Yes," Jack answered. "A bad guy pushed the pilot away and drove the plane to New York City. He drove it into a building. He didn't know there were people in the building and when he found out he was sad."

What I learned through this play episode was that not only did Jack know about the events of 9/11, but also that he had remade the tragedy into a story less horrendous and frightening. We see this often with young children, who mix fantasy and reality so easily: they take a piece of tragic news they've heard and transform it into a more positive story—one easier to understand and cope with.

When I went to El Salvador during the war there (as a member of a Sister City delegation; my city of Cambridge, Massachusetts, paired with the town of San Jose Las Flores), I spent time with children who had witnessed horrors; every child I met had lost family members to the violence. I realized early on in my stay that playing with building toys, reading books, and drawing pictures helped the children talk about or reenact what they had gone through. Using these symbolic materials gave them an avenue for expression, offering protection from reexperiencing the trauma of war too vividly while still allowing them to process their experience. Eight-year-old Dora, one of the children in the village I stayed in, drew a picture of Swimmy, the little fish in Leo Lionni's book of the same name, who struggles with his family to survive the appetite of a giant fish. Dora talked as she drew.

We roamed in the mountains all together just like the little fish Swimmy that roamed with his brothers. The airplanes were dropping bombs on us and we would run to the holes very scared that they were going to kill us. When we went to school the soldiers shot at us. The soldiers killed whole families, the same as in the Swimmy book.

Dora, like many of the children I met in Las Flores, was able to talk about her life during the war when she used a story and drawing as vehicles for expression. Other children in the village talked very little, but used blocks and Legos to reenact violent scenes they had lived through; fortunately, there were adults present who were supporting these kids as they played. I have seen throughout my life with children everywhere that open-ended materials like blocks, play dough, and drawing, which we discussed in depth in chapter 3, offer children powerful tools for reordering their experience and restoring inner balance.

After the events of September 11, I worked closely with Susan, a first-grade teacher in Boston. The children in Susan's class seemed preoccupied with the terrorist attack and talked about it with a high-pitched kind of energy. Sue put some small airplanes in the block area and watched as the children built tall towers, then flew the tiny planes into them, knocking them down, only to rebuild them and knock them down over again, playing and replaying the event. Some children put miniature play people in their buildings who got buried in blocks when the "towers" fell. One child put a small pony and a gorilla in there, too. After several days of all this building and crashing play, Susan asked, "What can we do to help the people and the animals?" Alonso said, "Get an ambulance!" So Sue brought an ambulance and a police car into the block area. Then she asked, "What else do we need to help the people who're hurt?" And Ada said, "We need doctor stuff." Some of the children began pretending to rescue and "save" the people, listening to their hearts with an improvised stethoscope and wrapping them in bandages. They built a hospital and beds for the people, and gave food (color cubes) to the animals.

Susan's gentle prodding helped the children begin to transform their violent reenactments into scenarios of healing and resolution. Parents can do this kind of intervention, too, by asking a simple question or by making suggestions that encourage constructive play themes like "rescue" or "hospital." When we watch children playing, we can often sense when such small suggestions might be timely. Gently guiding children in this way can support their sense of security and encourage positive social skills as they figure out how to help others. And well into the elementary school years, play and artistic expression can continue to serve children as they seek to make meaning of their experience.

Engagement, Hope, and Empowerment

I was sitting on the couch recently with my grandsons Jackson and Miles, now ages nine and seven, and the daily newspaper sat on the table in front of us. Miles pointed to the large color photo on the front page and asked, "What's that?" It was a picture of the coffin of a U.S. soldier surrounded by grieving loved ones. A little boy, wearing a photo of the soldier pinned to his jacket, stood next to the coffin, crying. I explained the picture to the boys simply and answered their questions about who the little boy was. Miles said, "It's sad," and Jack sat quietly, saying nothing. Right after this, as I turned on the TV to put in a short DVD for the boys to see, the weather channel came up showing coverage of a tornado-ravaged area. A resident was describing the devastation as I was scrambling to put in the disc. Jackson said, "Please stop! It's making me cry." (I thought he was referring not only to the tornado, but also to the newspaper story he had just seen.)

The violent and tragic news so many of our children hear about today can make them feel sad and hopeless. But child development theorists have long stressed that children need to feel like active, competent agents within their surroundings. This is why I believe that today, as many children hear increasing amounts of discouraging news, we should be especially mindful of how important it is for them to feel empowered through doing. Helping children take constructive steps to positively affect their world will help others, and it will also help them. One way to begin is to point out stories of what other people have done that can inspire and uplift children. Libby, a fourth-grader I talked with in a local school, for example, learned about her mom's friend, who had acted to protest the racism in a video game. Libby was bright and animated when she told me what her mom said her friend had done.

> There's a video game that has a villain, and there's cars going by and the villain shoots the people in the car. And you're the police and you're supposed to get him and kill him. And the villain is Haitian. My mom's friend at work is Haitian and she wrote a letter. Because it makes kids think that all dark-skinned people are bad and they kill people. But that's not true.

In this vein, I look for examples in the news to share with my grandchildren of positive actions people take on behalf of others. I brought them the newspaper article about Wesley Autrey, for instance, the fifty-year-old construction worker in New York City who jumped onto the subway tracks to save a stranger from being crushed by an oncoming train. Jack and Miles were amazed by this story and had many questions about what Mr. Autrey had done and why. I also told them about volunteers in Cape Cod, Massachusetts, who came out in the freezing cold last winter to save a group of dolphins beached on the sand. More recently I showed them a news photo, reprinted in the *Boston Globe*, of Kathy Switzer, who dared to run the Boston Marathon (registered as "K.V." instead of "Katherine") during an era when women were not allowed in the race. She had tried to pass for a man in her sweatshirt and sweatpants, ponytail tied under a baseball cap, but in the photo she is being aggressively shoved off the course by three men at the fourth mile.

(She refused to be intimidated, went back into the pack, and finished the race, though she was officially disqualified.) Miles and Jack wanted to go back over this story several times. Why couldn't women run in the race? What if they still made it that way? (Their mom, Lori, ran the marathon last year.) They talked about how "brave" Kathy Switzer was to go out and break an unfair rule. When my own sons were young, I told them stories of the civil rights movement, of the courageous acts of Rosa Parks and Dr. Martin Luther King Jr. These great leaders so inspired my younger son Matt that, at the age of nine, he pinned a photo of Dr. King above his bed and kept it there throughout his school years. Especially today, when children are inundated with popular culture messages that glamorize money, looks, and celebrity, they need to know that people can be motivated by deeper values like love and a passion for social justice. The stories we tell children about the positive acts people take— and the beliefs and feelings behind them—can give them hope and feelings of optimism about living in the world they are inheriting.

Sometimes when children hear about distant and tragic happenings, they need some positive way to respond in the moment. Betty, the former school director, told me that when children came to her school having heard about an unsettling event, she would sit with them for a minute. "And then we would say, 'We send our best thoughts and best wishes to those who are suffering right now.' And it helps to light a candle or plant some flowers—to engage children in doing something active." And Meg, who teaches kindergarten in Cambridge, Massachusetts, helps the five-year-olds in her class "send kindness" to those in need. As part of their daily routine, Meg asks her class if they want to send kindness to anyone. One year the children in her class sent kindness to the children in Iraq, the people of New Orleans after Hurricane Katrina, and many others. Families can do this, too—we can think about others who are suffering or in need and send them kindness as part of a regular family ritual or during family meetings.

We can also find ways to help children take their own more direct steps to bring about a better world. Action steps that work best are those that matter to children and where they can see the effects of what they do, as in the next two examples. The first is of nine-year-old Maeve, who lives in Brooklyn, New York, and whom we met in the last chapter. Maeve loves animals and likes to frequent the neighborhood pet store, but she told me she got upset by what she saw there.

> When I went to the pet store—we went in a lot—I saw a hamster with a deformed leg that was running in circles and bumping into the wall—they didn't clean his cage. There were tiny guinea pigs, newborns, and other big ones in the same cage that were chasing them. One bird was bald except for a few feathers on its head. An eel couldn't move the bottom of its body in the tank and couldn't get any food.
>
> I went home and called the ASPCA—me and my babysitter. We said there's a pet store on Ninth Avenue between Fifth and Sixth streets and they torture the animals. They don't clean the cages or give them food, the hamster doesn't have water. One day some kids were throwing the hamsters. The ASPCA said they'd check it out as soon as they could and they'd call and tell us what happened. They said they'd give them a warning and then come back, or they would have to pay a fine.

I asked Maeve how she felt about calling the ASPCA and she said, "I felt really good 'cause I knew I was helping. When I grow up I want to turn my house into an animal shelter." Maeve was lucky that her babysitter had helped her do something positive about a situation that mattered to her.

In my second example, it was the child's parents, Ellen and Octavio, who decided on an action that would include their seven-year-old daughter, Ariela. As Ellen explained, they were accustomed to shopping at Wal-Mart, a store Ariela liked a lot, in their small town outside of Seattle, Washington. But Ellen and Octavio became sympathetic to the campaign in town to boycott Wal-Mart because of its labor practices. (Wal-Mart pays little to its workers and offers minimal health care—it tops the list of private companies in Washington State with the most workers on taxpayer-subsidized health care.)

Ellen explained that "as an immigrant from Mexico, Octavio has faced exploitation in his work, so we talk a lot at home about workplace justice and Ariela is part of these discussions. We decided not to shop at Wal-Mart and I said to Ariela, 'We don't like the way that store treats its workers. We really don't believe in what they're doing and we want them to change and be better, so we aren't going to go there until they do.'" Ellen told me that she and Ariela talked many times about taking this step and that, slowly, Ariela understood more about the boycott. Much to Ellen's surprise, she later discovered that Ariela was also talking with her second-grade friends about what her family was doing. When Ariela's friend Efraines came over to play, he said to Ellen, "You don't go to Wal-Mart, huh?" And Ellen answered, "No, we don't. Because we're worried about how Wal-Mart is treating the workers." "Yeah, I know," said Efraines. "I already talked with Ariela." During our interview, Ellen told me how pleased it made her to think of the playground talk changing from "Oh, I like your belt" to "Wal-Mart isn't being fair to its workers." And she told me, "I think Ariela feels really good that we are doing something about this as a family."

All of these examples represent ways in which we can help children maintain optimism and learn about how people can act to change things for the better.

A Widening Circle of Care

Throughout this book we have seen a multitude of ways to help children meet their primary need for positive relationships with family and peers. But, taken together, the suggestions in this book will also encourage children to extend the caring and compassion they feel for those they know to a wider web of humanity.

In the next story, we see that eight-year-old Russell is already beginning to care about those he has never even met.

Russell went to Washington, D.C., last year with his mom, Corinne, and they visited the Vietnam Memorial, the giant black wall that lists the names of every American soldier who died in the Vietnam War: there are 58,200 names on that wall. Corinne told me,

> The wall and all the names were very powerful to Russell. He said, "All these people died in just one war? There have been so many wars." We went closer to the wall so Russell could touch it. He began touching the names and counting them. He stood against it and tried to measure the wall using his own body. He determined that one hundred names were contained in about three feet of wall and most of the wall was taller than he is and some of it even taller than his dad and that he was a good counter but this was too big a number for him.
>
> I read him some of the names and he asked, "Are these just the names of the people that died on our side? Where are the names of the other side?"
>
> I felt amazed and a little awestruck by his simple question.
>
> The names of the Vietnamese who died were not included on our memorial and yet Russell had sensed their names and lives as he explored the wall. I said it was good to not just count the names on our side, that it was important to remember those who fought on the other side, and that if they were included here, the wall would be even higher and longer.

What both Russell and his mom do in this story gives us food for thought. Corinne's role seems simple but it is vital and profound: she supports Russell's attempts to make sense of the huge number of names on the Vietnam Memorial's wall in his own way. First she goes closer with him so he can touch the stone, and then she waits for him as he tries to figure out, using his body, how many names are recorded there. Then Corinne begins reading names to Russell, and as she does this, he puts forth a question—one that he has thought of on his own—a question deep enough to set his mother back: "Where are the names of the other side?"

This question comes from within Russell. It is not something that he answered for homework or that he memorized to get right on a standardized test. What does it take for a child to be able to ask an original question like this—one that comes from deep within his own consciousness? I believe that the answer lies in all of the pages of this book that have led us to this point. When children have the opportunity, one that is diminishing for most kids in the United States today, to build their own ideas over the course of their childhood and in the context of relationships that are based on mutuality and love, they become capable of thinking for themselves, of being connected to their own feelings and to the feelings of others. The world our children are inheriting will need citizens who can think like this—in creative, new ways that embrace a wider humanity—if we are to solve the awesome global problems that face our planet

STEPS YOU CAN TAKE

▶ Recognize and sit with your own feelings about raising children in these uncertain times.

▶ Try to protect younger children as much as possible from exposure to violence, war, and terrorism in the news.

▶ When talking with children of any age about world events, ask open-ended questions to learn more about what they understand and what they are concerned about.

▶ Help young children feel a sense of hope and empowerment about their world—emphasize the proactive, concrete steps adults are taking to make the world better and safer.

▶ Help children process and express what they've heard about world events through play and art, using open-ended materials, and gently intervene to encourage scenarios of healing and resolution.

▶ Tell children about the positive actions people take and why they take them.

▶ Encourage children to send "thoughts" and "kindness" to those in need.

▶ Help children learn how to take their own action steps to bring about a better world, especially actions they can take that involve things that matter to them and which might have concrete results they can see.

▶ Support children in every way possible to become original thinkers whose caring and compassion for others will gradually expand to include all people everywhere.

CHAPTER 11

Small Acts, Big Changes

Taking Action in the Wider World

The true measure of a nation's standing is how well it attends to its children—their health and safety, their material security, their education and socialization, and their sense of being loved, valued, and included in the families and societies into which they are born.

—"Child Poverty in Perspective,"
UNICEF Report, 2007

The quote above comes from the opening of a recently released first-of-its-kind United Nations report on the well-being of children in the world's most developed countries.

How true, I thought as I began to read the report. What better way to know the character of a nation than by looking at how it cares for its children? Then I went on to read the document's findings, summarized in a chart ranking the twenty-one countries included in the study by evaluating children's well-being along such lines as poverty, health and safety, education, and peer and family relationships. I was disappointed but not surprised when I saw that the United States sat second from the bottom on the list. Obviously, as the report mentioned, there was no relationship between a country's wealth and the well-being of its children—after all, the United States is first in the world in terms of GDP (gross domestic product).

The steps to take back childhood that we've discussed thus far—to reclaim and promote healthy play, to foster a sense of security and competence, and to help our kids learn how to resolve conflicts peacefully and form loving relationships with others—are things we can do every day with the children we interact with directly in our own personal lives. But as long as we live in a country where all children's basic needs are not well met, and in fact are often undermined by negative societal forces, our efforts to support children will feel like a hard struggle against the tide. What is needed, of course, is for those of us who care about these issues to extend ourselves, each in our own way, to not only take action as individuals but also to join together to advocate for change on a larger scale, so that all the nation's children, not just our own, can thrive.

When I step outside of my familiar circle to take action in the wider world, I like to remember the words of the anthropologist Margaret Mead, whose particular interest was in child and adolescent development across cultures: "Never doubt that a small group of thoughtful people can change the world. Indeed, it's the only thing that ever has." Here are some of the ways you can become involved outside home.

Join Organizations That Advocate for Children on a Wide Variety of Issues

The Children's Defense Fund (www.childrensdefense.org) grew out of the civil rights movement under the leadership of Marian Wright Edelman and has become the nation's strongest voice for children and families since its founding in 1973. CDF's leadership has played a crucial role in many of the policy victories that have occurred for children over the last three decades. You can join their "Leave No Child Behind Movement" to get access to resources and to receive updates on breaking news events that affect children and action alerts on how you can help.

Stand for Children (www.standforchildren.org) is a newer organization with a mission to teach ordinary people like us how to join together to win concrete, long-lasting improvements for children at both the state and local levels. With a belief and a strategic plan grounded in grassroots participation, Stand for Children has already had a powerful positive influence in several states with regard to government policies that affect kids' lives. By joining this advocacy group you can participate in selecting "Stand for Children" issues and find out how to contribute through taking action as an individual.

MomsRising (www.momsrising.com) is another new citizen advocacy movement mobilizing mothers, and all those who have mothers, through grassroots organizing online across the United States, with the goal of creating a cohesive force for promoting family-friendly state and federal legislation. This fledgling but growing effort already has fifty thousand members and links to over fifty other organizations, many of which have not previously partnered. Together they are working on issues such as paid family leave, after-school programs, health care for all kids, improvements in quality and availability of childcare programs, and living wages. You can sign up now with MomsRising to read facts and statistics, find resources, and get information on action steps to take in your community on a wide range of topics vital to children's well-being.

(See the appendix for a fuller listing of similar organizations.)

Combat the Commercialization of Childhood

The UN study quoted at the beginning of this chapter did not include a comparison of the protections countries provide children against harmful media and marketing forces, but these are another important indicator of children's well-being. The United States has far fewer such protections for children than do most other industrialized countries. As noted in chapter 1, the federal regulations once in place to protect children from overcommercialized TV were systematically dismantled in the mid-1980s, during the Reagan era, opening the floodgates for big business to market freely to kids through television, Hollywood movies, video and computer games, fast-food chains, and even schools. Other countries, however, still provide significant protections against the exploitation of their children by commercial interests. For example, Norway and Sweden ban all advertising to children under the age of twelve; in Greece, the advertising of toys to children on television is prohibited between 7:00 a.m. and 11:00 p.m., and advertising war toys is banned at all times; in Italy, no ads are permitted during the broadcast of children's cartoons; and Denmark prohibits the use of figures and puppets that appear in children's programs in any advertisements.

Meanwhile, here in the United States, we have a climate of commercialism that favors big business and not families—a climate that allows many of the negative societal trends we've discussed in this book to flourish. But it is also the case that a growing number of parents, citizens, and organizations are fed up with the impact this has on our children and are advocating, in all kinds of creative ways, for a more child- and family-friendly society—and they are gaining allies and momentum. Here are some examples and some specific efforts you can take part in.

Campaign for a Commercial-Free Childhood (www.commercial freechildhood.org) is a national coalition of health-care professionals, educators, advocacy groups, and concerned parents who counter the harmful effects of marketing to children and launch continuous campaigns that aim to push back against the rampant commercialization of childhood we see in the United States today. On the CCFC website, there is a model you can use to start a local chapter in your own community.

The Citizen's Campaign for Commercial-Free Schools (www.scn.org/cccs) is a grassroots organization that started in Seattle, Washington, and is dedicated to stopping corporations from using public schools as a vehicle for marketing to children. Parents in that city organized and carried out a walk-through of thirty of the city's schools to identify all forms of commercialism and put what they found into a report for fellow parents. After three months, CCCS got the Seattle school district to rescind a new policy allowing the selling of wall space to advertisers. After another five years of hard work, the advocacy group succeeded in getting an anticommercialism policy passed by the Seattle public school committee prohibiting most kinds of commercial activities, including Channel One, wall ads, and ads on vending machines—it is the strongest policy against commercialism in schools in the United States. CCCS is now working in twelve other communities in the state to develop similar policies. CCCS can help you organize a chapter and begin to make your schools commercial-free zones.

An organization called Commercial Alert (www.commercialalert.org) has many campaigns aimed at stopping the commercial assault on our nation's children. One of these is called the Parent's Bill of Rights—it's a set of nine legislative steps that are needed to stop corporate marketers from negatively affecting children's values, health, and education. You can download the Parent's Bill of Rights from the Commercial Alert website and send it to your members of Congress and state legislators, asking them to turn these provisions into laws that would protect children from commercial exploitation. You can also sign up at the website to stay informed of relevant news and action alerts. Or you can become a volunteer and help promote Commercial Alert's campaigns.

Inform Others about Media and Marketing Trends That Harm Children

You can talk to teachers and school administrators about sponsoring a discussion night on the media and consumerism for parents at your child's school. One parent I spoke with, Mei, volunteered to show a video to parents about media violence, made by the Media Education Foundation (www.mediaed.org), that she found in her local library. Mei also put together a handout filled with facts about media and media violence. Another parent, Marc, told me that he had put together his own "dog and pony show" on media and marketing for parents. "I volunteered to present it in the public schools in my city, and four schools took me up on it. I started off by talking a bit about marketing in general. Then I gave some statistics on professional wrestling and showed parts of a DVD, reminding parents to think about the developmental stage of their child and how [he or she] would interpret the messages. Then we moved on to video games. I showed another short video and then we talked about tips for parents and had a general discussion—it [lasted] about two hours." CCFC and the Media Education Foundation are examples of organizations that have developed materials to help you get started doing outreach presentations like Mei's and Marc's in your own community.

One father told me that he went to the website of Teachers Resisting Unhealthy Children's Entertainment (www.truceteachers.org) and found a gold mine of resources and handouts waiting to be downloaded and distributed. He got the administrator of his son's afterschool program to make copies of these valuable materials for each classroom. Teachers posted the TRUCE printouts for parents to see and encouraged them to try out the ideas they offered at home.

You can go to the websites of these and other organizations mentioned above or listed in the appendix—or contact them by mail or phone—to find a treasure trove of valuable material to share with others.

Take Action to Protect Children from Violent, Stereotyped, and Sexualized Material

The previously mentioned Campaign for a Commercial-Free Childhood launched an effort in Massachusetts to ban ads for violent video games from public spaces. CCFC protested against posters on Boston subway cars for the game Grand Theft Auto: Vice City Stories. The group's action resulted in a policy change by the local mass transit authority and a new ruling precluding the marketing of video games rated M or AO (adults only) on public transit.

And don't forget that individual action can also be effective. Next time you go into your local video store, ask them if they have a policy against selling or renting M-rated video games to minors. If they say they do, ask them how they enforce it. Lewis, one dad I spoke with, told me that he asked to speak to the manager at a video store because the person at the cash register didn't know how the policy on renting to minors was enforced. Lewis said he asked the manager to make sure everyone working there knew about the policy and took steps to enforce it.

Keeping with the same issue, as a voter you can approach local officials about banning the sale of violent and sexually explicit video games to minors in your community. This can be a viable step, although businesses have used the courts to push back against such ordinances; still, about twenty states and municipalities have either passed game-related laws or are considering them. Two single dads from Washington, D.C., Jauhar Abraham and Ronald "Mo" Moten, were behind the legislation passed there. Worried about the violent video games their children and other kids were playing, these dads went to the mayor and the city council and asked them to back legislation that would ban the sale of M-rated games to children. Disgusted with game creators and stores that don't take responsibility for selling such brutal, often racially stereotyped images to kids, these two dads decided to picket local chain stores that were selling this kind of product and to protest outside the Manhattan headquarters of the makers of the extremely violent Grand Theft Auto, which we've mentioned several times before in this book and which they chose as a symbolic example. Eventually they convinced the mayor of D.C. and most of the city council to back legislation that would ban the sales of any M-rated games to children.

To find out what's happening nationally with video game legislation, you can go to www.gamepolitics.com/legislation.htm.

Push for Antibullying, Conflict Resolution, and Peer Mediation Programs in Your Local School

You can organize parents, speak with administrators and teachers, and tell school boards that you want programs in your schools that will prevent bullying and teach children how to resolve conflicts creatively. Many programs like this, designed by educators who know that parents are hugely influential in shaping children's social behavior, also include sessions for them. In one school district in New Jersey, a conflict resolution program was threatened with a major budget cut until a group of parents wrote a joint letter to the school board and circulated it throughout the district. On the night the board met to vote on the budget, these parents also came out and spoke up passionately about the positive changes they had seen in themselves and their children as a result of this program, and when the votes were counted its budget remained intact.

Two highly respected national organizations that disseminate conflict resolution, mediation, and bullying prevention programs are Educators for Social Responsibility (www.esr.org) and the Morningside Center for Teaching Social Responsibility (www.morningsidecenter.org). You can call ESR or the Morningside Center and ask for help in trying to bring these positive social programs to your school.

Distribute the "Call to Action on the Education of Young Children" Petition

An organization called the Alliance for Childhood (www.alliance forchildhood.net) takes on public education campaigns that focus attention on children's play, learning, and healthy development. They have issued a "Call to Action on the Education of Young Children"—a petition that has been signed by more than 125 of our nation's leading voices in child development, psychology, and pediatrics—calling for a reversal of current trends in early education. The call to action states that political pressure is fueling an emphasis on standardized tests and unproven methods of academic instruction in early education that can damage children's healthy development and undermine their learning. The signers want to see education in the early years that emphasizes hands-on learning, creative play, and caring human relationships. Many parents have downloaded the statement and distributed it in their communities; some have brought it to PTA meetings, to school committee hearings, and to parent conferences. If you find that it addresses your concerns, you might try sending it to your local paper, along with the organization's press release, and asking for it to be printed.

Hold a Fair Trade Fund-raiser at Your School

You can initiate a fair trade fund-raiser as an alternative to or a part of a traditional school fair. Holly, a parent we heard from in chapter 6, organized such an event with other parents at her daughters' school, where they sold Equal Exchange coffee, tea, and sweets to friends, families, and co-workers, many of whom were excited about the opportunity to support socially conscious fair trade products and raise money for their school at the same time. Equal Exchange (www.equalexchange.com/fundraiser) offers a fund-raising kit and educational tools to use in classrooms so children—and adults—can learn about fair trade issues that farmers face around the globe.

Take Action to Protest Products Harmful to Children

You can protest against products you believe are harmful to children by writing letters as an individual and/or by joining up with other people and groups to strengthen your effort. A campaign against Hasbro's planned line of blatantly eroticized dolls based on the Pussycat Dolls—a real-life burlesque troupe turned music group famous for its sexualized lyrics and dance routines—to girls as young as six got its start from one parent, Lisa Flythe, the mother of a four-year-old girl. Lisa first wrote to Hasbro herself complaining about the Pussycat dolls to be, and then alerted the national organization Campaign for a Commercial-Free Childhood to the problem. CCFC joined forces with Dads and Daughters (www.dadsanddaughters.org), a group dedicated to maximizing the power and potential of father-daughter relationships, to initiate a grassroots letter-writing campaign urging the toy company to reconsider. The response to th.is call to action was tremendous and resulted in Hasbro announcing the cancellation of the line.

Here are some other success stories. Parents and grassroots groups around the country joined together during the holiday sea-son of 2002, when a toy called the Forward Command Post—which was, unbelievably, a fully outfitted bombed-out toy house—appeared on the market. The campaign was directed at JCPenney, one of the chains that carried the toy, and in response to the protest, the company removed the toy from its website. To cite another example, a group of parents protested the marketing of thong underwear with the words "Eye Candy" and "Wink Wink" printed on them to ten-year-old girls and got Abercrombie & Fitch to stop selling these items. And sometimes just one act by one concerned parent can bring about a positive change, as when a father wrote a letter to the head of Campbell Soup to complain about a commercial that showed preteen girls on a diet. A few days later he heard back from the CEO, who told him that the commercial had been pulled. If you're concerned about a toy, product, or program you see, write to register your complaint and/or (better yet) contact an advocacy group to find out if they can help you mount a protest.

Use Your Consumer Purchasing Power to Advocate for Kids

When you go to a grocery store, a video store, or a toy store, choose items that will support children's needs and healthy development and steer clear of those things that undermine creative play, teach violence, or promote harmful stereotypes. Let store managers know which products you prefer and why. If you see a product marketed to children that seems inappropriate, make the effort to talk to the store manager or write to the manufacturer and complain. These may seem like small actions, but the more of us who take them, the more difference they will make.

Speak Out for More Family-Friendly Workplaces

Let employers (and political candidates) know, however you can, that we want and need their help in balancing work life and family life. You can talk about issues such as the need for more flexible hours, parental leave, and release time to attend a child's school activities. Remind your employer that family-friendly workplaces make for a healthier and more productive environment for all employees.

Work for Candidates Who Advocate for Children

Working for political candidates who advocate for policies that will improve the health and well-being of children on many levels is another important way we can effect change. Parents make up about one-third of the electorate and we can use our power as voters to help America's children. You can support candidates who speak out for better child welfare laws, improved day care and after-school programs, policies to limit the harmful affects of media and marketing to kids, and schools that are adequately funded and commercial-free, schools that also promote hands-on activities, social and emotional learning, and the arts.

Participate in the National TV-Turnoff Week

Families all across the country have participated in TV-Turnoff Week, an annual event that began in 1994, to raise awareness about the role the media play in our lives, organized by the nonprofit TV-

Turnoff Network (www.tvturnoff.org), a branch of the Center for Screen-Time Awareness. More than sixty-five national organizations support this illuminating experiment, and parents and kids alike attest to the new discoveries that come from turning off the tube and finding other ways to spend their time. You can join the TV-Turnoff Network, receive its newsletter, organize a TV-Turnoff Week in your community, distribute the group's enlightening fact sheets, and have fun exploring the hundred and one "Screen-Free Activities" offered on its website.

Support Rating Systems That Are Consistent across All Media

The film, television, and video game industries each have their own separate rating systems, systems that most parents find confusing and hard to use—and for good reason. These industries prefer self-regulation over external monitoring because it allows them to control their own standards, which will ultimately translate into greater profits for them. But, clearly, the self-regulation scheme has not worked for children and families. What we need is an independent ratings board that operates outside of industry control and that extends across all three areas of entertainment—television, film, and video and computer games. We need ratings that give parents information about actual content in a way they can understand and use, and that are strictly enforced.

You can look for ways—with friends, advocacy groups, and policy makers—to discuss how inherently flawed our current entertainment rating systems are, and you can push for a better system that will provide real, understandable standards that parents and families can use to protect their children from potentially harmful material.

Support Media Reform and Regulations to Protect Children from Aggressive Marketing

Free Press (www.freepress.net) is a national organization working for a more diverse and public-oriented media system with a strong nonprofit and noncommercial sector. Free Press wants to get to the root of the media problems we have in our country today, including those that shape children's media (i.e., most of our TV and radio stations are owned by giant corporate conglomerates that don't represent the views of most Americans and which make huge profits off the public airwaves). You can sign up with Free Press to receive information about their latest campaigns and learn about the many action steps you can take toward a more just and participatory media system in the United States, one that could vastly improve the quality of media programming for children.

Many of us who advocate for media reform want to see regulation of commercial broadcasting that will protect children from exploitation by media and marketing forces. The transnational conglomerates dominating our media will do anything they can to generate the biggest, easiest profits unless we hold them to a higher standard of public service. We citizens have a clear legal right to do this because the airwaves are owned by the public and by law the broadcasters who get licenses are overseen (theoretically at least) by the Federal Communications Commission.

First, advertising should be strictly regulated or removed altogether from all children's programming. The American Psychological Association has called for a ban on advertising to children under the age of eight; it cites research showing that before that age most kids don't understand persuasive intent, so advertising to young children exploits them (many of us would rather see a ban to the age of twelve, as in Sweden and Norway). Second, we need regulations that prohibit the marketing of toys and products directly tied to TV shows, like the ban that existed in the United States before 1984. And third, as the Federal Trade Commission has already recommended, there should be no more marketing to young children of action figures, toys, and other products linked to movies rated for older viewers. Such a law would eliminate, for example, selling toys, underpants, and toothbrushes tied to the *Spider-Man* movies (rated PG-13) to little kids.

Implementing these three regulatory policies would go a long way toward protecting children from a media climate that is currently undermining their healthy play, exposing them to far too much violent and sexualized content, and immersing them in a culture of consumerism. You can help to educate others about the need for media regulations: write letters to the editor, push politicians on the issue of regulating marketing to children, join groups working on media reform, organize a PTA meeting or parent group to focus on media reform—in short, try to keep these issues in the forefront of public dialogue whenever and wherever you can.

Use Your Power of One, a Few, or Many to Make a Difference

Parents, caregivers, and citizens working together can make the well-being of children a new national priority for the United States. By taking the steps outlined in this book, both inside and outside our homes, and by reaching out to others in our communities to do the same, we will eventually be able to effect changes that will make our nation into one that truly does "attend to its children," not just by speaking empty words, but with effective and enforceable public policies that provide for children's basic needs and protect them from exploitation. I am optimistic about this effort. As historian

Howard Zinn, in his memoir *You Can't Be Neutral on a Moving Train*, reminds us,

> We don't have to engage in grand, heroic actions to participate in the process of change. Small acts, when multiplied by millions of people, can transform the world.
>
> To be hopeful in bad times is not just foolishly romantic. It is based on the fact that human history is a history not only of cruelty, but also of compassion, sacrifice, courage, kindness. . . . If we remember those times and places—and there are so many—where people have behaved magnificently, this gives us energy to act, and at least the possibility of sending this spinning top of a world in a different direction.

I believe that you and I, with our heightened awareness of what children need and the impediments they face in this country today, can act on children's behalf, each of us in our own individual ways, to bring into being a society and world that truly does nurture and nourish the young.

Appendix

Organizations Helping to Take Back Childhood

Alliance for Childhood
P.O. Box 44
College Park, MD 20741
www.allianceforchildhood.net

American Academy of Pediatrics
Department C-TV
141 Northwest Point Boulevard
P.O. Box 927
Elk Grove Village, IL 60009
www.aap.org

American Medical Association
515 North State Street
Chicago, IL 60610
312-464-5563

American Psychological Association
750 First Street
Washington, DC 20002
202-336-6046

Campaign for Commercial-Free Childhood (CCFC)
Media Center
Judge Baker Children's Center
3 Blackfan Circle
Boston, MA 02115
www.commercialexploitation.com

Center for Media Education
1511 K Street, NW, Suite 518
Washington, DC 20005
202-628-2620
www.cme.org/cme
e-mail: cme@cme.org

Center for the New American Dream
6930 Carroll Avenue, Suite 900
Takoma Park, MD 20912
www.newdream.org

Children Now
1212 Broadway, 5th floor
Oakland, CA 94612
www.childrennow.org

Children's Defense Fund
25 E Street, NW
Washington, DC 20001
www.childrensdefense.org

Citizens' Campaign for Commercial-Free Schools (CCCS)
Seattle, WA
www.scn.org/cccs

Commercial Alert
P.O. Box 19002
Washington, DC 20036
www.commercialalert.org

Dads and Daughters
2 W. First Street, Suite 101
Duluth, MN 55802
www.dadsanddaughters.org

Educators for Social Responsibility
23 Garden Street
Cambridge, MA 02138
617-492-1764

Equal Exchange
50 United Drive
West Bridgewater, MA 02379
www.equalexchange.com

Free Press
100 Main Street
P.O. Box 28
Northampton, MA 01061
www.mediareform.net

Media Education Foundation
60 Masonic Street
Northampton, MA 01060
www.mediaed.org

MomsRising
www.momsrising.org

Morningside Center for Teaching Social Responsibility
475 Riverside Drive, Suite 550
New York, NY 10115
www.morningsidecenter.org

Peace Games
280 Summer Street, mezzanine level
Boston, MA 02210
www.peacegames.org

Stand for Children
516 SE Morrison Street, Suite 410
Portland, OR 97214
www.truceteacher.org

Teachers for Resisting Unhealthy Children's Entertainment (TRUCE)
P.O. Box 441261
West Somerville, MA 02144
www.truceteachers.org

TV-Turnoff Network
1200 29th Street, NW, lower level #1
Washington, DC 20007
www.tvturnoff.org

Notes and References

A Note to the Reader

You will find two kinds of notes in this section. First, there are references to articles and books that contain the studies and facts mentioned in the book. All of these are indicated by the page numbers and phrases from the text to which they refer. These phrases should have enough information to allow you to find them easily in the text. Second, there are notes that provide more detail or information about the people and ideas mentioned in the book and these are preceded by a black dot (•) followed by key phrases from the text.

Chapter 1: Taking Back Childhood

3 • *from Jean Piaget's work on play and learning to Mary Ainsworth's ideas on attachment to Erik Erikson's articulation of the stages of life:* Jean Piaget, born in Switzerland in 1896, developed the most comprehensive and compelling theory of children's intellectual development in all of psychology. Mary Ainsworth was born in 1903 and grew up in Toronto. Ainsworth studied patterns of attachment in babies both in Uganda and the United States and is often credited with having done the most important research on attachment. Erik Erikson, born in

Germany in 1902, expanded on Sigmund Freud's psychosexual stages of development with his renowned theory of the eight stages of life, where he introduced new and original concepts to explain children's relationship to the social world.

4 • *child development theorists, from Lev Vygotsky and Jean Piaget to Anna Freud and Erik Erikson, saw play as vital:* Lev Vygotsky, born in Russia in 1896 and a Marxist, believed that human development had to be understood in its social-historical context. His writings on play have contributed greatly to our understanding of how children learn through play with others. Jean Piaget wrote extensively on children's play, which he saw as an essential aspect of symbolic thought and cognitive development. He began outlining his theory of play in his early book *Play, Dreams, and Imitation in Childhood.* Anna Freud, youngest daughter of Sigmund Freud and founder of child psychoanalysis, was born in 1895 and grew up in Vienna. Her observations of children during World War II documented how children use play to work on difficult life experiences. Erik Erikson, who also wrote extensively about children's play, emphasized its value in helping children cope with traumatic events. According to Erikson, play offers children a healing resource as they resolve anxieties through dramatic reenactments of life events.

6   *studies . . . have shown that . . . kids' play has become far less creative:* D. E. Levin and N. Carlsson-Paige. 1995. The Mighty Morphin Power Rangers: Teachers voice concern. *Young Children* 50(6): 67–72. N. Carlsson-Paige and D. E. Levin. 1991. The subversion of healthy development and play: Teachers' reactions to the Teenage Mutant Ninja Turtles. *Day Care and Early Education* 19(2):14–20.

6   *today, eight- to eighteen-year-olds spend an average of nearly six and a half hours per day consuming media:* D. F. Roberts, U. G. Foehr, V. Rideout. 2005. *Generation M: Media in the lives of 8 to 18 year olds.* Menlo Park, CA: Kaiser Family Foundation, 3.

6   *American Academy of Pediatrics recommends that children under the age of two not watch television at all:* American Academy of Pediatric website, Television and the Family. www.aap.org/family/tv1.htm.

6   *Kaiser survey found . . . 68 percent of all children under two use screen media. . . . Twenty-six percent . . . have TVs in their bedrooms:*

V. Rideout, E. A. Vandewater, and E. A. Wartella. 2003. *Zero to six: Electronic media in the lives of infants, toddlers and preschoolers.* Menlo Park, CA: Kaiser Family Foundation, 4.

6–7   *the typical child . . . exposed to . . . the current average of forty thousand commercials per year:* S. Linn. 2004. *Consuming kids: The hostile takeover of childhood.* New York: The New Press, 5.

7   *In 1978, the Federal Trade Commission (FTC) . . . decided to ban advertising to children under the age of eight:* S. Linn. 2005. The commercialization of childhood. In S. Olfman, ed., *Childhood lost.* Westport, CT: Praeger, 108–9.

7   *in 1984 . . . the Federal Communications Commission (FCC) . . . removed all of the regulations it had put in place over earlier decades:* N. Carlsson-Paige and D. E. Levin. 1990. *Who's calling the shots?* British Columbia, Canada: New Society Publishers, 11.

7   *Corporations spend $15 billion annually on marketing targeted at children . . . more than they spent in 1992:* J. B. Schor. 2004. *Born to buy: The commercialized child and the new consumer culture.* New York: Scribner, 21.

12   *study by the American Medical Association . . . 75 percent of parents . . . concerned about . . . violence shown on children's television:* American Medical Association. 1996. *Physician guide to media violence.* Chicago: American Medical Association.

12   *Kids are exposed to more violent content in children's programming than adults are in all of prime time:* Parents Television Council. 2006. *Wolves in sheep's clothing: A content analysis of children's television.* Los Angeles: Parents Television Council, 1.

13   *exposing children to violent images can have a similar impact to "physical abuse or living in a war zone":* A. Poussaint. 1997. Taking movie ratings seriously: The risks faced by children allowed to watch film meant for adults are as real as those from alcohol, tobacco, or abuse. *Good Housekeeping,* April, 74.

13   *There is a growing body . . . research showing . . . frightening media . . . increased fearfulness:* J. Cantor. 2006. Why horror doesn't die: The enduring and paradoxical effects of frightening entertainment.

In J. Bryant and P. Vorderer, eds. *Psychology of entertainment*. Mahwah, NJ: Lawrence Erlbaum, 315–327.

14   *62 percent of parents . . . said that their child had been frightened by something he or she saw in a TV program or movie:* D. A. Gentile and D. A. Walsh. 1999. *MediaQuotient: National survey of family media habits, knowledge, and attitudes.* Minneapolis: National Institute on Media and the Family.

15   *a recent study from the Harvard School of Public Health found a "ratings creep" . . . by the Motion Picture Association of America:* Kimberly M. Thompson and Fumie Yokota. 2004. Violence, sex, and profanity in films: Correlation of movie ratings with content. *Medscape General Medicine.* Cambridge, MA: Harvard School of Public Health.

16   *in the 1970s, 61 percent of mothers stayed home full-time. By the year 2000 . . . two-thirds of the children . . . had working moms:* J. T. Bond with C. Thompson, E. Galinsky, and D. Prottas. 2002. *Highlights of the national study of the changing workforce.* New York: Families and Work Institute.

17   *Diaries . . . reveal that American children . . . now spend almost twice as much time in supervised, structured settings:* S. Hofferth and J. Sandberg. 2001. Changes in American children's use of time. In T. J. Owens and S. L. Hofferth, eds., *Advances in life course research series: Children at the millennium: Where have we come from, where are we going?* New York: Elsevier Science, 193–229.

17   *the television that is on during mealtimes for 63 percent of American families:* E. A. Vandewater, D. S. Bickham, J. H. Lee, H. M. Cummings, E. A. Wartella, and V. J. Rideout. 2005. When the television is always on: Heavy television exposure and young children's development. *American Behavioral Scientist* 48(5):562–77.

23   *Compared to the average American worker in 1969, today's earners put in an additional 163 hours per year:* Juliet Schor. 1991. *The overworked American: The unexpected decline of leisure.* New York: Basic Books.

24   *thirty-year period, parental time with children . . . declined by 13 percent:* The economic status of parents in postwar America, 1996, paper prepared for the Task Force on Parent Empowerment, 9.

Chapter 2: Through Their Eyes

29–30   *a 2001 landmark survey sponsored by Zero to Three . . . found that . . . parents and adults . . . lack . . . child development information:* J. R. Lally, C. Lerner, and E. Lurie-Hurvitz. 2001. National survey reveals gaps in the public's and parents' knowledge about early childhood development. *Young Children* 56(2):49–53.

45   *bullying . . . on the rise nationwide . . . showing up among younger children:* Indicators of school crime and safety, 2002: Nonfatal student victimization—student reports. National Center for Education Statistics. Available at nces.ed.gov/pubs2003/schoolcrime/6.asp?nav-1. Accessed June 13, 2007. Primary school bullying on increase. 1999. BBC Online Network. Available at news.bbc.cd.wk/1/h1/education/433279 .stm. Accessed June 13, 2007.

47 •   *He asked about the popular videos for infants called* Brainy Baby: For more information on baby videos, their effects on infant development, and the movement to halt marketing to babies and toddlers, go to the Campaign for Commercial Free Childhood website at: www .commercialfreechildhood.org/factsheets/facts.htm.

48   *watching DVDs and videos . . . language development:* F. J. Zimmerman, D. A. Christakis, H. N. Meltzoff. 2007. Associations between media viewing and language development in children under age 2 years. *Journal of Pediatrics,* vol. 120. Available at www.emedicinehealth.com/ script/main/art.asp?articlekey=83086. Accessed August 2007.

Chapter 4: No More Time-Outs

78 •   *Jean Piaget, along with other theorists writing on children's moral development . . . about the effects on children . . . adult power over them:* For more about moral development and parental use of power see J. Piaget. 1965. *The moral judgment of the child.* New York: The Free Press; L. Kohlberg. 1984. *The psychology of moral development.* New York: Harper & Row; and A. Kohn. 1990. *Punished by rewards.* Boston: Houghton Mifflin.

83   *Daniel Goleman . . . American kids are getting worse at cooperation, at being able to work things out, and at controlling their impulses:*

S. Munro, M. U. O'Brien, J. W. Payton, and R. P. Weissberg. 2006. Common ground: Cooperative learning helps create the essential skill of working (and compromising) within a group. *Edutopia*. Available at www.edutopia.org/magazine/ed1article.php?id=Art1616&issue=sep06. Accessed September 2006.

87   *a national survey . . . 61 percent . . . it's appropriate to spank a child as a regular form of punishment:* J. R. Lally, C. Lerner, E. Lurie-Hurvitz. 2001. National survey reveals gaps in the public's and parents' knowledge about early childhood development. *Young Children* 56(2):49–53.

89   *Dr. Alvin Poussaint . . . hitting kids . . . prone to depression, feelings of alienation, use of violence toward a spouse, and lower . . . achievement:* A. Poussaint. 1999. Spanking strikes out. Available at www.nospank.net/psnt.htm. Accessed April 29, 2007.

89   *Several definitive studies . . . spanking . . . increases the chances . . . serious psychological and behavioral problems:* M. Straus. 1994. *Beating the devil out of them: Corporal punishment in American families.* New York: Lexington Books, 83–88.

Chapter 5: From *Spider-Man* to *Smackdown*

96   *educators and child development experts agree . . . play has become more imitative, less imaginative, and more violent:* D. E. Levin and N. Carlsson-Paige. 2006. *The war play dilemma.* New York: Teachers College Press, 3–14.

105   *Studies . . . children are scared by TV and films even more often than we adults think they are:* J. Cantor. 1998. *Mommy I'm scared: How TV and movies frighten children and what we can do to protect them.* San Diego: Harvest, 24–26.

109 • *The Federal Communications Commission was created to play this protective role, but it has . . . abandoned this responsibility:* For more information about the history and role of the FCC see R. W. McChesney. 1999. *Rich media, poor democracy: Communication politics in dubious times.* New York: The New Press.

110 *In the summer of 2000 . . . Six major medical and mental health groups . . . issued a joint statement on media violence:* American Academy of Pediatrics. 2000. *Joint statement on the impact of entertainment violence on children,* presented at the Congressional Public Health Summit, Washington, DC.

111 *researchers have shown that patterns of aggression at age eight are . . . correlated with aggressive behavior in adulthood:* L. Eron and R. Slaby. 1994. "Introduction" in *Reason to hope: A psychological perspective on youth and violence,* eds., L. Eron, J. Gentry, and P. Schlegel. Washington, DC: American Psychological Association.

114 *children of all races . . . associate positive qualities . . . with white characters on television and negative characteristics . . . with minority characters:* Children Now, May 1998. A different world. Children's perceptions of race and class in media. Oakland, CA: Children Now.

114 *human characters were almost exclusively white in video games for young children and . . . nearly all heroes were white:* Children Now. December 2001. Fair play? Violence, gender and race in video games. Oakland, CA: Children Now.

Chapter 6: All Ads, All the Time

123 *In 1983, corporations spent $100 million on television advertising directed at kids; today . . . 150 times that amount:* New American Dream. 2006. Facts about marketing to children. Available at www.newdream .org/kids/facts.php. Accesssed on June 19, 2007.

127 *this country . . . 4.5 percent of the world's population . . . 45 percent of the global toy production . . . kids get an average of seventy new toys a year:* J. Schor. 2004. *Born to buy.* New York: Scribner, 19, 27.

128 *"We're teaching them that if you don't have product X, you're not worthy":* As told to economist Juliet Schor by a marketer and reported in: K. Kelly and L. Kulman. 2004. Kidpower. *US News and World Report,* September 13, 4.

129 *American Psychological Association Task Force . . . report on the sexualization of girls:* Report of the APA task force on the sexualization of girls. 2007. Washington, DC: APA.

129 *the more a young girl is exposed to the media, . . . dissatisfied with her body, her appearance, and herself:* D. Hargreaves and M. Tiggermann. 2002. The effect of television commercials on mood and body dissatisfaction: The role of appearance-schema activation. *Journal of Social and Clinical Psychology* 21, 465–77.

133 *"All of our advertising is targeted to kids. You want that nag factor":* K. Stitt, senior brand manager at Heinz. 2001. *Wall Street Journal*, October 24.

133 *children ages four to twelve influence some $565 billion of their parents' purchasing each year, and children's influence on adult spending is growing at . . . 20 percent per year:* J. Rowe and G. Ruskin. 2003. The parents' bill of rights. *Mothering*, January/February. Available at www.mothering.com/articles/growing_child/consumerism/bill _of_rights.html. Accessed June 19, 2007.

133 *the more kids buy into the culture of getting and spending, the worse their relationships are with their parents:* J. Schor. 2004. *Born to buy.* New York: Scribner, 160–75.

133 *studies tell us that children . . . more materialistic are not as happy . . . fewer positive relationships with their peers than those . . . less caught up by consumerism:* T. Kasser. 2003. *The high price of materialism.* Cambridge, MA: MIT Press.

135 *when interactions with others are based on materialistic values, . . . relationships are more shallow and superficial:* T. Kasser. 2003. *The high price of materialism.* Cambridge, MA: MIT Press.

138 *minimize the influence of commercialism . . . if we reduce or eliminate television:* J. Schor. 2004. *Born to buy.* New York: Scribner, 169.

143 *A Gap shirt made in El Salvador . . . sells in the United States for twenty dollars . . . workers receive just twelve cents for making it:* B. Peterson. 2002. Planting seeds of solidarity. Weaving world justice issues into the elementary classroom. In *Rethinking globalization: Teaching for justice in an unjust world*, eds., B. Bigelow and B. Peterson. Milwaukee: Rethinking Schools, 22.

144 *40 percent . . . secondary students . . . required to watch Channel One, a ten-minute daily news show with two minutes of commercials:*

The Center for Commercial-Free Public Education. Channel One. Available at www.ibiblio.org/commercialfree/channelone.html. Accessed on June 14, 2007.

144   *seventy-seven of these classroom kits . . . nearly 80 percent . . . biased in favor of the sponsoring company or its agenda:* Consumers Union, 1998. Captive kids: A report on commercial pressure on kids in school. Washington, DC: Consumers Union. Available at www.consumersunion.org/other/sellingkids/inschoolpromo.htm. Accessed June 14, 2007.

Chapter 7: Might Does Not Make Right

148   *one of the biggest research studies . . . conflict resolution . . . children can learn these skills . . . to use in resolving conflicts peacefully:* L. Aber, J. L. Brown, and C. C. Henrich. 1999. *Teaching conflict resolution: An effective school-based approach to violence prevention.* New York: National Center for Children in Poverty. Electronic version of the report is available at www.nccp.org.

154 • *A second bedrock communication skill . . . is called "active listening":* Both active listening and "I" statements/messages have been part of conflict resolution programs for at least thirty years. I first encountered these two ways of communicating with children in 1972 when I took an effectiveness training course for parents developed by Thomas Gordon.

156   *The Buddhist monk Thich Nhat Hanh . . . a deep practice requiring the full presence of our whole being:* T. Nhat Hanh. 2001. *Anger: Wisdom for cooling the flames.* New York: Berkley, 89–98.

166   *Marshall Rosenberg . . . explores anger . . . nonviolent communication (NVC) approach:* M. Rosenberg. 2005. *Nonviolent communication: A language of life.* Encinitas, CA: PuddleDancer Press. M. Rosenberg. 2005. *The surprising purpose of anger: Beyond anger management: Finding the gift.* Encinitas, CA: PuddleDancer Press.

168   *Daniel Goleman and Linda Lantieri . . . calming strategies with parents and kids:* L. Lantieri and D. Goleman. 2008. *Building emotional intelligence: Techniques to cultivate inner strength in children.* Boulder, CO: Sounds True.

Chapter 8: Love Above All

171   *Daniel Goleman . . . these "human skills" . . . better predictors of suc-*
      cess and well-being than any other single factor: R. Stern. 2007. Social
      and emotional learning: What is it? How can we use it to help our chil-
      dren? NYU Child Study Center. Available at www.aboutourkids.org/
      aboutour/articles/socialemotional.html. Accessed March 14, 2007.

171– *field of neuroscience . . . social and emotional factors . . . affect brain*
172   *development . . . we can . . . do a lot to influence and strengthen . . .*
      neural connections: D. Goleman. 2006. *Social intelligence: The new*
      science of human relationships. New York: Bantam Dell, 4–12.
      D. Siegel. 2001. *The developing mind: How relationships and the*
      brain interact to shape who we are. New York: Guilford Press.

181 • *John Bowlby called, in his book* Attachment and Loss, *a "secure base":*
      John Bowlby's "attachment theory," created in the 1940s and 1950s,
      was a major contribution to our understanding of the development of
      attachment and affectional bonds, and the consequences of their dis-
      ruption. Bowlby demonstrated the importance of early attachment in
      determining a person's later security and success in forming relation-
      ships with others.

184 • *children . . . have a hard time seeing someone else's perspective:* De-
      velopmental theorist Robert Selman, building upon the moral devel-
      opment theory of Lawrence Kohlberg, described stages children go
      through as they learn to take the perspective of others. A good refer-
      ence for reading about Selman's stages is R. K. Selman, "Social-
      cognitive understanding: a guide to educational and clinical practice,"
      in T. Lickona, ed., *Moral Development and Behavior* (New York:
      Hold, Rinehart & Winston, 1976).

Chapter 9: When to Step In

191   *we have seen an increase in aggression among children . . . and*
      more of it at ever younger ages: R. Goodman and A. Gurian. Ag-
      gression. New York University Child Study Center. Available at
      www.aboutourkids.org/aboutour/article/aggression.html. Accessed
      June 18, 2007.

209 *when peers . . . step in, bullying . . . stops 57 percent of the time within ten seconds:* D. Pepler and W. Craig. 2007. Binoculars on bullying: A new solution to protect and connect children. Available at www.voicesforchildren.ca. Accessed June 18, 2007.

209 *Bullying . . . escalating problem in U.S. schools today:* See National Center for Education Statistics. *Indicators of school crime and safety.* Available at nces.ed.gov/pubserch. Accessed June 18, 2007.

209 *more than 16 percent of U.S. schoolchildren said they had been bullied . . . during a school term:* N. Ericson. 2001. Addressing the problem of juvenile bullying. Fact Sheet # 200127. Washington, DC: Office of Juvenile Justice and Delinquency Prevention.

Chapter 10: When Real Life Intervenes

219 *almost four in ten parents say their children . . . frightened . . . something they've seen in the news . . . concerned . . . could happen to them or their families:* J. Cantor and A. Nathanson. 1996. Children's fright reactions to television news. *Journal of Communication* 46(4):139–52.

219 *children today feel less safe than kids did in the past:* J. Garbarino. 1995. *Raising children in a socially toxic environment.* San Francisco: Jossey-Bass, 64.

223 *one study . . . 43 percent . . . in the fourth through sixth grades thought it was "likely" that they would be kidnapped . . . in their lives:* J. Price and S. Desmond. 1987. The missing children issue: A preliminary examination of fifth-grade students' perceptions. *American Journal of Diseases of Children* 141:811–15.

Chapter 11: Small Acts, Big Changes

239 *United Nations report on the well-being of children in the world's most developed countries:* The United Nations Children's Fund. 2007. *Child poverty in perspective: An overview of child well-being in rich countries.* Florence, Italy: The United Nations Children's Fund, 1.

240 • *Margaret Mead . . . "Never doubt that a small group of thoughtful people can change the world":* Margaret Mead, who was a pioneering

anthropologist, wrote numerous books on various cultures and on contemporary issues such as education, the women's movement, and ecology. This quote was accessed at www.quoteb.com/quotes/1821.

241   *comparison of the protections countries provide children against harmful media and marketing forces:* C. Hawkes. 2004. *Marketing food to children: The global regulatory environment.* Geneva: World Health Organization.

252   *The American Psychological Association has called for a ban on advertising to children under the age of eight . . . kids don't understand persuasive intent:* American Psychological Association. 2004. *Report of the APA task force on advertising and children.* Washington, DC: American Psychological Association. Available at www.apa.org /releases/childrenads.html. Accessed June 19, 2007.

253   *Federal Trade Commission has . . . recommended . . . no more marketing to young children of action figures, toys, and other products linked to movies rated for older viewers:* Federal Trade Commission. 2000. *Marketing violent entertainment to children: A review of self-regulation and industry practices in the motion picture, music recording and electronic game industries.* Washington, DC: Federal Trade Commission, 54.

254 •   *"We don't have to engage in grand, heroic actions . . . and at least the possibility of sending this spinning top of a world in a different direction":* Howard Zinn is a historian, playwright, and social activist who has authored some twenty books, among them his epic masterpiece *A People's History of the United States,* which tells the true history of our country and in so doing, gives us hope now and for our future. The quote used here is from Zinn's memoir *You Can't Be Neutral on a Moving Train* (Boston: Beacon Press, 1994), 208.

Index